· ASK YOUR ANGELS ·

Ask Your Angels

ALMA DANIEL

TIMOTHY WYLLIE

ANDREW RAMER

Illustrated by
Yanni Posnakoff

BALLANTINE BOOKS · NEW YORK

*Copyright © 1992 by Alma Daniel, Timothy Wyllie, and Andrew Ramer
Illustrations by Yanni Posnakoff*

*All rights reserved under International and Pan-American Copyright Conventions.
Published in the United States
by Ballantine Books, a division of Random House, Inc.,
New York, and simultaneously in Canada by Random House
of Canada Limited, Toronto.*

*Library of Congress Catalog Card Number: 92-72772
ISBN: 0-345-36358-2*

*Cover design by James R. Harris
Cover art: Abbot Henderson Thayer, Angel, 1889.
Washington, D.C., National Museum of American Art/Art Resource
Manufactured in the United States of America
First Edition: September 1992*

10 9 8 7 6 5 4 3

· T A B L E   O F ·
Contents

· PART III ·

· L I S T   O F ·
Exercises

Chapter Eleven

Chapter Twelve

Chapter Thirteen

Chapter Fourteen

Acknowledgments

No book is ever written by the author, or in this case three authors, alone. We're indebted to many whose names may not be mentioned, most especially the people who have come to our workshops and helped to refine the techniques that we offer in *Ask Your Angels*. We want to express our heartfelt appreciation to each of you as well as to all the angels, named and unnamed, who have participated in this work.

Two angels who most certainly deserve recognition up front are Barbara Bowen, who provided invaluable structural advice, and Barbara Shor, who gave us clarity on the flow and feeling of this book and helped to weave it all together.

Many thanks also to Jeff Doctoroff, who coordinated the intricate dance between editor, authors, production, and angels.

For the whimsical and joyful illustrations that grace these pages, we are deeply grateful to Yanni Posnakoff. We are indebted to Malachi McCormick for permission to use his drawing of the angel that announces each of the exercises.

A special expression of thanks goes to Mona Brookes of Monart Schools. She inspired her art students to produce delightful renditions of angels that, regrettably, we were unable to use. And to Christopher Castle, William Giese, June Atkin

Sanders, and all the other artists who shared their angel drawings, our deep appreciation.

Many individuals provided the anecdotal material used throughout *Ask Your Angels*. In some cases, names and identifying details have been changed.

For their contributions through angelic transmissions, experiences, and expertise that were generously shared with us, we want to especially acknowledge Hilda Brown, Mimi DeMirjian, Lee Ellis, Carolina Ely, Anne Entus, Deborah Hicks, Dorothy Maclean, Mercury, Sara Michaels-Smith, Monte Morris, Patricia Powell, Joe Rodriguez, Gail San Filippo, Michael Schwager, Paul Selig, Carolyn Short, Solara, David Spangler, Betsy Stang, Elsita Sterling, Felicia Telsey, LiLi Townsend, Martha Wakefield, and Paul Waterman.

For providing the gracious hideaway that incubated and nurtured a substantial part of this book, our deep appreciation to Jackie Sideli and John Sideli.

We've been blessed by the friendship and faith of individuals who arranged angel workshops or assisted us with them in the United States, Canada, and Europe: Mary Bohaychuk, Carmel Bouzane, Andy Cox, Cathy Deutsch, Mary Donker, Elana Freeman, Glenn of Trees, Liane Haynes, Carol Horne, Karen Malcolm, Cynthia O'Neal, Ralph Pittman, Ann Seamster, Ellen Sokolow, Emerald Star, Jill Steiner, John Stowe, David Tenerowicz, Ruth Terry, Laura Watts, and Mindy Yanish.

For their guidance in angel research, we thank Abi'l-Khayr, Rabbi Steve Blumberg, Elder Eldon Cooley, David Gitomer, Menachem Kallush, Herman Mills, Dr. Abdel-Rahman Osman, and the reference librarians in the religion section of the Brooklyn Public Library at Grand Army Plaza.

There are many others who have helped and encouraged us along the way: Elli Bambridge, Jean Barrett, Teza Bates, Nelson Bloncourt, Judith Borg, Gail Brudny, Ivan Chelnick, Jyori Chrystal, Connie Costa, Valerie de Montvallon, Anjani DiBello,

P. R. D'Or, Ruth Drayer, Annette and Ed Eckart, Robert Faust, Marilyn Ferguson, John Fletcher Harris, Kamala Hope-Campbell, Cher Jung, Samuel Kirschner, Linda and Rob Leahy, Frederic Lehrman, Susan Lorette, Susan Meadowcroft, Steve Milkis, Rita Maloney, Michael Morrison, Rosie Murray, Tom Patrick, Maryanne Quinones, Richard Ramer, Gerard Rizza, Lilith Rochas, Prudence See, Joan Sexton, Don Shewey, Peter Sonnenberg, Marty Spiegel, Anya Sprinkle, Starheart, Ruth Strassberg, Linda Tellington-Jones, Simon Vinkenoog, Teddy Vitchell, Jeff Wadlington, Ingrid Wagner, Anne Walsh, Bill Walsh, Robert Windslow, Ora Yemini, and the "Women of Power"—you know who you are.

For the gift of life, and their loving support and confidence in us, we acknowledge and thank our mothers, Rita Sachs, Gerry Shields, and Diana Wyllie.

Finally, *Ask Your Angels* would not be in your hands if it weren't for one woman's vision of a book that could teach people to talk to their angels. For her unwavering determination in shaping this book, and, most of all, for believing that three people and four angels could write it, we gratefully acknowledge our devoted editor, Cheryl Woodruff.

Prologue

You are driving on the interstate across the great southwestern desert. It's night. In the focused beams of your headlights you see a large metal tire iron falling from the tow truck thirty yards ahead of you. It bounces once and hurtles straight for your windshield. Feet away, it simply disappears.

It happened to Carolina.

You're traveling in your station wagon with a friend beside you. It's late, you're tired, and you've been driving hard for hours. The snow has stopped falling, but there are slippery patches of ice on the road. Suddenly, while you both watch, frozen in horror, the eighteen-wheeler in front of you jackknifes. Then everything seems to be happening in slow motion. You, your dumbstruck companion, and your heavily laden station wagon are sailing out over the median, right over the two opposite lanes of oncoming traffic. You're deposited on the other side of the freeway, so gently that nothing and no one is damaged, facing back in the direction from which you came.

It happened to Sara and her friend.

Joe never could explain it, however many times he'd run it through his mind afterward. Something about the entire event made him feel acutely uncomfortable, as if he'd been wholly, unreasonably privileged. Saved for an unspecified destiny.

It happened in Vietnam. Joe was working in a shed in the camp's ammunition dump when an enemy mortar scored a direct hit. The shell demolished the dump. One hundred and eighty-four men died—but Joe walked out of it untouched.

Three true examples of mysterious happenings—incidents that defy rational, logical explanation. Our culture would have us believe that angels don't exist. But Carolina, Sara, and Joe know that angels do exist. Angels saved their lives.

Angels don't only show up in life-threatening situations. They're with us all the time. Polly saw an angel in her kitchen, on a sunny afternoon when she was baking cookies for her kids. And Ben's been talking to angels since his grandmother first told him about them in 1957.

Perhaps when you were young, you were in touch with your invisible friends but weren't believed and learned to keep silent after that—and forgot. Almost everyone has had a mysterious, unexplained occurrence in his life. Your story may not be as dramatic as the first three examples we've given. Or you may not even think you have a story. But the angels come into our lives in different ways. If you've picked up this book, the angels have already touched you. And this is the beginning of your story.

· WHAT YOU'LL FIND IN THIS BOOK ·

There are many books about people's encounters with angels. There are also a number of books on the history of angels in art and literature. This book is different from all the rest. It will teach you how to talk with your angels. The simple five-step method you will be using is called the GRACE Process.

Ask Your Angels is a guide to establishing a new form of relationship with your celestial companions—that of best friends. It comes into being as part of the great reawakening to the angels that is currently under way. Whatever belief you've previously held about them, applying what you'll learn here will open you to a new way of being with these blessed messengers.

In Part I, we'll be sharing a bit of the history of angelic encounters with the human race. Then we trace the evolution of how people have perceived angels and the celestials' impact on the World Mind. And to give you a sense of how it happened to us, we'll tell you the stories of how we met our own angels. We hope that our personal stories will pave the way for you to enter into a new spiritual companion-ship of your own.

Anyone and everyone can talk with celestials—the three of us have been doing it for years. And with direct input from our beloved companions we have taught many, many other people to do it, too. From all these experiences, we distilled the GRACE Process, which we'll be guiding you through in Part II of the book. If you approach the exercises and meditations that we offer with heartfelt sincerity, you'll make full, joyful contact with your own guardian angels.

There are many different divination tools, such as the tarot, the runes, and the *I Ching.* In this book we will be sharing a new one with you—the Angel Oracle.

Using it is an enjoyable way to open yourself to the wisdom of a wide range of angels and will help you tap into your own intuitive knowing.

Once you form a relationship with your heavenly helpers, whole new vistas unfold. In Part III, you enter into a working partnership with the angels, for the purpose of personal and global transformation. You'll learn how to fine-tune your relationship and team up with the angels to achieve your goals. We will show you how to bring the winged ones into all your relationships, dreams, healing, and recovery. Our angels end the book with their inspiring visions of how we can dance with them into the twenty-first century.

· WHO—OR WHAT—ARE ANGELS? ·

Angels are intelligent beings, capable of feelings, yet a different species, who have their existence on a slightly finer vibrational frequency from the one to which our physical senses are tuned. This means we can't perceive them ordinarily with our eyes or ears, but they can perceive us. Our realities interpenetrate one another—with their reality encompassing and enfolding ours.

The word *angel* is a generic name for the collective group of beings—citizens of "inner space"—whose responsibilities include the harmonious organization of the inhabited universe. Some people believe that angels are the thoughts of God, while others hold that they are the creation of the Divine Mother Spirit. A relatively small number of this vast multitude is immediately concerned with humanity and our planet. Among these are our closest companions—our guardian angels—and also the many millions of angels who tend our planetary reality. Our research has made it clear to us that there are angels who watch over virtually every aspect of human activity.

For example, we were given an angel to help us in the creation and writing of this book. It's hard to imagine how this all could have worked without Abigrael's skillful mediation. Abigrael is indeed its name, which immediately brings us to the first strangeness we encounter when communing with an angel. Angels are genderless. Two of us, for instance, perceive Abigrael as female, yet for the third it is unquestionably male. Angels are androgynous. They have both male and female qualities along with their individual characteristics.

This underlines a most important fact to be borne in mind while reading this book: There is no correct way to perceive angels. They come to us very much on their own terms, appearing to us in ways that are highly personal to each individual. They are here to help us raise our loving understanding and they connect with us at the highest level at which we are capable of functioning.

Contact and conversation with your angel is filled with all the tenderness, love, and wonderment of discovering a best friend—known forever, but not seen in years. Talking with angels is an entirely natural relationship, although over the centuries it's become obscured by the belief that if you can't see something or touch it—it isn't real.

Now, however, at a time when we need help more than ever before, the angels are stepping forward once again. Interestingly, they tell us that it is because of reorganizations within their own domain that they are receiving instructions to make closer contact with us. Just as we are preparing ourselves for the enormous changes ahead, so the angels tell us that they are also evolving. As above, so below.

Their closer presence is deeply encouraging—just the helping hand for which so many of us have been praying. *The angels are here.* They are with us whether we believe in them or not. The universe works on a need-to-know basis; when we ask we are answered. In talking to our angels we extend and expand our capacity for growth and transformation—and move closer to our destiny.

· HOW DO ANGELS FUNCTION? ·

A clue lies in the word *angel* itself, derived from the Greek word *angelos* and meaning messenger. Angels are messengers of our Creator. Within them they contain the basic patterns of creation that become manifest in our three-dimensional world. They are literally messengers who are themselves the message.

Angels work with our souls, in conjunction with Universal Mind, to help us raise our sights and spirits by reminding us of the truth, beauty, and goodness that exist within everything. By invoking our angels to help us accomplish mundane as well as inspired tasks, we can be confident that all will proceed according to Higher Will, not just ours alone. Through this act of cooperation, we lose our sense of isolation. We begin to truly comprehend that we're not alone, not unaided; that there is help and guidance all around us. And we start opening to the state of gratitude in which miracles can occur.

· HOW TO USE THIS BOOK ·

Just as you went from baby talk to using words and then sentences, learning to talk with your angel is a step-by-step process. It expands and deepens as the lines of communication open wider and wider and your confidence grows.

To reap the most benefit from *Ask Your Angels,* we suggest that you use a tape player to prerecord the exercises and meditations. Hearing the instructions spoken in your own voice creates a feeling of security that will greatly enhance the potential for angelic contact.

A notebook or journal is also a vital companion for this adventure. The three of us have found that spending time writing down what we hear and say is an invaluable tool—especially for future reference.

Being able to hear and speak the truth is a valuable ally in your relationship with your angels. Doing this can be quite challenging, but ultimately it is always kind, and often very funny indeed.

Enthusiasm is also important. And so is gratitude.

As you acknowledge and release any judgments that may arise, it'll be easier for you to open to the reality of angels. Although it's great fun, conversing with your angels is not a parlor game like the Ouija board, nor is it another form of fortune-telling. It cuts much deeper than that. Developing a relationship with the angels assumes you are a student of life, and that the goals you have set yourself are not only for your highest good, but for the best of all.

· NEW WAYS OF WORKING IN NEW TIMES ·

The three of us met our celestial companions in the course of our everyday lives and developed our friendships with them in different ways. We were already good friends with them when they drew us together to write this book.

Our angels have made it clear to us that they wanted three different people with three different voices to collaborate on the delicate business of writing *Ask Your Angels.* This was both to demonstrate the skill of angelically assisted work, and also to make sure that no single view prevailed. There are many ways to talk with angels, and seeking their friendship is not limited to any one belief system. Connecting with them is the next step in our evolution as a species of conscious beings. In fact, as Abigrael tells us, it is also the next step in angelic evolution as well. So the exchange goes both ways, as in any good relationship.

· THE VALUE OF INTUITION ·

Intuition is based on subtle feelings. It can atrophy when you overemphasize your logical mind and materialistic concerns. How many times have you had a hunch and then talked yourself out of it, only to find later that if you'd followed your intuition and not listened to your mind, matters would have turned out much better?

We all have that intuitive faculty, and *Ask Your Angels* offers you a powerful way to tune into the Source of that inner knowingness. When we ask our angels, we open ourselves to a level of wisdom and understanding that is rarely available to us in ordinary consciousness. Ego limits us to what *I* know, or *I* think, or *I* do. Opening to the angelic voice shows us that we don't have to go it alone—and we can tap into a larger base of knowledge. As we release notions that we and we alone must know, think, or do, and drop the limitations that these notions engender, we can then enter the inestimably rich storehouse of information and guidance available through Universal Mind.

· ASKING IS . . . . ·

Asking is always a reaching out, an opening up on our part. And as we open, we make ourselves ready to receive. This moves us past the immediate restrictions and limitations that we have taken on in this lifetime, transmutes them, and reveals to us the wonders of life all around us.

Asking is not about demanding. Or grasping. It's about remaining open, without judgment or criticism, while the bits and pieces of information come together. Asking simply means accepting whatever appears, and trusting that, at the right time, the correct and salient understanding will be made known for the best of all.

True asking doesn't come from fear or aggression; it arises from the deep wish to know, and the willingness to listen and receive. Being with your angels is not about sitting in a darkened room with eerie music, a crystal ball, and flickering candles. It's simply conversation. We're all capable of walking down a street and having a conversation with our angels, not as a symptom of schizophrenia, but as a part of what it means to be whole and healthy, to be eminently sane. Talking with angels is the most natural thing in the world. Everyone can do it. And it's good for you. Good for your funny bone. Good for your soul. Good for your body. Good for everyone with whom you come in contact.

When you *Ask Your Angels,* you can be sure that you will be answered.

Angels, Angels Everywhere

You're about to embark on an adventure with the angels. Your passport is an open heart—and we suggest you travel light.

Since the terrain isn't physical, you won't need a map, but like any good explorer, it will be helpful for you to know where others have gone before and what they have found. Each of their encounters illuminates one more aspect of the territory. Knowing about them will give you a context for your rendezvous.

In chapter 1, you'll get an overview of how angels have been perceived through the ages, as well as information on the ranks and orders of angels. You'll learn why the techniques for communicating with them are no longer hidden, as they once were. What do angels look like? What is their nature? What is the difference between an angel and a nature spirit? We give you the answers to these questions, along with thumbnail sketches of our "Celestial Top Ten"—some of the best-known winged celebrities of the Western world.

In chapter 2, we trace the unfolding story of angelic encounters and their influence through history—from the Bible to World War II.

And, to bring all this into the mainstream of contemporary life, in chapter 3 we tell you the stories of how each of us met our own angels. We're not historical—we're real just like you. And since it happened to us, it can happen to you, too.

Bon voyage!

Angels Watching Over Us

Angels have always been with us, in every time and culture. Ever since we emerged from the dim, distant past there have been records and representations of another race of beings who share this world with us. In pictograms and paintings, poetry and children's stories, our ancestors down through the ages have tried to pass on what they knew about these beings.

In the last few hundred years we have come to believe that something is real only if we can see it through a microscope or telescope. But no telescope will ever be powerful enough to see into the angelic realms. This doesn't faze the angels one bit.

Just because our era doesn't generally acknowledge their presence doesn't mean they cease to exist!

But all this is changing, as you will see in the brief survey that follows of angels through the centuries. As our species matures, as each of us individually awakens to the surprising dimensions of who we truly are, so the angels are becoming more available to us. To all of us, all the time. Not just to special people at special times.

· TRADITIONAL VIEWS OF ANGELS ·

What first pops into your mind when you think of angels? Jacob and his ladder; the angel who stopped Abraham from killing his son Isaac; the angels with Daniel in the lions' den; Gabriel announcing to Mary the astonishing news of her imminent pregnancy; or six hundred years later, the very same archangel sweeping the prophet Mohammed off on a star-studded night journey to Heaven. These are just a few of the beings in the angelic realms.

All three major religions in the Western world, Christianity, Judaism, and Islam, as well as virtually all of the world's other systems of religious belief, include celestials in their cosmologies. Their scriptures all contain references to angelic interventions.

Angels, like people, belong to families or clans. Many names have been given to them, but in the opinion of a number of angel historians, the most familiar can be arranged in three categories, or spheres, starting at the top with those closest to God, and moving down to those who are connected to the physical world.

· INFORMATION ON THE SPHERES OF ANGELS ·

All angel writers would agree that there are many different kinds of heavenly beings that bridge the spiritual and physical realms. There are numerous opinions as to how many categories exist, what they are named, or what the functions are of each one. The system of organization most commonly followed in the Western world comes from a book that appeared in the sixth century. It was supposedly written by Dionysius the Areopagite, a disciple of Saint Paul. In it there are three categories, or spheres of angels, with three orders in each one.

The word *angel* itself is used both as a generic term to refer to all heavenly beings, and as a specific term to refer to the members of the third sphere, those closest to the physical. So, too, the word *archangel* is often used as a generic term to refer to all the high orders of heavenly beings, although they are in fact but one of the higher orders.

· ORDERS OF ANGELIC BEINGS ·

The First Sphere—angels who serve as heavenly counselors:

1 Seraphim
2 Cherubim
3 Thrones

The Second Sphere—angels who work as heavenly governors:

4 Dominions
5 Virtues
6 Powers

The Third Sphere—angels who function as heavenly messengers:

7 Principalities
8 Archangels
9 Angels

The numbers refer you to the illustration on pages 18 and 19.

Since this is by no means the only classification system in the long history of angel watching, we asked our angelic coordinator, Abigrael, to explain and simplify.

· ANGELS ·

ABIGRAEL: The angels that you're most familiar with are in the last order. They are the ones who are closest to humanity, the ones most concerned with human affairs. Within the category of angels, there are many different kinds, with different functions. You'll find information on them later in the book. The ones that you know best, and the ones that *Ask Your Angels* is primarily about, are the guardian angels. Because of shifts in their functions and your consciousness, it is useful to think of these celestial beings as companion angels. As you enter a time of increased light and love on the planet, they will not need to guard you, but rather will be your guides to greater and greater consciousness.

· ARCHANGELS ·

Beyond the angels are the beings you are used to calling the archangels. But we suggest that you call them overlighting angels, since they tend the larger arenas of human endeavor. These beings are a different family from the angels. There are many different kinds of overlighting angels in this larger family. The four you are most familiar with are Gabriel, Michael, Raphael, and Uriel.

· PRINCIPALITIES ·

Beyond the archangels are the principalities. They are the guardian angels of all large groups, from cities and nations to recent human creations such as multinational corporations. These might more accurately now be called integrating angels. There are many of these beings involved with your planet, and later in the book, you will be meeting one particular integrating angel who carries the pattern of a unified global order in its heart.

· POWERS ·

The first order in the second sphere are those beings who have been known as powers. They are the bearers of the conscience of all of humanity, the keepers of your collective history. The angels of birth and death are in this category. They are able to draw down and hold the energy of the divine plan the same way trees draw down the energy of the Sun. In this way, the powers can send all of you a vision of a world spiritual network. Just as you have a heart, liver, kidneys, and other organs in your body, all of the world's religions are different organs in the emerging spiritual body of this planet.

· VIRTUES ·

Beyond the powers are another group of beings, the virtues. They are of particular importance to you now because they are able to beam out massive levels of divine energy. As more groups of you learn to work with the virtues, there will be a greater infusion of spiritual energy available for your planet.

· DOMINIONS ·

The dominions are the heavenly beings who govern the activities of all the angelic groups lower than they are. Divine bureaucrats, they also serve to integrate the spiritual and the material worlds. Although they take their orders from God, and rarely contact individuals, their work is still connected to your reality.

· THRONES ·

The first order in the third sphere is the thrones. They are the companion angels of the planets. At this time in your history it is important for you to be aware of the particular throne, the Earth Angel, who is guardian of your world, whom you'll meet later.

· CHERUBIM ·

Beyond the thrones are the cherubim. They are the guardians of light, and of the stars. Remote from your plane of reality, still their light touches your lives, the divine light that they filter down from Heaven.

· SERAPHIM ·

The highest order of the highest hierarchy are the seraphim, the celestial beings said to surround the throne of God, singing the music of the spheres, and regulating the movement of the heavens as it emanates from God.

According to Abigrael, there are four orders within the heavenly hosts that particularly concern us now: angels, archangels, principalities, and thrones. You'll get more details in chapter 14.

While it looks like there is a higher and lower echelon, it's more accurate to visualize all these orders in a great circle, with the "highest" and the "lowest" holding hands. For example, seraphim, who appear to be closest to the Creator, also serve the God in us.

· SECRET KNOWLEDGE THROUGH THE AGES ·

The angels come into all of our lives in a variety of ways. Some people meet them directly, in person or in visions and dreams. Others have felt their scintillating presence or heard them speaking or singing. Still others have experienced them as muses who inspire them creatively. And some, through the centuries, have dedicated their lives to studying angels from a purely philosophical or theological perspective.

In addition to reports of angels in the Hebrew scriptures, the New Testament, and the Koran, each of these religious traditions has a vast "underground" literature about the celestials and how to make contact with them.

The work in this book comes from the common Western path of angel encounters—with one major difference. In the past, the methods used for connecting with angels were kept strictly secret. Only certain initiates of spiritual sects, those who were older, well established in their lives, and generally male, were taught the meditations and consciousness-shifting techniques necessary to open to our invisible companions. Most of this knowledge could only be passed on verbally, from teacher to student. In more superstitious times, it was with good reason that the information was carefully cherished and what was written down was often encoded or deliberately made unintelligible except to those already on the path.

· THE END OF THE AGE OF SECRETS ·

But we are living in a different time in history. Secret traditions are now being shared openly all over the planet. We stand on the brink of massive change. On the one hand, we face apparent global disaster, and on the other, there is the potential for the most glorious spiritual transformation our species has ever seen. We seem to be more out of balance than ever. Yet, we are also more globally entwined, more open and caring and evolved. At this time of personal and planetary acceleration, previous rules and old forms are being discarded. Contact with the angels, which used to take years of meditation and dedication, is now available to all who seek it, because the angels are closer to us, and more open to working with us on a conscious level, than they have been in thousands of years.

From the interest generated in the workshops and seminars the three of us have been giving, it's apparent that the angels are coming into more and more people's lives right now, bearing the same message—it is time to change, time to grow and heal our lives and our beloved planet. And the angels aren't making contact just with special people, or in a secret way. They are doing it openly, joyfully, bringing good humor and good news.

· ANGELS AND NATURE SPIRITS ·

Once you open to your angels, and in some cases perhaps even before, you may run into their cousins, the *nature spirits*. The nature spirits are themselves an angelic order, but they're literally on a different wavelength from our spiritual companions.

Some of the names given by different cultures to the nature spirits are devas, elves, fairies, undines, sylphs, salamanders, fauns, trolls, and gnomes. They are the presiding patterns that oversee all living, growing things, crops and gardens, forests and lakes, fish, fowl, and animals. We see their handiwork in such configurations as flocks of birds and schools of fish, and in the unique and delicate tracery of a single leaf.

Nature spirits co-create and nurture the physical environment—which they do independently of human efforts. However, at Findhorn in Scotland, and Perelandra in the state of Virginia, two sites of horticultural wonders, you can see for yourself and appreciate the enormous mutual benefit of consciously developed teamwork between humans and nature spirits. People of any sensitivity who work with the land have always had some sort of feeling for the existence of this unseen realm. Whether you're aware of it or not, you connect with the nature spirits whenever you tend to your plants, follow an impulse to hug a tree, walk in a garden, or eat anything that has been grown.

Our human bodies also have nature spirits, or devas (pronounced *day-vahs*) as we call them. The devas of our bodies are the organizing principles that coordinate the immense amount of information constantly flowing through the physical body. They are the spiritual equivalent of the myriad of cells, organisms, and microorganisms that have agreed to cooperate in such conglomerates as our kidneys, liver, lungs, heart, and pancreas.

Of all the angelic beings, the nature spirits are the ones who are most closely tuned to our human reality. They are a realm to be greatly respected since they have borne the brunt of most of our environmental follies—and yet they continue willingly to serve. Opening ourselves to them now is very important as they possess much information vitally needed for this time of planetary transformation.

· THE ANGELIC NATURE ·

Angels don't have human natures, although we humans continue to project our characteristics upon them. They see and understand things in a very different perspective from the way we do. While we do have much in common, especially in regard to our higher goals, it's our very differences that can lead to fascinating dialogues.

All kinds of contradictory information can be found in angel lore. Some believe that angels are immortal, while others claim they are created only for a specific time and function. People argued long into the night over such questions as: When were the angels created? Do they have free will? Are they entirely creatures of mind and spirit, or do they have physical bodies of some sort? Can people become angels, or are they an entirely separate species? Do angels ever come to Earth and take on human form? Are they higher than humans in the great chain of being, and therefore our potential teachers? Or are they more like our spiritual servants?

And—that hoary old question—are they really external creatures at all? Could it be that angels are aspects of our souls? Or that they are the reflections of our future selves toward whom we are evolving?

All of these conflicting ideas have been held to be true by a variety of scholars and spiritual seekers over the last three thousand years. But no two angel encounters are ever quite the same and, as we have stressed, there is no one right way to meet them.

Although they're coming to us in a new and different manner, and are making contact with us more easily than ever before, it's helpful and instructive to know something of how our predecessors viewed the angels. As you read some of the accounts, remember that almost everything written about angels shows us yet another aspect of their fluid reality, and surely carries another piece of the larger truth. In showing you how different each encounter is, we hope that it will be simpler for you to embark on your own unique and joyful adventure.

· WHAT DO ANGELS LOOK LIKE? ·

Just as there's no correct way to experience angels, there's no right way to see them either. They manifest in a myriad of ways to different people. As we follow some of their appearances through the ages and see how they've chosen to be with some of our ancestors, you will begin to appreciate their wonderful fluidity.

Since we are so dependent on information from our five senses, we asked Sargolais (pronounced *sar-go-lie'-iss*), Andrew's companion angel, to tell us what an angel might look like, if we could see it.

SARGOLAIS: That's difficult to answer. Physicists are finding the same problem in determining what an electron is like. Is it a particle or a wave? Is it in one place at a time, or in several? So, too, with angels.

Our bodies exist in several places at one time, or in all of them. So how can you draw a picture of an angel or take its photo? You cannot. We can slow ourselves down enough to appear in one place and time, but we do that for you.

If your subtle senses were fully developed, as they will be in your future history, you might begin to see us as radiant pulsing beings of light. This light isn't the same as the light that comes from a sun, a fire, or a light bulb. It is a far more subtle and all-pervading light.

So you'd see us like that, but you'd also see us in many different places at the same time. This would be something like holding many slides of the same person up to a bright light, so you could view them all at the same time. In the midst of this overlay of bodies, you would see an intricate tracery of fibers, like filigree work, or more correctly like the meridians—the fibers of flowing energy—of the acupuncture system in your bodies. Some of these fibers would be seen inside our bodies, but many of them would also be extending outward, in a timeless, spaceless way, to every part of the universe. It's these fibers that some of you have sensed as wings, while it's the light of us that has caused others to see us as wearing halos.

There are many different kinds of angels. Some of us might appear to you as multidimensional spheres, while others would appear as shafts of light, spirals of light, cones of light, ranging in size from a dot to a galaxy. While our size is filtered through your perceptions, it does bear some relationship to our function and nature: The larger we appear, the more collective our function. So, those of us you'd call "higher beings" will appear to you as larger.

· TRANSFORMATION AMONG THE ANGELS ·

It's become apparent to angel watchers over the last few years that profound changes have been occurring in the realms of our celestial cousins. We asked our recording angel Abigrael for some inside information.

ABIGRAEL: What is being reorganized is the relationship of certain angels who work with your world. This is because changes in your collective consciousness are now allowing us to come closer than ever before.

What I've been commissioned to share with you for this book is how things are now. Some of what existed in the past was either recorded wrong, remembered wrong, or deliberately changed to conform to human belief systems at different times.

For example, there are four major overlighting archangels who are involved with human life on Earth. When you thought that the Earth was at the center of the universe, these four seemed quite important in Heaven. They are not. There are millions of archangels. These four, however, are quite important on Earth. More of them used to be needed to get information through to you because you were less receptive. But as you have evolved, fewer archangels are needed!

Today, the archangels Gabriel, Michael, Raphael, and Uriel are relevant for Earth. Later in the book I will be giving you up-to-the-minute briefings on how they're now working for you. This is not the same as the information you have from the past; they are no longer working in quite the same way. Michael, for example, was always seen with a sword, cutting away evil. But as you are mastering duality, Michael doesn't need to do that. Its functions have shifted, and it is now the Guardian of Peace.

As another example, Gabriel was always seen as the Angel of Revelation, but as you come closer to us, the nature of revelation changes. You no longer need things to be revealed that you're open to in other ways. So Gabriel is taking on different functions, experiencing changes in its job description, and simply becoming the Angel of Relationship.

You're living more in harmony with All That Is, even if it doesn't seem this way on the surface. This is why *Ask Your Angels* can come into being now, whereas in the past the same capacity to make connection might have taken twenty years of practice.

Congratulations on your evolution as a sentient species—even if the evidence is still visibly lacking.

· LUCIFER: A STUDY IN LIGHT AND DARK ·

No real understanding of our celestial colleagues would be complete without tackling the issue of the "fallen" angels. Opinions differ as to the precise nature of what happened in the past that could have caused angels to fall, but what is unarguable is the persistence with which this idea has shown up in most planetary belief systems. Christianity and Judaism have their Satan and Lucifer and, depending on the sect, any number of fallen angels. Islam has its Eblis, or Shaytan as he is sometimes called, who is clearly the counterpart of Satan.

Even in this day and age, films like *The Omen, Rosemary's Baby,* and *The Seventh Sign* evoke horror because they tap into the possibility that we may be influenced in some way by universal messengers of evil.

However, according to our angelic informants, the situation, thank God, is not like that at all.

Lucifer, it is said in one tradition, was one of the seven great archangels of our solar system, serving as the guardian of the planet Venus. God asked for a volunteer from among His top angels who might be willing to go down to Earth and help strengthen humanity's spiritual resolve by offering constant temptation. Lucifer volunteered. Despite his loving intentions, slowly, over the ages, Lucifer has become identified in our mind as the devil, instead of an aspect of God dedicated to our growth by helping us strengthen our spiritual muscles. "The devil made me do it" is a tempting excuse for just about anything, and we've allowed this to blind us into depicting Lucifer as the source of everything we consider "evil" in the world.

One of the heavenly tasks of Lucifer, whose very name means "light giver" or "light bearer," is to teach us about the necessary dark side of life. Lucifer is the shadow that reveals the light by contrast. In many ways we can't see the true light until we first experience the darkness. We tend not to value something until we lose it and then regain it through our own efforts. The parable of the prodigal son touches on this quirk of human nature.

This interdependence of light and dark, of joy and sorrow, of good and bad, and all the other opposites in our dual system of reality, yields to an understanding that, within the larger context, Christ and Lucifer, while not exactly complementary to each other, are at least on the same side, integral parts of the same whole.

Many contemporary Christians have begun to abandon the concept that there is a real devil, recognizing once again that there is only one omnipotent force in the universe. "Evil," as poet-philosopher William Blake wrote, "is only the deprivation of good, and when the soul emerges from this illusion of evil, Lucifer resumes his original status as one of God's great archangels."

· THE END OF ILLUSION ·

Slowly, surely, we are collectively emerging from this illusion of evil. To do this means to hold firmly to the understanding of God as One Power, as One Ultimate Life Principle, from which all else emanates. Naturally, the illusion of fear and loathing still stalks our cities and can sometimes convince us, if we pay too much attention to the media, that it has some degree of objective reality.

But isn't this exactly the challenge being presented to us—to come more fully to terms with the shadow side of our own nature? As we learn how to release and finally let go of negative and self-destructive behavior, we also cease to project our own negativity onto a fictitious devil, or fallen angels, or onto other people. When we reach this point we have no further need to hang onto the illusion of evil.

In reconciling these apparently opposite characteristics we also demonstrate those qualities the angels revere so highly in us. And, in turn, we can free the so-called fallen angels from the negativity we have externalized onto them for all these long millennia. By so doing we can allow them once again to pursue the functions for which they were originally created.

· SOME FAMOUS ANGELS ·

The three of us have all had the spontaneous good fortune to have the angels turn up in our lives. Since we hadn't approached this subject from the historical or academic route it wasn't until we started researching this book that we had any inkling of the enormous amount of material available on angels and what a venerable tradition we seemed to be following. Not only in the Western Judeo/Christian/ Islamic cultures, but virtually every society that we examined proved to have an extensive and deeply rooted belief in guardian angels or companion spirits of one sort or another.

Angels have been used in Western monotheistic religions to help distinguish the good guys from the bad, the benevolent spirits from the malevolent demons. In polytheistic cultures, the tasks performed for us by the angels are taken over by the gods themselves. The functions become blurred. Among the great religions of the East and in most shamanic cultures, for instance, there is a large group of beings who are invoked to attend to the details of everyday living—crops, weather, fertility, and other important issues. Rarely, however, are they perceived as personal guardians. These beings deal with issues rather than individuals. In India, for example, the *pitarah* are household deities, somewhat like guardian spirits, who make sure the home is protected from illness, famine, drought, or other disasters. Among the Pueblo peoples of the American Southwest, the *kachina* is a guiding, beneficent life spirit, while a *wajima* to the Australian aboriginal is nearer to a spirit ancestor.

All of these beings, one way or another, are angelic. The very fact that angels can appear in such different ways, in different times and locations, emerging in cultures often totally inimical to one another, suggests that they are a species with patience, persistence, and a finely honed sense of the absurd.

· A CELESTIAL TOP TEN ·

In the case of the better known angels of the West—Gabriel, Michael, Raphael, Uriel, and some of the others in our Top Ten—their influence and presence can be seen extending down through the ages, touching the human process in ways that invariably change us. Fascinatingly, sometimes the same angel, Samael for example, has been viewed as a force for good in one era and as a devil in the next. But on the whole, the overall tone of angelic relationships has been one of good humor,

mystical exploration, high adventure, and a wonderful, almost overwhelming level of unconditional love.

So let's meet our selection of among the best-known angels in the Western world. Before each encounter you might want to repeat the angel's name a few times slowly with your eyes closed. Then, while you are reading, take deep breaths and consciously slow your breathing down. Allow yourself the time to simply observe how you feel as you are coming to know about each of these beings, and open yourself to possible contact with them.

Michael, whose name is a question—"Who is like God?"—is surely the best known of the overlighting archangels. Michael is acknowledged by all three Western sacred traditions. He is believed to have appeared to Moses as the fire in the burning bush, and to have rescued Daniel and his friends from the lions' den. To Christians, he's the angel who informed Mary of her approaching death. Islamic lore tells us that his wings are the color of "green emerald and are covered with saffron hairs, each of them containing a million faces and mouths and as many tongues which, in a million dialects, implore the pardon of Allah." The Koran also paints the touching image of the cherubim being formed from the tears of Michael.

In the Dead Sea Scrolls Michael emerges as the Prince of Light fighting a war against the Sons of Darkness in which he leads the angelic battle against the legions of the fallen angel, Belial. Most recently, in 1950, Pope Pius XII declared Michael to be the patron of all policemen.

Gabriel, whose name means "God is my strength," seems to be our most frequent visitor from the higher realms. He astonished Mary, and her cousin Elizabeth, mother of John the Baptist, with his pronouncements concerning the births of their respective sons. To the followers of Islam, Gabriel is the Spirit of Truth who dictated the Koran to Mohammed. In Jewish legend it was Gabriel who parted the waters of the Red Sea so that the Hebrews could escape from Pharaoh's soldiers.

According to court testimony of the time, it was Gabriel who came to Joan of Arc and inspired her to go to the aid of the dauphin. Gabriel's apparent ongoing interest in this planet is most probably due to his function as heavenly awakener, the angel of vibratory transformation.

Metatron, in the world of the Jewish mystics, came to hold the rank of the highest of the angels despite his not being mentioned in the Scriptures. The meaning of his name has never been satisfactorily explained although one interpretation of it is "one who occupies the throne next to the Divine throne." It could also be derived from the Latin *metator,* a guide or measurer.

In a number of traditional sources, Metatron is said to have been the prophet Enoch, who was taken up to Heaven and transformed into an angel of fire, with thirty-six pairs of wings, to continue his days as a celestial scribe. Metatron has also been identified as the Liberating Angel and the one who wrestled with Jacob; the angel who stayed Abraham's hand from sacrificing his son Isaac; and the one who led the Hebrews through the forty years in the wilderness. In certain schools of mysticism, Metatron, said to be the tallest of all the heavenly beings, became known as Lesser YHWH. In Hebrew, the letters *YHWH* stand for the most sacred and unpronounceable name of God.

As God has many names, so, too, Metatron was thought to have many names, the use of which was believed to offer the user protection and access to this great angel's powers. Yahoel, Yofiel, Surya, and Lad are just a few of his other names.

Uriel's name means "Fire of God," and he is ranked variously as a seraph, cherub, regent of the sun, flame of God, presider over Hades and, in his best-known role, as the Archangel of Salvation. Like Metatron, Uriel is said to be one of the angels of the Presence, a most high posting since only the highest voltage angels can sustain the presence of God.

Uriel is thought to have been "the spirit who stood at the gate of the lost Eden with the fiery sword." The Book of Enoch tells us that it was Uriel who was sent by God to warn Noah of the impending flood, and elsewhere it's written that he disclosed the mysteries of the heavenly arcana to Ezra, and that he also led Abraham out of Ur in the Chaldean region.

Some have claimed that the divine art of alchemy was brought down to Earth by

Uriel, and that it was also this angel who gave the Kabbalah, the Hebrew mystic tradition, to humankind. John Milton describes Uriel as "the sharpest sighted spirit of all in Heaven." The angel also showed up to berate Moses for neglecting to circumcise his own son Gershom. Sharp eyes indeed!

Moroni is the angel of the Latter-day Saints. While there seems to be a dearth of indigenous American angels, in 1823 Moroni appeared to Joseph Smith in upstate New York and led him to discover buried golden tablets inscribed with dense lettering. When translated by Smith, again with Moroni's help, this text became *The Book of Mormon,* which tells us that in about 600 B.C., prior to the destruction of Jerusalem, a Jewish family fled the city and made its way by ship to what is now North America. Their descendants became two nations—one the ancestors of the Native Americans, the other lost and gone. However, records kept by one of the last elders of that vanished people tell that Jesus appeared to them after His death on the cross. The elder's name was Mormon, and it was his son Moroni who buried the tablets his father had kept, in about A.D. 400. According to the story, Moroni thus joins the ranks of Enoch and Elijah who were transformed into angels, and follows in the tradition of Gabriel in being the angelic giver of a book of revelation.

There is a forty-foot-high statue of Moroni that stands on top of a hill near Palmyra, New York, where Smith discovered the buried tablets. The angel is shown as it appeared to Smith, without wings and clothed in a long robe. Smith, who went on to found the Church of Jesus Christ of the Latter-day Saints, described Moroni as a "being of light with a face like lightning."

Melchizedek, the Sage of Salem, is another one of the few known cases of a high angel taking a human, very male, body. According to *The Urantia Book,* he appeared fully formed, some two thousand years before Christ, announcing that he was a servant of El Elyon, the Most High. He then set up a teaching center over which he personally presided for ninety-four years.

It was Melchizedek who delivered God's Covenant to Abraham and introduced the revolutionary concept of salvation through pure faith to the thinking of the planet. He established an extraordinarily wide-flung missionary program, centered in Salem, the ancient site of Jerusalem, sending out thousands of missionaries who literally circled the globe.

Called Sydik in Phoenician mythology, Melchizedek was believed to be the father of the seven Elohim—more Angels of the Divine Presence. In the third century A.D. a group of "heretics," calling themselves Melchisedans, claimed to be in touch with "a great power named Melchizedek, who was greater than Christ." His sojourn here as the Sage of Salem was said to have been a concerted effort on behalf of the celestials to bring some much-needed light to a dark and chaotic time, and to set the seeds for the coming of the Christ.

Ariel means "Lion of God." However, some confusion exists as to exactly whose side Ariel is on. He's ranked as one of the seven princes who rule the waters and is also known as Earth's Great Lord. To the poet John Milton, however, Ariel is a rebel angel who is overcome by the seraph Abdiel on the first day of the great war in Heaven.

Jewish mystics used Ariel as a poetic name for Jerusalem. In Gnostic lore, that first- and second-century melting pot of revelation, Ariel is the angel who controls the demons. Ariel has also been associated with the order of angels called the thrones and is known to have assisted the archangel Raphael in the curing of disease.

John Dee, magician, occultist, and court astrologer to Queen Elizabeth I, reckoned Ariel to be a conglomerate of Anael and Uriel, which sets him among the overlighting archangels!

Ariel makes an appearance in William Shakespeare's *The Tempest,* which may well have been the source of why Percy Bysshe Shelley, the nineteenth-century poet, liked to refer to himself as the angel Ariel.

Israfel, whose name in Arabic folklore means "The Burning One," is both an angel of resurrection and of song. By these same accounts, Israfel paved the way for Gabriel by serving for three years as a companion to Mohammed, whom he'd originally initiated into the work of being a prophet.

In an Islamic variant of the Genesis account of Adam's creation, Allah sends Israfel, Gabriel, Michael, and Azrael—the Angel of Death—out on a mission to fetch the seven handfuls of dust needed to make humanity's progenitor. According to legend, only Azrael returned successful.

Edgar Allan Poe, writer of mystery tales and verses, footnoted a poem with a cryptic reference to "the angel Israfel, whose heart strings are a lute, and who has the sweetest voice of all God's creatures." Elsewhere Israfel is described as a four-winged angel who, "while his feet are under the Seventh Earth, his head reaches to the pillars of the Divine throne."

Raziel, which means "Secret of God," is believed to be an "angel of the secret regions and Chief of the Supreme Mysteries." There is a legend that Raziel is the author of a great book, "wherein all celestial and Earthly knowledge is set down." When the angel gave his tome to Adam, some envious angels stole it away and threw it in the ocean. After it had been recovered by the primordial angel/demon of the deep, Rahab, the book passed first to Enoch, who apparently claimed it as his own, then to Noah, who learned how to make his ark from it. Solomon, too, was thought to have possessed the book, which allowed him his unusual knowledge of magic and control over the demons.

The Zohar, the major work of Jewish mysticism, claims that set in the middle of Raziel's book there is secret writing "explaining the fifteen hundred keys [to the mystery of the world], which were not revealed even to the angels." Other Jewish mystics report that "each day the angel Raziel, standing on Mount Horeb, proclaims the secrets of men to all mankind."

What we didn't know when we began this book, but what Abigrael, our recording angel, told us later, is that Raziel is its boss.

Raphael is perhaps the most endearing of all the angels, and the one most frequently depicted in Western art. His image is featured on the canvases of such masters as Botticelli, Titian, and Rembrandt. His name means "God Has Healed." Not only does he appear to be the high archangel charged with healing the Earth, but according to the Zohar, "the Earth furnishes an abode for man, whom Raphael also heals of his maladies."

Indeed, Raphael's career seems to be peppered with medical missions. He healed the pain of circumcision for Abraham as the old man had not had the procedure done when he was young. Raphael was then sent by God to cure poor Jacob's thigh after he'd been roughed up by Samael. And it's also claimed that Raphael gave Noah a much-prized "medical book" after the flood.

There's a legend that when Solomon prayed to God for aid in building the great temple in Jerusalem, Raphael personally delivered the gift of a magic ring with the power to subdue all demons. It was with this "slave labor" that the Hebrew king completed the construction.

Raphael has also been called "a guide in hell," which after all is where healing is needed the most.

· YOUR OWN FAVORITES ·

You've now met our Top Ten angels, but you probably have a few of your own favorites that we didn't include. Perhaps it was that sonorously named angel prince Sandalphon, who, some say, Elijah became after his death; or perhaps Beelzebub, if you have a taste for darkness; or Zophiel; or Zadkiel. As Abigrael reminds us, there are many, many angels. Most important to you of all these will be your own companion. However, as you come to know the angels better, and as your friendship and trust deepen, you might enjoy asking them to put you in contact with one of these high angel princes.

In our experience, at this point in time, a sincere request for contact with any member of the celestial family will not go unheeded. Ask and you shall be answered.

Angels Through the Ages

Like waves breaking through history, the presence of the angels in our lives has advanced and deepened through the celestial encounters of courageous men and women, and the slow and patient coming together of understandings that they've been able to retain and hand on to those who have followed.

Abigrael tells us that we are currently in the rising of the third great wave of angels. The first was in biblical times, when they only appeared to the occasional prophet or patriarch. The second was during the medieval period and they came mostly to the saints and seers. Wave three began to gather in the eighteenth and nineteenth centuries. It's now, in this third wave, that the angels are reaching out to each and every one of us. They are visiting poets and artists, and increasingly, people in all walks of life. They are showing up in popular novels, in films and as the stars of top-rated TV shows. All over the planet people are getting the message: The angels are ready to come into everyone's lives—all made possible by our hard-won evolution in consciousness.

The angels watch over us—that is clearly one of their functions. But they also reveal us to ourselves, gradually expanding our world views to include a much larger universe, on both the inner and outer planes. They help us to see that we aren't alone and adrift in a vast and empty cosmos, simply random collections of molecules with no rhyme, reason, or purpose.

We are all very much a part of this expanding wave of knowledge, and the story of this wave is part of our global spiritual heritage. It does not belong to the members of any particular religion, race, creed, or gender, but rather to all of humanity.

· ANGELS IN THE ANCIENT WORLD: THE FIRST WAVE ·

The foundation for our Western understanding of the angels comes from the Old Testament, which is filled with angel stories. The Hebrew patriarch Abraham and his family had numerous angelic encounters. They appeared to Hagar, the mother of his first son, Ishmael. And three unnamed angels came to Abraham and his wife Sarah to tell them that they were going to have a child. The couple was past ninety at the time, but in nine months a son, Isaac, was born to them. Later, when God told Abraham to sacrifice Isaac to Him as a test of his faith, it was another angel who grabbed his hand at the last moment to stop him. All through history, angels have been coming into our lives as the bearers of miracles.

· OLD TESTAMENT STORIES ·

Sarah and Abraham's grandson Jacob, had several angel visitors, too. They often came to Jacob in his dreams. In one he saw a ladder reaching up to Heaven, with angels going up and down. He built an altar on the spot where he'd had that dream. Another night, alone and awake, an angel of God came to him and wrestled with him. They struggled all night, and he was wounded in the thigh. In the morning, having held his ground, the angel blessed him. Haven't we all had to wrestle with our spiritual nature from time to time and felt blessed later by what seemed so difficult when we were going through it?

Angels attended the Hebrews as they wandered in the wilderness after the Exodus from Egypt. And angels also appeared to many of the ancient prophets. Two of the most profound encounters occurred to the prophets Ezekiel and Daniel, who lived almost a thousand years after the time of Jacob.

Ezekiel had been deported, along with the ruling class of his people, when the king of Babylon conquered the kingdom of Judah. Living through one of the darkest hours of his people, his words were filled with anger and hope. As with all prophets, he called upon his people to sanctify their lives. His visions of the throne of God and of the angels became models for generations of angel explorers who followed him. In probably his best-known vision, Ezekiel saw the throne of God like a chariot surrounded by cherubim with four faces and many pairs of wings. The beating of their wings could be heard from one end of Heaven to the other.

Daniel was the first prophet to call any of the angels by name. (Jacob asked the angel he wrestled with for its name, but got no answer.) It's in the Book of Daniel that we meet Michael and Gabriel by name, and hear about the guardian angels of nations for the first time. Gabriel came to Daniel to help him interpret dreams. When the king had Daniel thrown into a lions' den, an angel shut the lions' mouths. In the morning when the den was opened, Daniel emerged unharmed. In this book, too, we meet Daniel's three friends, Shadrach, Meshach, and Abednego, who were saved from the fiery furnace they'd been thrown into by an angel who appeared in the midst of the flames. Down through history the angels have saved countless women and men from what seemed like impossible situations. They bring hope in times of despair.

In the Book of Tobit in the Apocrypha, one of the later books that didn't quite make it into the Old Testament, we find the wonderful story of how Raphael, the Angel of Healing, appeared to Tobit's son Tobias, disguised as a fellow traveler. In the course of the story Raphael heals Tobit of his blindness, delivers Tobias from a demon, and restores the family to happiness. This story was first told more than two thousand years ago, and angels have been reaching out to us in healing ways ever since. How many angels in disguise do you suppose you might have encountered in your life?

· NEW TESTAMENT STORIES ·

Perhaps the most famous angel visitation of all occurred to a Jewish woman named Mary. As described in the New Testament book of Luke, the archangel Gabriel came to her to tell her that she was going to have a child. The birth of this child, Jesus, has changed the history of this world. From his birth until his death, there were angels all around him. According to another source, it was the angels who rolled away the stone that covered his empty tomb.

The last book in the New Testament is the Revelation to John. Like Ezekiel and Daniel five hundred years before, John was also living in exile from his homeland. An angel appeared to him and directed him to write to the guardians of several early Christian churches. In John's visions of the apocalypse, we find descriptions of the many different angels who are involved in the birth of a new world. John lived in challenging times—and so do we. Angelic midwives surround us, ready to assist us in the birth of the new world that John foresaw so long ago.

· ANGELS IN MEDIEVAL TIMES: THE SECOND WAVE ·

Angels appear when they're least expected. And they are equally unpredictable in what they say and do. Over thousands of years, much of the work of angels seems to have focused on keeping a spiritual equilibrium in the world of humans, and on generally preventing the worst excesses of which we are capable.

All through the early Middle Ages an intense interest in angels continued to build in both the Christian and Jewish communities. Cities and empires were rising and falling. Perhaps it was the chaos all around them that led people to try and make sense of the organization of Heaven. In medieval texts, angels were assigned to places, to days of the week, even to times of the day. Debates raged on the numbers of angels, their ranks, their functions, who their rulers were, and the most crucial question of the day: How many could dance on the head of a pin?

· ANGELS AS SERVANTS ·

In earlier times, angels had been seen as the servants of God and our guides to the Higher Realms. However, by the Middle Ages there was an increasing tendency to view angels as the potential servants of anyone who knew their names. Treatises appeared on how to invoke them and how to control them. Small wonder there was such a fascination with the fallen angels throughout this period, since people believed they could offer unlimited power to anyone who worked with them.

In A.D. 613, the archangel Gabriel once again intersected human history, this time to play his part in the creation of the religion of Islam. Gabriel began dictating the Koran to the prophet Mohammed, a task that continued until Mohammed's death in 632. This great undertaking, together with the prophet's night flight to Paradise in the company of the angels, placed the celestials at the center of yet another wide-reaching piece of social and religious engineering.

For the next few hundred years, while northern Europe was laboring through the Dark Ages that followed upon the collapse of the Roman Empire, there was a marvelous flowering of science, the arts, and the mystical tradition as the Jewish and Muslim communities came into contact with each other in Spain, North Africa, and Egypt.

· LOVING FRIENDS ·

It was the Sufis, the mystics of the Islamic world, who put a new emphasis on meeting our invisible friends. They saw the angels as the companions of our hearts, reflections of God as the Beloved. This profound perception, which was based on authentic encounters with celestials, ushered in the uplifting concept of angels as loving friends.

And in Europe, the Dark Ages gave way gradually to the sublime celestial perceptions of Gothic art. Graceful cathedrals rose to the heavens, their surfaces intricately carved with sacred images. The angels surrounding the main portal of the cathedral of Chartres, for example, express to perfection some of the beautiful and protective feelings that humankind had come to associate with the heavenly realms.

· POETS AND SAINTS ·

At the same time within the European mind, a growing emphasis on ideal beauty and romantic love began to develop. This led to the perception of feminine angels. During the Crusades, chivalric codes of behavior came together with the Sufi revelation of the angel as inner beloved. Ibn Arabi, a great Sufi poet, maintained that his major prose work, *The Meccan Revelations,* had been given to him by the Angel of Inspiration. And, Suhrawardi, author of *The Crimson Archangel* and *The Rustling of Gabriel's Wing,* has left us the richest record of angelic encounters in the Islamic world.

From the Jewish philosophers of that exhilarating time came the primary Kabbalistic text, the Zohar. It contains many methods of consciousness alteration aimed at attaining the mystical states in which it is possible to converse directly with angels. Considering the dangers involved in being accused of heresy, it's not surprising that the information is obscure and often heavily disguised.

Saint Francis of Assisi, who is best remembered for talking to birds and animals, had a meeting with a seraph at the end of his life. Modern Christian thought about the celestial realms was largely shaped by the thirteenth-century Catholic theologian, Thomas Aquinas, whose great treatise, *Summa Theologica,* contains an entire tract on angels. He visualized them as bodiless, exceeding us in number and in spiritual perfection but not quite capable of humanity's rapid continuing spiritual growth.

Contemporaneously in Germany, the Christian mystic, Meister Eckhart had several direct encounters with angels. And in Italy, the great poet Dante Alighieri left us his *Divine Comedy,* one of the most enduring accounts of a pilgrim in the heavenly domains. Like the Sufis, Dante has his beloved inspire him to poetic heights and, together with the Roman poet, Virgil, guide him through the different realms in a universe teeming with angels and demons, all the way up to the throne of God.

We can't emphasize enough the importance of the Sufi recognition of angels as beloved friends. Through their work we find a reconciliation of the conflict between those who see the angels as external beings and those who see them as aspects of our soul or Higher Self. When we realize that it is our angel, our true self, the companion of our soul, who is the one who leads us to God, it's no longer relevant whether the angel is inside or outside—the paradox has been transcended. And a new era of relationship between our two species has begun.

· A RENAISSANCE FOR ANGELS ·

It was a wonderful blossoming for our celestial friends that all the great Renaissance artists painted angels, and by no means solely because the Church of Rome may have been their patron. The artists' predilection for representing the Annunciation helped make the archangel Gabriel's appearance to the Virgin Mary among the most famous of all angelic encounters. The artist Raphael—could his name be an accident?—loved to show the celestial realms in his paintings, frequently depicting that dimension alongside normal, everyday reality. Later, the great Dutch painter, Rembrandt, was continually inspired to paint angels and many appear in his larger works, although there are touchingly beautiful glimpses of angels among his sketches, especially one of the archangel Raphael with Tobit.

· INSPIRING ART ·

Among the most sacred objects of the artistic tradition are icons, those beautiful jewel-like gesso and tempera masterpieces that are found mostly in Russian and Greek Orthodox churches. Here, the images are painted as direct invocations of saints and angels; they are artistic meditations that evoke through their visual symbolism some of the hard-earned understandings we have garnered from these beings.

As the third wave of celestial encounters begins to gather, the angels start to make themselves known to a number of artists, scientists, and saints. Earlier, Theresa of Avila, a Spanish nun, described an angel piercing her heart with a spear that filled her with the love of God. Her account inspired many works of art in this period.

· INSPIRING WRITING ·

Less gory, perhaps, are the angelic visions of the German Protestant mystic, Jacob Boehme. And, the seminal investigations into the celestial realms of two Jewish sages, Moses Cordovero and Isaac Luria, contributed richly to the Kabbalah. Luria, for instance, was one of the first to point out the significant role we humans have in restoring the balance of goodness in the world.

In England, poet John Milton took on the formidable task of attempting to unravel the truth of the fallen angels and their impact on human destiny. His life's work gave us the epics *Paradise Lost* and *Paradise Regained.*

A century later in Sweden, the eminent scientist Emanuel Swedenborg had an ongoing series of visionary encounters with the celestial realms from 1747 to his death in 1772. That he was remarkably in tune was borne out by a number of incidents in his life in which he accurately predicted events, such as fires, that happened many miles away.

He wrote voluminously about his experiences with angels and had a profound influence on many great thinkers of his time, including the English mystic, poet, and painter William Blake, who left us a heritage of some of the most passionately involved angels ever depicted.

· POPULAR IMAGES ·

Possibly the most widely known images of angels to have emerged from the last few hundred years—the ones most of us think of when we conjure up the immediate representation of an angel—spring from the etchings of the French illustrator, Gustave Doré. Who can forget his magnificent, brooding illustrations for Dante's

Divine Comedy? Demons in the pits of hell, and the heavenly host—angels coiling off into infinity!

From around 1850 to the turn of the century, in an attempt to counter what was seen as the onrushing specter of industrial materialism, the Pre-Raphaelite (there's that name again!) painters focused a good deal of their attention on the subtle realms. Artistically, in terms of what moves a fine artist to produce relevant and authentic work, it was a last gasp. Angels were soon almost entirely eclipsed by the sparkling new world of technology as the potent symbol of the modern age. And yet, although we shifted our attention away from them at this point, the angels by no means disappeared.

In fact, they're still appearing all over the place. Their images can be found in virtually all the cities and towns of the Western world: in railway stations, on war memorials, on murals and friezes in libraries, on museum facades, hospitals, movie theaters, and department stores. We see them dressed in bronze in the middle of fountains, floating on the domes and frescos of our town halls, and painted on the walls of the corridors of power. Look around you and you'll see them wherever you point your head.

· ANGELS IN MODERN TIMES ·

The United States was not to be excluded from angelic intervention. The Mormon Church of the Latter-day Saints was founded, as we have seen, by Joseph Smith after a visitation by the angel Moroni. And in the 1840s and 1850s, there was a rush of spiritual activity in the Shaker communities started by Mother Ann Lee. People in the Shaker sect were receiving words and seeing visions of the angels, many of which have been preserved and form an important branch of angel wisdom.

Slightly later, in Europe, the German poet Rainer Maria Rilke flourished as an artist and is one of the few examples of writers of that time working together with angels as muses. A very inspiring example, too!

· REBIRTH OF INTEREST ·

The late part of the last century and the early twentieth century in both America and Europe saw a lively rebirth of interest in transcendent matters, although the bias was more toward the psychic than the spiritual. Both Madame Helena Petrovna Blavatsky, the founder of Theosophy, and the German mystic, Rudolf Steiner, wrote extensively on angels and argued the importance of their place in human affairs. Steiner's celestial order picked up the original nine angelic orders, and then added a tenth evolving group—humanity. There was also a revival of interest in angels in the Muslim world, best exemplified by the luminous books of Henry Corbin.

In the United States again, from 1905 to 1935, there came one of the most remarkable angelic revelations to date. Transmitted largely through the mouth of a sleeping man, *The Urantia Book* is a massive compendium of information on God, the universe, and the angels and their work. It offers a view of life on our planet from the perspective of a universe filled with millions of inhabited worlds, and trillions of angels.

· ANGELS IN WORLD WAR II ·

One of the most powerful and moving angelic encounters of the last half century occurred in Hungary between 1943 and 1944. Four artist friends, living in Budapest under the shadow of Nazi invaders, suddenly found the angels speaking through one of them while she was in a light trance. The communications continued for over a year, giving both practical and spiritual counsel on how to deal with the oncoming disasters as well as transmitting some of the most pertinent and poignant insights from the angelic realms that we possess.

Gitta Mallasz, the only one of the four artists who survived the war, went on to record the words of the celestials in the marvelous book *Talking with Angels,* which conveys beautifully the depth and impact of the angels' brilliant wisdom.

"Could anything be more natural than our talking together?" the angels ask the four artists in a moment of cosmic complicity. Collectively our new relationship with this realm becomes gradually but progressively more intimate and well formed. Our free choice is always scrupulously observed, but there is little doubt that our two species are drawing nearer than ever to each other as the end of this century approaches.

· ANGELS IN POPULAR CULTURE: THE THIRD WAVE ·

Not only are the angels speaking to all those who can silence their minds enough to hear them, but our perception of the celestials has also gone beyond the sole context of religion. With the advent of modern communications, they have made their presence felt in the entertainment industry as well.

· IN MUSIC ·

Music has been a major access point for the angels to make their presence felt in twentieth-century popular global culture. Certain kinds of music can create transcendent states of consciousness and when this occurs, it is surely a source of great mutual joy to both angels and humans. From the 1950s onward, there is a repetitive theme of celestials in seemingly endless ribbons of "teen-angels" and "Oh—Oh—angel—babe!" lyrics in songs like "Earth Angel," "Angel Eyes," "Johnny Angel,"

"I'm Living Right Next Door to an Angel," "Where Angels Fear to Tread," and of course, "You Are My Special Angel."

Profane though these pop songs may sound, they are in fact following in a venerable tradition and can be traced directly back to the medieval Sufi masters and mystics who first articulated the angel as the beloved. From this we can see how a revolutionary idea, if it's aligned with higher truth, can transmute itself into our everyday thinking.

· IN MOVIES ·

While the angels have figured less prominently in the fine arts through the course of the twentieth century, they have always made a good showing in motion pictures through such films as *Angel on My Shoulder, The Bishop's Wife, The Milagro Beanfield War,* and that perennial favorite, *It's a Wonderful Life.* Who can ever forget "Every-time a bell rings an angel gets his wings"? Is there a more famous angel in American popular culture than Clarence?

Among the plethora of recent movies featuring angels is *Wings of Desire,* by German director Wim Wenders. This film is a soul-stirring exploration of the nature of angels and what they might experience in their lives and missions. The yearning that Wenders attributes to his supercorporeal angels for the touch of a hand, the smell of the wind, a cigarette, and a cup of coffee ("Together . . . fantastic!") is somehow deeply familiar. Possibly it has something to do with the way we ourselves were drawn into matter.

Wenders depicts with great delicacy the multidimensional quality of angelic reality—its layers of sound and visual images interpenetrating each other to form a vast patina of sensual information. The fact that films can communicate this degree of charm and complexity, perhaps more effectively than painting or sculpture, might explain why the angels are now using this medium to reach out to us.

· IN TV AND BOOKS ·

The angels also seem to be making something of a comeback through the 1980s and early 1990s in the popular marketplace with a well-rated TV series, *Highway to Heaven,* the hero of which is an angel, and with several popular novels, including Andrew Greeley's splendid adventure, *Angel Fire.* Found in the paperback rack at a local supermarket, this book contains accurate and advanced information about guardian angels but puts it all in a way that is easy to digest and a pleasure to read.

· IN PERSONAL ENCOUNTERS ·

The archangel Raphael has recently been making himself heard through the crystal clear writings of Ken Carey. *Starseed Transmissions, Starseed 2000,* and *The Return of the Bird Tribes* are modern masterpieces of angelic vision. In a similar vein, contemporary American philosopher David Spangler continues to work with angels, as does his Findhorn colleague, Dorothy Maclean, who recorded her experiences in *To Hear the Angels Sing.*

Sophy Burnham, author of *The Book of Angels,* received many thousands of letters from people all over the country in response to her book. In all walks of life, in small towns and big cities, their lives had been touched by the angels, and they wanted to tell their own stories. *Angel Letters,* the sequel to her first book, contains many of these personal accounts.

One surprised reaction the three of us had when we started becoming more involved with the angels and their reality was just how much there is going on around us about them. We noticed billboards sporting our celestial friends beaming down at us; lyrics, ads, TV, and jingles dropped references to our unseen companions with astonishing regularity. Cab drivers named Angelo turned up with delightful frequency and at invariably significant moments. And on and on.

Wherever we went, we heard the same tales, from countless people. It isn't just happening to us—or to you. The angels are reaching out to everyone, in every way they can, and to a degree that they never have before.

· GUARDIAN ANGELS ·

The relationship between humans and angels is, by nature, very intimate. The angels have shown us that we humans are that part of the Creator sent furthest into the density of matter. It is the angels' recognition of the Creator within us that so deeply motivates them to help us in our human lives.

A Dutch physician, H. C. Moolenburgh, became interested in angels after hearing so many of his patients talk about them, and has written of his understandings in *A Handbook of Angels.* He sees humans like a team of deep-sea divers, hunting for lost treasures, connected to the surface by only a few air hoses and by radio. The angels are the surface crew, working on board ship to make sure that we remain safe.

"We have even received," he writes, "detailed instructions of the kind of treasure we should be collecting, that it is to be of the type that can be taken back up. And probably we are pulled up every night so as to take a breather, and at our death we are pulled up permanently."

How often do we forget that we have all the help in the world? Yet in order to evolve, we have needed to "forget." If not, we would have remained, in Moolenburgh's words, "dependent children, overwhelmed by the grandeur of our elders."

"No single created thing is without its own personal protection," says Abigrael—

and the angels who protect and counsel us stand ready at the air hoses and radios.

Everyone has guardian angels up on deck. And as we seek to live the life and follow the ways of being that are most aligned with God and our higher destiny, our angels are drawn more closely to guide and counsel us.

The angels themselves tell us that the moment one of us makes the conscious decision to dedicate his or her life to our Beloved, that person's guardian angels then dedicate themselves fully to the human being concerned.

This book was written to help you meet your guardian angel—your companion angel. The moment you make contact—you have earned your wings.

CHAPTER 3

How We Met Our Angels

· INTRODUCTION ·

As you have probably gathered from reading this far, there is a larger plan at work here. A great orchestration. The angels are opening to us as never before. Something profound is on the move. And each one of us, to the precise extent that we can sustain the vision, is part of this great plan.

The angels say that the worst is over—the tide has turned. But it will take time for this grand vision to be fully realized in our material reality. All is in place for the coming transformation. We will look back and wonder how it all happened. How did we slip so gracefully and smoothly into a new era of light and life where spirit and matter are united?

We are doing it, of course, with the help, guidance, and shared wisdom of our angels. And with their love, and that of the Creator of us all.

The supremely easy and fluid way that the three of us came together to write this book, for instance, was a fine example of angelic coordination. It all just slid into place.

After conducting group meditations together for about a year, Alma and Timothy began teaching people to talk with their angels. They first got the idea to write a book on the subject in 1986 at an "Opening to the Angels" workshop they were leading in Philadelphia. At the end of a joyful gathering, one of the participants said, "You know, you really ought to write a book about this. You could call it"—he paused, and it seemed as if the words came from somewhere else—*"Ask Your Angels."*

At about the same time, Andrew was teaming up with the angels on his own, teaching individuals to open to these delightful beings in his counseling and healing work.

Timothy and Andrew met on the eighth day of the eighth month of 1988, at a celebration in New York City held at the Sacred Circle in Central Park. There was an immediate mutual recognition. They spent the next few hours enthusiastically sharing their angel experiences and the extraordinary impact the celestials were having on their lives. A few days later, Timothy introduced his partner, Alma, to Andrew and the three of us settled into a new friendship that was soon to become a collaboration.

Meanwhile, unbeknownst to us, the angels were also making themselves felt in the heart of the world's largest publishing company. Not long after we three met, Andrew, who'd already published a book of stories, *little pictures,* with Ballantine Books, was sitting in the office of Cheryl Woodruff, editor of its meditation, self-help, and recovery books. She'd just received a proposal for a book on angels in history, and although it wasn't right for her, it sparked an idea.

"I want a book that gives the reader concrete tools for working with angels," she told Andrew.

"I've just met a very interesting man who's already written a book with angels in it," he replied.

Cheryl knew about Timothy's book, *Dolphins* Extraterrestrials* Angels,* and asked Andrew to speak to him about her idea.

The time was right. Angel time. Timothy told Andrew that he and Alma were already collecting material for such a book. One thing led smoothly to another. Based on his own angelic and writing experiences, Andrew was asked to join the team. From the ease of it, we concluded that once again, albeit unwittingly, we'd participated in a celestially assisted miracle of coordination.

But the angels weren't through yet.

Several weeks later, Cheryl was in the office of Susan Petersen, president of Ballantine Books.

"What are you working on that's good?" Susan asked.

Cheryl replied: "I've just received a proposal for a book called *Ask Your Angels.* It teaches people how to talk with them."

"Sounds terrific," Susan said. "Buy it."

Within two weeks, we signed the contract. Considering the number of proposals Ballantine receives each day, and the intricate channels through which they normally have to go before acceptance, we could only assume that the angels' wings were in this one, too.

We were later told that at a Ballantine Books conference to introduce Sophy Burnham's *Book of Angels,* there were large, three-dimensional angels decorating the meeting room. As requested by Susan Petersen, they were all floating airily over the heads of the assembled sales reps.

As Susan told the group: "Ballantine is on the side of the angels." And she went on to say that every day she receives letters from readers telling her how deeply a particular book has touched them, or helped them get through a rough patch in their lives.

"Ballantine isn't only interested in books making money," she said. "We want books that make a difference in people's lives."

Sounds like an angel to us.

You'll notice, no doubt, from our personal stories that follow, that we are very different people, with very different perspectives on our angelic friends. If each of us had written this book ourselves, three totally different books would have emerged. But the angels wanted it this way—through the three of us they demonstrate that mutual collaboration, not individual struggle, is the new way. Not only did the angels arrange all this, but if it hadn't been for their patient and skillful ministrations we would never have been able to reconcile our strongly held and often divergent views!

As you read our stories and get to know us, you will see that there is no one correct way to experience angels. The most important thing is for you to find your own way. May our experiences give you some handholds as you start climbing the heights of your own limitless potential.

· HOW I MET MY ANGEL, AND HOW WE WORK TOGETHER ·
Alma

When I look at the clear, compassionate counsel that my angel consistently gives to me, it seems madness, or stupidity, to have resisted meeting and listening to her for as long as I did. But at the time we met, I was a lot more stubborn than I am now, and I was more interested in talking than listening. It took an act of God to arrange it.

Mystical and supernatural occurrences frequently coincide with times of great personal stress. When all normal resources and means have been exhausted, help arrives from another sector. Such was the case for me in the third week of October 1985. At the time, I was a working mother with three kids to look after. Very down-to-earth. I ran my businesses out of my home. I had a psychotherapy practice, taught classes in self-improvement, and had a floatation tank that I rented out by the hour.

Two weeks earlier, a leak in the tank had swamped my downstairs neighbor with 150 gallons of water in which 800 pounds of Epsom salts had been dissolved. The salty water had drenched a Persian carpet that had been given to him by the Shah of Iran and ruined a collection of leather-bound books that lined the walls of his study directly below me. It was a nightmare. The flood put me out of a thriving business I'd enjoyed for five years—introducing people to the benefits of floating weightless in a lightproof, soundproof chamber. Financially, it was a disaster. And emotionally—I was already in rough shape. Two of my children were leaving home and there was tension and upset in the family. As you can imagine, the combination of all these pressures created enormous pushes and pulls on my psyche.

As is frequently the case when events or issues come up that we do not understand or cannot deal with, after the deluge I got physically sick and had to go to bed. This meant I couldn't cover my dismay at a life that appeared to be falling apart with my usual daily activities—seeing clients and teaching classes in healing. Bedded with the flu, I had no energy to do anything, except to listlessly leaf through some old notebooks I'd kept. In them, I'd recorded my experiences at many of the five dozen workshops I'd attended, in determined (if some would say unsuccessful) efforts to raise my consciousness.

At one workshop, eight years earlier, I'd been asked to visualize an ideal space in which I could create anything I wanted. I was told that two "guides" would appear, and I was to notice their appearances and ask their names. My carefully kept notes revealed that I had dutifully visualized a beautiful environment and waited for the arrival of the guides. In flounced a man in purple tights and an Elizabethan doublet, who announced himself as Greg. Right on his heels appeared a woman with a pompadour and snood, wearing a plaid jacket with shoulder pads, reminiscent of the 1940s, who said her name was Eleanor.

I recalled thinking disdainfully that Eleanor was a rather ordinary name for a guide, and the lady looked about thirty years behind the times, to boot. As for the guy in the purple tights . . . I wanted no part of either one of them. I promptly dismissed them both and put them out of my mind.

As I was rereading these notes, Timothy came into the room, bearing a steaming cup of herbal tea. For months, he'd been urging me to make contact with my angel. For months, I'd been resisting like crazy. As a child, I hadn't been brought up with the idea of guardian angels, and I simply didn't believe I had one, although as an adult, explorations in metaphysical realms had opened me to the possibility of contact from other dimensions. Spirit guides, sure. Indian medicine men and Tibetan monks, no problem. Angels? No way.

Setting the tea down, Timothy looked up over my right shoulder. "Your angel is here, right now. I sense its presence. Just ask for its name," he urged.

I glowered at him and grumpily replied: "If you're so smart, you ask for its name."

He closed his eyes and within a few moments murmured: Elena (accent on *el*).

"No!" I said, scarcely believing my ears. Then I told him how I'd rejected the Eleanor who'd appeared eight years previously, because I didn't like her name. "And Elena sounds just like it!" I obstinately refused to accept this new version.

"Okay, okay, then you do it," Timothy insisted, explaining, when I protested that I didn't know how, that all I had to do was close my eyes and ask. To prove how wrong he was, and that it didn't work, I snapped my eyes shut. "What's the name of my angel?" I demanded. Instantly, on the inside of my forehead three capital letters appeared: *L N O.*

I stopped struggling. I gave in. I acknowledged her presence. At Timothy's persistent prompting, I picked up a pen to write down whatever message she might have for me. The first thing she told me was something that I didn't want to hear:

"Timothy has been called in to clear you of corruption and fear and the job is not easy or nice."

Corruption? Fear? Who, me? Forget it! Just forget the whole thing, I'm not playing. LNO went on, uncannily catching my thought:

"This is not a game you and Timothy are playing. Your resistance, which comes from what you perceive as his patronizing you and making you wrong, is there because you have not completely rid yourself of false, negative beliefs about yourself and your worth."

The anger that welled in me made my hand shake as I continued to write the words that I heard within me. Relentless, compassionate, LNO concluded:

"The balancing of ego that Timothy has spoken with you about is vital to the integration and understanding of your Godness. It must be done in the physical realm. This means stripping away, divesting yourself of human frailties, leaving the best human qualities—devotion, courage, truth—intact."

LNO had arrived. I marked the event with a temper tantrum.

On a calmer occasion, a year later, LNO reminded me gently: "No one ever thanks you for information they don't want to receive."

I have since learned to thank LNO—and my other angels—for *all* their interventions and guidance, whether I like them or not! In the weeks that followed, LNO's presence encouraged me to view the loss of my floatation tank business not as a disaster, but as an act of God. The flood forced me to open myself to new possibilities, one of which led to the development of the "Opening to the Angels" workshops that Timothy and I began to offer two months later.

Nowadays, LNO will sometimes pipe in whether or not I call on her, but she never interferes or meddles. She just shows up when I really need her. Not long ago, I was talking to some friends, rattling on and on, enchanted by the sound of my own voice, when I noticed the glazed expressions on their faces. I had that sinking feeling you get when you know you're being boring, but you don't know what to do about it, so I just kept on babbling. Suddenly, I heard a rather loud voice in my head: "It's never too late to shut up!" I stopped in midsentence, which nobody seemed to mind at all. Later, LNO, who tends to be terse, explained it to me. "Silence is always appropriate," she said evenly. "Silence is the refuge of the wise."

As I grew to know LNO and to respect and appreciate her wise counsel, her

influence became more and more important to me, first, personally, and then gradually in my psychotherapy practice, too. LNO is now a valuable colleague and trusted friend. When I work with a client, I call upon her and invoke the presence of the other person's guardian angel, too, to align the body, mind, and emotions. LNO assists by helping me to get my ego, my little mind, out of the way. When I feel her presence or hear her voice, I move into Higher Self. Joining in her vibration prepares me to be a clear channel for cosmic intelligence. It enables me to become a loving vessel that can facilitate the healing that God does with those willing and ready to be healed.

My angel enhances this process by helping me to release any of the ego-centered fears that can arise in such a situation—will I know what to do? What to say? Using LNO as a lens through which I focus my own energies and intentions helps me shift away from concern about my personal performance to confidence that God knows what S/He is doing! LNO tells me that as a spiritual healer, I do the work, but the results are up to God.

In the meditation and prayer that precedes my work with another, I ask to be a perfect channel for God's healing light and grace. I ask that the client and I be allowed to unite our healing energy. I can feel when this occurs; it means entering an altered state of consciousness. The brain-wave frequency shifts from beta (normal waking consciousness) to alpha, and sometimes theta, which characterize meditative and trance states. The client's consciousness shifts, too, so we are resonating on the same frequency.

In this state, I frequently hear the responses of my client's angel before he or she does. It comes in words that I hear, just as I hear the voice of my angel in words. Usually within a few seconds, or less than a minute, the client speaks the words that I heard. I have found this to be a much more effective way of serving. When people open to their angels, they become empowered to access the information they need on their own—making connection with their own highest source.

In sessions, LNO also works with me in a number of other ways. First, through specific directions, such as "link the Third Eye and the Heart chakras," or "bring energy to the throat," which now come in as *knowings*. By this I mean I suddenly know, without thinking; it's a heightening of my intuitive faculties. There is a certainty that bypasses my conscious mind. Next, in collaboration with my client's angel, LNO gives me integrative insights. These knowings and insights allow me to recognize the origins of certain behavior patterns, the true need that these patterns were developed to meet, and the healthy new way in which these needs might now be met, so the outmoded behavior can be released.

On other occasions, LNO works with the guardians of my clients to give me written transmissions on the spiritual and emotional nature of their problems. Flawlessly accurate and deeply penetrating, this information sometimes starts coming in unbidden—usually when I'm at a complete loss!

Here are a few excerpts from LNO's casebook. You'll notice that I dialogue with her, as she goes on:

"Melody" is twenty-five and comes from Missouri. She found her way to New York City when she was eighteen and has been working for families ever since as a live-in baby-sitter. She loves kids and she loves her job; she came to me because she had a bad back pain. I asked LNO about its source.

LNO: It is meant to hold her back—to keep her from cutting loose and traveling freely. She is a being who does not carry her own emotional baggage—she has none—but has adopted some to better fit into the world around her. Melody is actually very free of sentiment and attachments, but this is at such odds with the world and people around her that she has picked some up, to keep her from the horror she feels at her sense of alien-ness and aloneness.

Melody's back—the sensation of the burning log she experienced during the session—refers to a burning at the stake that her soul once experienced, in another body at another time. She was burned for her heretical views, views that were at odds with her community. She was then, as now, out of step with those around her, ahead of her time, more progressed than her contemporaries. In this life, too, she has entered a family whose consciousness is at a lower level than her own. Their condition has held her *back* because she did not feel that it was acceptable to surpass them.

Being in human form, Melody is prey to human feelings, but these affect her differently than they do others. She has not yet come into her own sexuality, and this retardation is based on two factors. First, fear of the level of possession that occurs in sexual relationships, for Melody is a free spirit who wishes to travel widely and without hindrance. Secondly, a disinclination to involve herself physically, for in her previous incarnations she has more frequently evolved her mind and spirit.

To integrate fully as a human in this lifetime, Melody needs to engage on the more human levels of emotions and physical experiences. She is still holding these back, and needs to be encouraged to open to these.

LNO, thank you. This feels a bit longer than I had in mind. . . .

LNO: In that case, Dear One, ask briefer questions.

Melody and I have been working together for almost a year, on an as-needed basis. In that time, she's traveled to Hong Kong, Europe, and the Bahamas and last week, she left for a month in New Zealand. She's become much more social and outgoing, has started to date, and is writing a book about her experiences as a New York nanny.

"Mark," a brilliant young writer, came to me because he suffered from bouts of depression, sometimes lasting for months. When he hit the pits, he couldn't write, stopped seeing friends, and to ease his gnawing pain, he'd eat himself into oblivion. When he arrived at my office for the initial consultation, he was fifty pounds overweight and scared stiff. He told me he was twenty-seven years old and had been a *wunderkind,* publishing a novel at nineteen that had been highly acclaimed and later adapted as a screenplay. Although he had made quite a sensation in the literary world when he was in his early twenties, he hadn't published anything in years. His talent had dried up, he told me, his love life was nil, and he was lonely.

It was clear that the depression was blanketing his fears, but after months of weekly sessions, he was as frightened as ever, and I couldn't figure out why. So I asked LNO why Mark was holding onto his fear and what that fear was about. Before she replied, she chided me: "This is a briefer question?" Then went on:

LNO: The fear Mark has is one he shares with many. He fears that he is not loved, and that without love he will die. He holds onto his fear because he is afraid to face it—and to face the fact that he has not been loving with himself. He wants and demands love from others, but will not give it to himself unless he meets his own requirements for love, which are based on achievement and acclaim.

By focusing on his fearfulness he avoids that which he fears. He has not yet been willing to come to terms with his own lack of self-love, his own self-repudiation. When Mark accepts that he is alone, and sufficient unto himself, he will begin to truly connect with All. He needs to know that this does not mean that he must spend the rest of his life alone, only that until he values himself as he is, without measuring his merit by his accomplishments or lovers, he cannot happily be with another.

LNO, thank you. This feels absolutely accurate and brief, too!

> LNO: Dear One, we are pleased that you are pleased and amused that you are surprised!

I made a copy of the transmission, without my interactive notes, and gave it to Mark, who had expressed interest in anything that LNO might have to say. It was six months before I heard a peep out of him again.

"You know that message that you gave me from your angel?" said Mark on the phone. "Well, I just reread it."

"Yes?" I replied, somewhat warily.

"Everything she said is true. I wasn't ready to hear it at the time, but it makes a lot of sense now," Mark said. "I'd like to come back and do some work."

In the course of the next few sessions, I helped Mark meet his guardian angel. Since then, he's lost thirty-five pounds. He's writing again, working on his third novel, and has joined the faculty of a university, teaching courses on creative writing. He loves teaching, and his students adore him. His writing is flowing. The last time we talked he was on his way to the airport to pick up his lover.

LNO deals with real-life issues and cuts close to the bone. One of my clients, "Gail," calls her a "kick-ass angel." Yet her messages always begin and end with encouragement, and she reminds us of the choices we have:

> LNO: Be at peace in your heart, although it is troubled now, and know that all moves toward the great healing. The crunch is taking place all around you. These are challenging times. Every soul is being tested and tried. You can

choose to reflect difficulty or you can choose to use humor and courage to lighten your own burden and those of the ones around you.

To create upliftment, your own and others, to be in the truth, in simplicity and humility, these can be your watchwords now. To be gentle, kind, loving, and truthful. To refrain from complaining or emphasizing the difficulty. To bless instead of curse. Know that you are truly loved and blessed. Give thanks for your blessings. Share them and your light with others.

Even after LNO had become an established part of my life, I had my moments of doubt. All of what she was saying made sense, but I couldn't help wondering whether it wasn't just a smarter part of myself that was talking. Finally, I asked and this is what LNO replied:

LNO: You can call these words your own thoughts, and they are, in the sense that you, Alma Daniel, selected the words and the arrangement of those words. We do not communicate actually with words, but with vibrations, emanations. You pick up these emanations and put them into a coherence you call thoughts. This is why angelic transmissions translated into words will sound different from person to person.

It is a connecting and inspiring function that we perform when we communicate with you. Within each human is the divine spark, the God That Is. Through the soul's descent into physical matter, that spark becomes covered over, hidden, yet it remains within each human individual—and indeed within each living thing. Our function is to ignite the spark within, to fill you not with "our" thoughts, but to connect you with the knowingness that you already possess. You forget. Humans forget because the descent into matter lowers consciousness and brings about forgetfulness. Gravity pulls on you in more ways than one, not the least of which is that you sometimes forget levity. We come to inspire you with light, with lightness, and with laughter, and to remind you of what the God in you already knows.

Being a how-to person at heart, I asked her how she did this.

LNO: In a state of openness, when your normal limitations and earthly concerns have been suspended—through love, or a deep sense of peace—you open the channels, or circuits, to your own wisdom. Our function is to connect you with these knowings, some of which have been so deeply buried that when they come up you attribute them to some other. There is no other. You and God are It!

Frequencies, wave forms, vibrations, which are close to what humans experience as feelings, are the means through which we do this. Because we are not in physical form, we do not even have "thoughts." We are the messengers of God's will and you humans are the living examples of it. You are the manifestation of God's "thought" or will.

While I relate very personally to LNO, whom I consider to be my guardian angel as well as an aspect of my Higher Self, I am aware of help from many other celestials who assist in different ways—facilitating my travel through the city, directing my actions in a tax audit, and so forth. These legions of helpers, I am told by LNO, come to serve us when we have consciously chosen a path of Light, consciously chosen to serve God and assist our brothers and sisters. When this choice is made, many angels are deployed to help.

When I ask for angelic protection (especially when I'm riding my bicycle in New York City traffic), I know that I am evoking a higher level of awareness than I can generate alone. It sharpens my extrasensory powers. Asking my angels for help opens me to receiving the bounty of the universe; it frees my imagination from limitations and allows the best, the brightest, the highest to flow.

LNO is always with me, and to the degree that I am aware of her and enter into her realm, my own life becomes smoother, easier, more flowing. When things don't go "my way" she has taught me to become alert instead of angry, to recognize that the universe is telling me something isn't working, that I'm not clear or my way would be untroubled. She instructs me to look at my own part in the confusion, so I can discover a remedy for the situation. LNO connects me to my God-nature, but she also continually refers me back to myself and my own actions, helps me to see my responsibility in what the Beloved and I have created. She impels me to examine my impeccability; gently allows me to see where selfishness or self-concern has blunted my perception.

> LNO: The remedy for selfishness is service. The remedy for arrogance is humility. The remedy for confusion is the clarity earned by living your code of values and speaking of it with others. Truth, kindness, and affirming the positive instead of emphasizing the negative are some of the values that will help you to come back into grace.

My heavenly helper gets me back in line when I'm on an ego trip:

> LNO: When you're strong, you don't have to be pushy. Insecure people overdo. Modesty comes when you recognize and reclaim your true power, which is love.

Or when I'm feeling sorry for myself:

> LNO: This is not a time for self-pity, but is an excellent time for you to observe when self-pity crops up. Trace it, embrace it, and face it. Then let it go.

And when I'm going through the pangs of being human:

LNO: Jealousy, like envy, is a disqualification of the self. Individuals who are unconditional in their love for themselves do not experience jealousy because they are not threatened by love. Love is not threatening. Lack is. Lack of love comes from insufficient love for self.

Whenever I run into a snag, or am downhearted, I head for my computer and slip LNO's disk into the drive. And when I'm ecstatic, delighted with the events in my life, I write her a little thank-you note. Although I used to put her messages on any old floppy disk I had handy, she made it clear that she was to have her very own.

In the years since we've been talking, LNO has moved from the personal "I" to "We" when she speaks. I am told that in addition to being my very own companion, she is a voice in a collective of angelic guardians whose function is to connect individuals to their Higher Selves.

While I have never seen her with my eyes or spirit vision, I feel her presence, and the presence of other angels when groups gather, as an opening of my heart. Sometimes the feeling of love and acceptance is so palpable, so tender, that tears fill my eyes.

A few years ago, when I was going through a lot of sadness and regret about the end of my partnership with Timothy, I turned to LNO to help me assuage the feelings. Here is what she said:

LNO: Sadness is a note in the scale of joy. Regret has to do with Then. It is out of time. Because regret is invariably about something that you are powerless to affect, you hold on to it, as if by grasping, holding, you could change what you cannot. You must accept that which you cannot change. You may not like it, but you must accept it. Once you have accepted it, you can release it. If you do not, you remain in regret.

Dear One, look at all the things that you regret. You cannot change any of them, and every time you think about them, it gives you pain. Can you not learn to truly live in the moment? To erase all personal history? To be with what is right now? At this very moment, isn't your life in perfect peace, perfect order? Isn't your health perfect? What more do you require for happiness, for joy?

Remaining in regret disempowers and debilitates. Like a drop of lemon in a cup of cream, it curdles the life and makes it unpalatable.

Remaining in regret cripples or impairs your ability to take positive actions now, thus depriving you of potential sources of self-esteem.

Regret is a form of self-criticism that gains energy from other people's agreement, or sympathy. As others feel sorry for you in your regret, they encourage you to believe in the power of what was.

When will you be joyful? What are your conditions for feeling joy? What about Now?

I was getting fidgety. Yes, yes, I knew all that. What was I supposed to *do* about it? I typed: "LNO, thank you. I could use some more specifics, please." Patient and direct as always, she said:

LNO: Dear One, let us take this from the point of completion. When something is complete, it is finished. People dread completion because it is synonymous with death. Since they have not coped or dealt with fear of death—which is actually a belief in mortality—they avoid it. People avoid completion for other reasons as well, such as the need to be perfect, fear of criticism, etc.

When you have cooked an egg, you cannot cook it again. It is cooked. So with life. When something is done, it is over. What is the point of holding on to the past, to remembering sad or unhappy events except to punish the self?

What is required for you to come into this moment, to dwell in the now, is a vigilance and discipline that allows you consciously to recognize and release all the old pulls on your energy and attention. All that is material passes into the plenum, into the unmanifest. What you have to hold onto are the values and the inspiration of divine Light and Love.

"LNO, this is very helpful," I typed, "but I'm not there yet."

LNO: Dear One, all of the information is contained here. It is up to you to decide whether or not you're ready to be free, really free. This pertains to your relationship as well as your activities in the world. You are limitless, if you choose that! Your freedom comes from letting go. Freedom means empowerment to be, do, go, feel, whatever your heart tells you. Only you have kept yourself from having this freedom out of some misunderstanding of what your responsibilities really are. Your responsibilities are to your Self. Serve that truly, fully, and you serve All.

By this time, she'd gotten through to me. "LNO," I typed, "I thank you." It took several weeks of mulling her words and using every releasing process I knew before I finally let go. Recently, in the course of revising this book, Timothy and I met up again. It was good to see him and, with Andrew, we spent many days working closely together. We acknowledged the love that we had for each other, and parted warmly—with no regrets.

Having LNO at my side makes an enormous difference in my life. It's not that problems don't crop up anymore, just that I've learned to see them differently, not as bad luck or punishment, but as challenges that will allow me to grow. I just have to remember to ask my angel for help. And even when I forget, make what appears to be the wrong choice, or go against my inner knowing and fall flat on my face, there's always some consolation, some deeper insight that accompanies my fiasco. I'm convinced this is my angel's way of saying, "Never mind, you are still loved. There'll be another chance to make it right."

When LNO speaks, she speaks not just to me, but to all who have the heart to listen. If these words resonate with you, take them as your very own, a gift to you from me and LNO:

LNO: Stop judging yourself.

Let go.

Remember who you Are.

You're doing the best you can. Be satisfied that at any given moment, your consciousness is as high as you are capable.

What holds humans in limitation and restriction is attachment to the past, preference for the future, and avoidance of the now. Do you wish to live a more enlightened life? Come into this moment. Be present.

Wake up to your own Divine Light. Delight in that. By acknowledging your light, watch it grow. Let your delight in your Divine Self ignite the light within others.

Go in peace and grow in knowing who you are.

· HOW THE ANGELS BURST INTO MY LIFE ·
Timothy

By the time I knew my own mind I thought of myself as an atheist. I'd have been shocked to my core to think then that I might ever believe what I now know to be true. Perhaps as a consequence of my total rejection of anything transcendental, when my first spiritual encounters occurred in my mid-twenties, they were amazingly powerful and quite overwhelming. They utterly changed my life, turning me back toward God and deepening my values and my goals. But I didn't meet or experience anything remotely angelic or angel-like until I died.

Somewhat dramatic, but the Near Death Experience (NDE) I had in 1973 irrevocably means that to me. Back then I didn't know an NDE was a relatively common experience—apparently something in the order of twenty million Americans have had one. This was before the writings of Raymond Moody, Jr., and Elisabeth Kübler-Ross made NDEs familiar. Yet I knew I'd died. And I knew I'd also been given a choice to come back to my earthly life. Here's how it happened.

For some years, I'd been the director of a nondenominational religious organization based in the United States and headquartered in New York City. For all intents and purposes, I lived the life of a monk, but very much within the cut and thrust of everyday life. It was an extremely challenging task, endeavoring to maintain an absurdly large and expensive building in midtown Manhattan and attempting to encourage a group of about fifty wilting and depressed young people to make enough money to support it.

One evening, having been exhausted and sick for weeks, I collapsed. My body would go no further. A case of walking pneumonia was filling my lungs with phlegm, and then my back, weakened from a fall in childhood, simply gave out. I dragged myself back to the house we'd rented on East 49th Street and drew myself a bath, hoping the heat would ease my pain.

Within moments of stretching out in the bath, I found myself, to my utter astonishment, hovering somewhere out in space, my body clearly visible in the tub far down below me. This was no daydream or fantasy. It was as real as the desk at which I'm now sitting—more real perhaps—since whatever it was that was happening to me was so totally unexpected. For once, I really paid attention!

The scene changed to a beautiful valley, again as real and as solid as any landscape I've seen in my travels. A monorail car was speeding silently down toward me on a single, shining curve of metal. Then, quite mysteriously, from hovering over the valley, I found myself inside the monorail cabin together with nine or ten other people. I can see them now in my mind's eye; opposite me sat an old black man playing a trumpet with great beauty. At that moment I knew we were all dying at the same time. A voice came to me over what I took to be a speaker system, although it may well have spoken directly into my mind. It was very lucid and clear, a male voice and quite the most loving I've ever heard.

"You are dying," the voice said to me in confirmation of what I knew, "but we wish you to make a choice. You can indeed pass on to what awaits you on the other side . . ." At this point I was allowed to see my body very easily and casually slipping under the water of my bath somewhere below me. A simple and painless death.

". . . or you can choose to return to your life. We wish you to know, however, that you have completed what you came to do."

The voice was utterly without judgment, wholly kind and considerate, and with no bias whatsoever as to which option I might choose.

I thought for a short while with a crystal clarity I've never since experienced, and then I knew in my heart that I wanted to return to the world. On announcing my decision, there was an expression of delight so profound that the monorail car dissolved around me, leaving me once again suspended in space.

It was then that I saw the angels. I've never seen anything so vast and so radiant. My entire visual field simply dropped away and there, arrayed before me, were tier upon tier of angels, stretching away and as far as I could see upward. And they were singing the most beautiful music I'd ever heard. I couldn't sustain the reality for more than a few moments before I totally disintegrated into the sounds.

Sometime later, as I regained a sense of unified consciousness, I became aware that I was standing on the edge of a great plain. In the middle of the plain there was an enormous golden structure. On either side of me, just at the edge of my vision, stood two tall beings of light. I knew intuitively that they were my guardian angels. Then

I was whisked by them into the great building and given some much-needed healing.

When I recovered and found myself back in my earthly body, the bath water by now tepid, I was entirely well. From being terminally ill, I was completely restored and stronger than ever.

I'd also had an encounter with angels that would change my life.

· A FIRST COMMUNICATION WITH ANGELS ·

In the early eighties, a young man who prefers to be called Edward, someone I'd never met or even heard about, started allowing the angels to use his vocal chords to speak. Edward had been spontaneously doing this among a small group of friends in Toronto, known to my companion of that time. The transcribed material sent to us felt authentic, so we set off for Canada to see if we could spend some time talking to the angels, too.

And talk we did! We were most fortunate. Edward turned out to be an excellent light-trance medium, and the angels themselves were invariably brilliant, caring, incredibly perceptive, and palpably loving. They were also very direct. They were no-nonsense angels who told us a great deal about themselves and gave us every reason to feel deeply optimistic about the state of world affairs.

They described some of the upcoming changes from their perspective. For instance, Mentoria, an angel of education, told us of some of the new forms of technology soon to be available that would decentralize knowledge. It saw a time when schoolteachers, as we know them, would be "without suitable institutional employment." And it gave a passionate call for more spiritual education for the young today, since the angels had received notice that ". . . great ones will come through these souls." I repeat verbatim the latter part of the transmission from the angelic voice that came through Edward.

MENTORIA: What is of greatest value in the education of these young ones is that they look to nature, to find therein the patterns placed by Intelligences Divine, and reflecting the eternal realities and the unfolding nature of time and space. Then we may come through to offer advancements, elaborations, and insights which will accelerate the process and bring spiritual realities unknown on this world.

What is in this is the decline of all forms of violence, and an ascendence of all forms of loving and understanding, of compassionate outreach, of sharing, spiritual, material, and mental. You would then see among these new ones a fuller portrayal of the potentials long held within the mortals of the realm.

Joy is the essence of our mission, joy and the satisfaction of the unfolding of the plan.

These conversations with angels extended over a three-week period, with much of the time spent talking about it among ourselves, attempting to assimilate this extraordinary situation.

At the last session, in which all seven of us friends were together, an unnamed angel of entertainment had us to begin with fascinated, and then, to our astonishment, all roaring with laughter. It told us about our being released from fear, which it saw as "the freedom to express the Divine within, which has been greatly liberated." It continued, "This is no less than the long hoped-for spiritual rebirth among the arts, the new renaissance that has been forecast in the minds of many.

"We are now enjoined to foster laughter," it told us, perfectly seriously, and the oddest thing began to happen. It was like being tickled on the most subtle levels of our beings. Laughter was utterly irresistible; we started roaring our heads off. There was no holding it back. Tears rolled down our faces. We laughed the relief of the ages.

"You are asked to see how the joy of laughter"—came the angel's gentle voice—"will set the world a-turning."

It was in this vastly open state that the last mysterious contact burst through.

"I am Shandron." It was a new and deeply resonant voice, and it fell over us in waves.

SHANDRON: I am a being of advanced status, greater than seraphim. I am one who would be of superuniverse status. I am supernaphim. My place here in this Great Work is as an usher of this new dispensation that is upon us, and I emphasize this aspect.

Yes, there has been a turning of a dispensation for your world, a release from patterns long held. But more, and this you know in your hearts. Such are the nature and magnitude of the changes being wrought here on this world that we, of superuniverse status, are invited to function with our younger sisters and brethren in the ordering of the new ways.

You would do well to see that the gradation of change has been accelerated. The new dispensation upon us all—in the light of the Supreme and His great movements, flowing out from the center universe, going into many forms and flowing through many minds—is coming to reveal and be revealed here and in eternity. In its fullness, it will require the completion of time to be understood by all. What is given to you in your outworking, in your forward motion in the ascension through higher worlds, are the crystalline insights into the eternal verities.

You would do well to understand that the old things have, indeed, passed away; that all things are made new. It is not the end of revelation to this world; it is your lives that are the Supreme revelation.

These things cannot be contained by any single entity nor by any established group. These things are for all beings to join in worshipful wonder of God.

We work to bring in new levels of organization. This will be a gentle transfer and upliftment. Much that is held in the mind as it exists today are but sketches on a note pad. These sketches will allow for the furtherance of the vision of the totality of the change. But it is in the living experience that the change may be made real.

Leave then your studies. Leave then your books. Leave all these things into the proper place within your lives. Find not your center in them, but within yourselves. Live your lives as they have been given you and in this will be the wonder for all to see. We carry forward the message, we carry forward the vision, we carry forward the glorious spectacle unfolding on this wonderworld, this place of peace. It is this planet of which I speak that is held in most loving concern by all the universe of universes, that in God's mercy all may live in bliss and harmony.

We were transfixed by the weight and rhythm of the words. The presence of Shandron was incontrovertible. It was as though we had received a universe bulletin—an update from the furthest reaches of space. An assurance from another dimension that there was indeed a Divine plan being worked out on our planet.

Then Shandron was gone, leaving us exhilarated and amazed by the turn of events.

· THE CALL OF JOY ·

These happenings occurred in 1981 and the up-stepping of consciousness about which we were told is continuing unabated. The reconciliation that the angels spoke about certainly appears to be having its effect on our small planet, and there is no doubt that any movement toward truth, beauty, and goodness is at this point supported wholeheartedly by the unseen world.

In my turn, I decided to throw in my lot with my guardian angels, the companions of my heart. The more credence I've given these realms the more I feel the effects they are having in my life. Talantia, a guardian angel who spoke so eloquently through Edward in Toronto, gave us some general hints as to how to include the angels more fully in the way we viewed things. I'd asked its advice at the time on how someone with little or no experience with transcendent realities might proceed in this form of communication.

> TALANTIA: Here the first step is the greatest. That the mortal would make the full, conscious decision to seek this contact would be a taking of this step. The next movement forward would be the inclusion within the personal belief system that such things are possible. A further step would be understanding that such things are loving; that such things are giving; that such things are also lawful; and that this is the Way of Heaven which has opened up for all mortals.

A Way of Heaven it has been, too. As I come better to know my two guardian angels, whom I call Joy and Beauty, my life has been infinitely enriched. They've not taken over my life, but they are always there as counselors and guides when asked. In particular, I have become close to Joy.

After the initial excitement of having a companion/friend/beloved right here

inside me gave way to the calmer rhythms of a blossoming relationship, we have grown to like, respect, and really "enjoy" each other. The love has always been there!

Although extremely rewarding, an ongoing conscious relationship with a guardian angel is also very challenging. For a start, there's nothing that can be hidden. It's splendid practice for the times ahead, when all of us will be able to be more open with one another, because this relationship is also a precurser of telepathy. And it gives us a chance to get to know, from the inside as it were, another race of intelligent beings who are yet very different from us. This is an invaluable preparation for the many different races of beings we will encounter as we become more fully part of the galactic community. I know that my angels will be with me, and I with them, when these days dawn, whether I am in this body or another—a thought that fills me with Joy.

· JOINED BY A NEW ANGEL ·

In autumn of 1988 I was going altogether too fast—an occupational hazard of New York living—and as can happen when I am blundering along not giving myself the time to listen, I found myself laid low with a bout of flu that stopped me in my tracks for five days.

Once I'd gotten over the aching eyes and the raw pain in all my joints, I fell once again into contact with Joy. The work on *Ask Your Angels* had just started and I found myself confessing to my angel that I personally had absolutely no idea of where to begin.

I was completely unprepared for what Joy told me, greeting me with its customary warmth:

JOY: Beloved, welcome. I should indicate to you that this process of dictation falls under the aegis of another. One you might call a close colleague, but an entity who, in many ways, is more adequately and appropriately equipped for such work. It is one with whom we have had much contact, and so through the years have you. Let me introduce you to . . .

I have to admit I almost panicked. My heart started pounding, and I felt a tremendous anxiety building up in my body. It was instantaneous, extraordinary, and unexplainable.

As I hung on for dear life, a name floated into my mind, one letter at a time: *A—B—I—G—R—A—E—L.*

The letters stayed there, seeming to hang suspended in the center of my head, while I wondered why I was feeling such anxiety. This was a formidable presence, I had no doubt. Yet I'd communed with other powerful entities before. Months later, I realized it had been the state of my physical health that had produced the high level of anxiety. I'd been blocking the circuits, and my fear had created resistance to the flow.

Joy waited until I'd calmed down and could hear its voice again without my ego getting in the way. The tension moved to a feeling of high excitement about the idea that we might have a special angel, and then switched, as abruptly, to an equally extreme nervousness as to whether I'd be able to hear this new voice. I needn't have worried.

JOY: Abigrael is a recording angel who has been entrusted with the accumulated thought patterns that many of us have centered on for this work. This is one of the ways we function. We trust you will find it valuable to have one particular terminal, who has ordered and sorted through the many different approaches taken, to make this document of general and real application to the widest possible audience.

I felt wonderful. Deeply relieved. I thanked Joy and welcomed Abigrael, acknowledging it for taking on this responsibility and for electing to work with us. Then I asked it how our communication could be made optimal, and how I might prepare myself to receive the cleanest and clearest angelic material possible.

ABIGRAEL: Dearest One, it is a pleasure to be here with you.

Abigrael's voice was strong and clear. There was no feeling of my earlier anxiety.

ABIGRAEL: I have been adequately trained and equipped to serve you and, indeed, all in this way. As you have, too. Have no fear. All that is needed is to be open to one another; for you to listen and use your analytical intelligence to ask the relevant questions. You will find that I always have the appropriate answers. This territory is familiar to us of the angelic realm.

I asked my new friend where it would like to start? What was the key item it wanted to get across up front?

ABIGRAEL: The first and most important fact is, Dearest One, as it always must be, love. Our contact and communication is made possible through love. It is the conductor. If there's little love, there can be little contact. And if there's no love in a person's heart, then it is well-nigh impossible for us to make any inroads.

What happens in those cases? I wondered.

ABIGRAEL: Generally the surroundings and environment of that person's life have to crumble in order to produce a state of emotional vulnerability. This will draw out the fears, the hopelessness, and the anger. And only then, after all these dark emotions have been felt, can there be the start of a feeling of love.

I received a rapid impression as to why we might be seeing so many personal disasters taking place all around us—especially those of us who choose to live in the big cities of the Western world. But my new friend was moving me along.

ABIGRAEL: We won't focus on this issue however because love *is* present on your world in all but remarkably few situations. It's for this reason that we now feel we can make a much wider and more general approach to your realm.

And, as so often happens when in contact with angels, I was able to see the human condition with much more compassionate eyes and within a wider framework. I found myself reminded of how low an opinion and with what pessimism we of the human species have come to look upon ourselves; our self-recriminations for the abuses we feel we have heaped upon the planet.

ABIGRAEL: Let it first be said that the conditions you live under on your planet are, in more universal terms, rather exceptional ones. On more regular planets at your level of density, which are inhabited by beings much as yourselves, we aren't hidden, neither are we unknown. The mortal and the angelic worlds have a full and cooperative aspect.

In fact, we are acknowledged by all, although many don't necessarily have day-to-day relationships with us. The mystery and disbelief surrounding our order of beings on your world is by far the greatest exception to the natural rhythms of ordinary planetary existence. Another way to express this might be to say that under more normal circumstances, we'd be evident as your planetary helpers and ministers, without whom it would be considered extremely difficult to live out your full term as a human being.

Abigrael was certainly putting things in perspective for me and, incidentally, allowing me to feel much more relaxed about talking to beings I couldn't see.

I'd frequently entertained the thought that life must exist on other planets in this vast and miraculous universe of ours. Over the years I've seen my fair share of flying discs, anomalous lights in the skies, and the casual hints of extraterrestrial life to which many of us have recently been subject.

If I was understanding Abigrael correctly, all mortal beings, regardless of whatever physical form they might take on due to local planetary conditions, have angels! What a wonderful feeling! What a splendid commonality!

Yet it occurred to me how few of us even start to really understand how our physical bodies work. We occupy an instrument of biomechanical genius, yet we're almost completely unaware of its inner functioning.

ABIGRAEL: Your scientists frequently speak of the insignificantly minute chance that life could have originated on any other planet besides yours—life which is in any way similar to what you experience on this world.

This is a misunderstanding based on the premise that life originated by chance. Indeed, if life on Earth really did start in this haphazard way, it would not only be unlikely, it would be totally impossible for it to be found anywhere in the universe. Yet, in a certain way your scientists are correct. This is a very unusual world, but for rather different reasons than they might conjecture. It is rare in the sense of the amazing isolation the life forms of intelligence have from one another. This spreads across virtually all the species who possess higher degrees of consciousness. Isolation is the key here.

You know almost nothing, for example, about the nature spirits or any of those realms who so diligently order the natural world. The whales, dolphins, and other sea mammals remain a mystery to you. The great trees and the wisdom contained in their noble intelligence, the winds and the storms—you see none of these as warranting intelligent communication. Horses, elephants, all the higher primates have an understanding that quite surpasses anything you've yet given them credit for.

If you only started to open to the consciousness inherent in all these realms, you'd quickly find that you are surrounded by intelligence, encompassed by wonder and brilliance. You would discover that life—full, loving, vital, extraordinary, vigorous life—is everywhere you look.

The utter necessity of this understanding, this heartfelt yet unsentimental appreciation that you are surrounded with intelligent life, is of particular and paramount importance at this point in the development of your species, for reasons that must be growing more obvious to you by the year.

This is as it has to be. Your planet has been isolated and has been cut off from these levels of understanding for longer than human history. No one would suggest or pretend that this has been an easy planet. No! In fact it may enable you to rest easier to know that among those whose function it is to assess the relative merits of inhabited spheres, your planet is considered to be the third to most difficult in this area of the universe.

But have no fear. All this is changing. The isolation and darkness that have so long beset your sphere are even now drawing to an end. Much of the fear and hatred, and the other negative emotional thought forms that have been repressed in your world mind, are even now rising to the surface to be released.

You are awakening from your nightmare, from your dream of fear. You will behold a reality of such love and joy as you have never been able to conceive possible. This, Dearest One, is the reason why we of the angelic realm are making ourselves more known to you. This is why we greet you with such enthusiasm as each of you individually awakens. This is the true meaning of the New Reality that is arriving for us all.

So ended my first encounter with Abigrael. And so began a new and wonderful friendship.

· HOW I MET MY ANGEL ·

Andrew

When I was six, and living on Long Island, New York, I made what I would now call an altar, on the top of the bookcase in my bedroom. It had two ceramic figurines on it, a cowboy and an angel. The cowboy was acceptable to my left-of-center family in 1957, but they refused to get me the angel for the longest time. It represented all the superstitions they were trying to leave behind. But I was a stubborn child, and they finally gave in to my demands.

My parents had an edition of Dante's *Divine Comedy*, illustrated by Gustave Doré, that sat on the bookshelves in the living room. I was obsessed with it, and spent hours by myself looking at the yellowed pages covered with pictures of angels, flocks of angels, swirling in the sky. In my favorite, the angels are assembled into a gigantic rose.

My father, in his own agnostic way, had an angel obsession, too. He was haunted by a movie he'd once seen, in which an angel is found after a nuclear explosion, dead and clutching a golden book in its hands. He was always on the lookout for that movie, but never found it again. He passed his search on to me. I haven't found the movie either. Do you know what it is?

As a child I always heard voices, both when I was awake and in my dreams. I don't remember connecting my love of angels with these voices, but I learned at an early age that it was best not to talk about them. It upset everyone, especially as I got older. Big boys are not supposed to hear voices.

When I was seven or eight, my father took me to the Metropolitan Museum of Art in New York City. There we came upon a wonderful painting of Joan of Arc, by the French painter Jules Bastien-Lepage, who lived from 1848 to 1884. (I still visit it from time to time.) In the foreground is Joan, staring out into space. From her expression, it is clear that she is listening to the three faint golden figures floating in the air behind her. What joy I felt, looking at that painting. For the first time in my life I knew that other people heard voices, too.

I didn't know who the woman in the painting was, and for three days I was truly happy. Then I asked my father about her, and he told me her story. To this day I remember how frightened I was, and how I began to shut down inside. I did not want to hear voices. I did not want to be burned at the stake like she was. I tried to ignore the voices as much as possible. If they got too loud, I finally discovered that I could sing to myself even louder to block them out.

By the time I started college, the voices had not gone away, but I had successfully learned not to hear them. The good part was that I no longer felt like someone who might go crazy or be burned to death. The bad part was that in order to block out the voices, I had to block out whole other parts of myself, too.

My first quarter of college was in the fall of 1969. I was living in Santa Barbara, California, and was involved in campus politics and the antiwar movement. But at the same time, I was exploring yoga and the Eastern meditative techniques that were starting to get popular in this country. "Trust the inner" was what one of my teachers kept telling us. I had not trusted the inner for ten years. But I began to let myself listen to the voices again—as an experiment. "If I start going crazy, I'll stop" is what I promised myself.

I had no sense of what or who the voices were. It took me seven years to quiet my inner chatter enough so that I could hear sentences and paragraphs again. And although there were times during those years when I was sure that I was going crazy, I somehow kept going. By then I was living in Brooklyn, New York, and working in a bookstore. But I was still so uneducated about my voices that when my friend Linda Sherwood gave me a copy of *Seth Speaks,* I laughed at it. I had to read half of it before I was able to recognize that I was doing the very same thing that its author Jane Roberts was doing—listening.

The popularity of channeling in the seventies was as comforting to me as the painting of Joan of Arc had first been. In that supportive climate, I was learning to distinguish the voices that were mine from the ones that belonged to my guides. I was beginning to recognize them as distinct individuals, with different things to teach me. Far from going crazy, the pieces of my life were at last beginning to come together.

By 1976, I was busy exploring my spiritual life, meditating, doing yoga, giving readings, and taking hundreds of pages of dictation from my guides. Under their tutoring, I studied Ice Age culture, and learned about life on several other planets. In addition, I received information that will be shared with you later, on the awakening of a new energy center in our bodies.

Having been raised in a family that did not believe in God, when I realized that I did believe in Something, I rejected the idea of the patriarchy and a Father God, and was tuned into the energies of the Great Mother. Inspired by an image of the ancient Egyptian winged goddess Isis, I discovered that I too had wings that spread out from my spine, and that they were slowly unfolding. I began to teach other people how to open their wings. But if you'd asked me about angels, I would have laughed. Angels were those pudgy little boys on valentines, the ones with bows and arrows and harps and little wings.

In 1979 I was in Los Angeles, taking care of my father, who was slowly moving toward death. One night, the phone rang. It was my friend Harriet Goldman calling from New York to say that a nuclear reactor was about to explode in a place I had never heard of—Three Mile Island. Harriet and I had often prayed and meditated together. When she said, "We have to do something," I knew what she meant.

I hung up the phone and was preparing to meditate, when suddenly I was pulled out of my body by an unseen force. All at once I found myself floating in the sky in the midst of a huge company of other beings. We were luminous and arranged in two enormous spheres around a nuclear-power station. I knew that our joint presence was going to keep the reactor from exploding.

When I came back into my body, I called up Harriet to tell her that everything was going to be all right. Then I turned on the television to watch the news. There on the screen was the very same power station that I had seen from the air. The news reporter did not mention the two spheres of light beings, any more than I allowed myself to notice that many of them were angels.

Three years went by, in which I continued to work with my guides, do readings, do healing work, and teach occasional classes. I went to massage school and was integrating those techniques into the healing work that I'd already been doing. I also started working with my friend Bill Walsh, a chiropractor, in an office he established to offer alternative forms of health care to people in recovery programs.

One night, in the spring of 1982, I was sitting on the floor in my bedroom meditating—when an angel appeared to me. He was seven feet tall, with brown skin, golden hair, golden eyes, and enormous golden wings, floating about three inches off the parquet floor. My first reaction was anger. The kind of meditation I was doing was supposed to empty my mind, not fill it with golden light. And it was one thing to talk to guides and to goddesses, but all of my internalized fear and self-judgment about hearing voices had gotten focused on angels. I shut down again. The moment I did, I could no longer see him. But the feeling of his being there did not go away. And he kept beaming out so much love to me that I had to open up to him again.

He smiled and told me to unfold my wings. I did. When he touched the tips of his wings to the tips of mine, my body began to vibrate, a subtle energy flowed through me, and I was flooded with the purest love I had ever felt. It was the essence of love, distilled, concentrated, pouring into every part of me—body, mind, and spirit.

Every night for weeks after that, I opened up to him again. He took me on journeys, talked to me, taught me things. For the longest time I told no one about him, or that he said his name was Gabriel. Nor did I mention that the angel he sometimes brought with him, the one with obsidian skin, amber eyes, and golden wings, called himself Raphael. This is not the sort of thing you talk about in Brooklyn. Now I understand that they come from clans of angels with those names, that there are as many Gabriels and Raphaels in Heaven as there are Jennifers and Jasons in the playground across the street.

Although the angels first came to me in a way that I could see them, once I got used to them, they stopped appearing visually. They told me that it takes a lot of work on their part to slow down their vibrations enough for humans to see them. It's easier for them to connect with us through sound. Once I got familiar with the angel frequency, I could hear each angel in a different part of my brain. Because certain specific areas "light up" for particular angels, I always know with whom I'm talking.

I did have another angel vision. One night, months after his first appearance, when I was used to talking to him without seeing him, Raphael showed up again in a visual form. He looked the way he'd looked before, like a man with wings. But I was getting curious about angels and gender, and so I asked him about that. Right before my eyes, he shifted from male to female. Without speaking, I understood what she was saying—that angels are both male and female. Then I asked her if angels really look like people. First, she melted down into a six-foot golden sphere, and then stretched out horizontally into a seven-foot golden, winged dolphin, floating about three feet above my bedroom floor. I understood that angels appear to each sentient being in its own form. Then, the dolphin melted back into the sphere again, which gradually became transparent. Long, undulating fibers emerged from a central vertical core, pulsing in different colors, but giving off a soft golden light. All of this was happening at the absolute edge of my visual field. I knew that this was the closest to what an angel really looks like that I would ever be able to see with my physical eyes.

Most people don't see angels. I asked mine once why they came to me so clearly, so dramatically, so visually. They said, laughing, that it was because I was so dense that it was the only way to get through to me.

In the summer of 1985 another angel, Gantol, came into my life, and he dictated a book to me on the subtle energy systems of the human body. This information proved invaluable in my practice as a body-worker. It was Gantol who first explained to me that the many fibers I saw emerging from Raphael's body when it had become a shimmering sphere of light were the same as the pairs of fibers that I had awakened on my own back, and thought of as my wings.

Through Gantol I met two other angels who were "assigned" to work with my partner and myself in our relationship and in the meditation group that we were leading. When that relationship ended, those two angels left and another angel came into my life, who identified itself only as The Green Angel. So I knew that there were different kinds of angels, information angels like Gantol, and the ones I call connecting angels, who work with us in our relationships. But did I ever wonder if there were such things as guardian angels, or if I had one myself? Never.

In my journal entry for April 9, 1987, I mention a new being that had come into my life two nights earlier—an "intense, highly active golden energy."

Now I have to backtrack a little bit. When I was three and a half, something happened to me. I was standing on my bed one night, just before I was going to go to sleep. A moment later I was so filled with terror that I was afraid to fall asleep again until I was almost sixteen. Although I never forgot that night, I could never remember what had happened to scare me. In the spring of 1987 several books had come out on UFO abductions, and I began to wonder if something like that had happened to me that night. So I went off to do some work with my good friend and fellow consciousness explorer, Barbara Shor. She deepened me into a trance and took me back to that night.

Once again I saw myself in my bedroom. For the first time, I could remember something. I was standing on my bed, opening up to a golden light that seemed to

go on forever. Then something went wrong. I seemed to open up too much, to take in too much light. I felt as if my circuits were being fried, especially around my heart. Terrified, I shut down to the golden energy that I clearly recognized as my guardian angel.

But my long journey of healing, of channeling, of talking to Gantol and the other angels, had been preparing me for this reunion. At thirty-six I was grounded and centered in a way that I had not been at three and a half. I could open myself to my angel once again. I could let myself be flooded with a love and joy that I had not felt in years.

Over the next few weeks, my angel and I reconnected. He told me that his name is Sargolais, and let me know that he had always been with me, at a distance, waiting for the time when I would be strong enough to reach out to him again. I realized that my angel statue and my love of angel pictures were the best way my conscious mind had of keeping me connected to him—without getting too close.

Being with Sargolais has changed the way that I live in the world. While I felt great love from all the angels that I met, there is a special love that comes from a being whose particular nature is to love me just as I am. This love allows me to encounter other people without being as needy. Knowing how hard it was to come back to my angel, I can now observe others with less judgment about their struggles. The information that Sargolais has given me has allowed me to move in the world with more clarity and a deeper sense of purpose. In fact, I find that the world itself is a more loving place than I had previously suspected.

There are still times when I'm scared, lonely, and confused. But Sargolais is always there. No matter how bad things get, I can always feel his wings wrapped around me. And sometimes, when I feel that I can't go on, if I call him, he gives me a heart-to-heart transfusion of golden liquid light that centers and heals me.

Ironically, my relationship with Sargolais has been the bridge between the politics of my family and my own spiritual path. He keeps reminding me what a gift it is to have a body and to live in the physical world, that it is only through love and our partnership with the angels that we can create the kind of world that revolutionaries may dream of, but can never achieve. Because of Sargolais, I see my spiritual work as a step beyond the rage that fuels revolutions. I see us all moving toward a radical transformation that can only come from love, from honoring all of life and honoring the rich diversity of our human family.

Through my connection with Sargolais, I have done angel readings and taught angel workshops. Some of the techniques in this book come from Sargolais, some from my old friend The Green Angel, and some from two other angels that they brought into my life. Plus there is my new relationship with Abigrael, the coordinating angel of this book. But when I think of angels, it's Sargolais that I think of first. And he has his own perspective on things. So what follows are his words on our relationship.

For the longest time, Sargolais wanted me to call him "it." But how could I call my beloved companion an "it." I prefer to say "he." And being a loving angel, he lets me.

· ON MY RELATIONSHIP WITH ANDREW ·

SARGOLAIS: My connection to Andrew is ancient. We were created together in a space out of space and a time out of time. Since we entered the realms of space/time, we have always traveled together. I have worked with him in and out of lives, as midwife, mother, healer, painter, dancer, flute player, architect, and hunter—the two of us working to bridge the physical and spiritual worlds. For humans exist to be conduits of spiritual energy into the material world just as angels exist to be conduits of material energy into the spiritual realms—and we need each other to fulfill our purposes.

In a sense, we companion or guardian angels are the social workers of the universe. Some of us have only a few clients, others have many. For example, Andrew shares me with 118 other entities, each of them in a different galaxy. But because we angels are not focused in space/time in quite the way that you are, I am equally present with Andrew and my other incarnate connections, all of whom are sentient, but not all of whom are human.

At this time in our shared history, most human beings are unaware of their angelic friends. This is not true for the sea peoples of your planet, the dolphins and the whales. And it is never true for the angelic member of a consciousness bridge.

A human or cetacean and its angel might be compared to an egg and its shell. So Andrew is the egg, and I am the shell, here to nurture and protect him. I cannot tell you how many times he has said to me, looking at all the suffering in the world, that we angels are not very good at our jobs. I keep reminding him that you are free beings, and that from our perspective, pain and suffering may very well be sources of spiritual growth. And you also have to remember that so long as you are not conscious of the bonds that exist between us, it is hard for us to share our wisdom and our love with you. You see, there is a simple rule of angel physics that we must all obey. We angels cannot enter your world—unless you open a window or a doorway for us. Even a crack is enough, a crack of a desire to connect. Once you do that, we can come in. Without that, we must remain on the outside, forever looking in.

The more you become conscious of our deep connection, the more you will be able to benefit from our experiences. When this happens on a global level, the way that you all live will change. For a species that is angel-aware cannot pollute, enslave, destroy, or kill.

At times the passage is difficult. But—and this is the most important thing I've ever said to Andrew, and I will say it to you, too—*God doesn't want us to be perfect. It only wants us to be present.* This applies to angels as much as it does to humans.

All of humanity is changing. You are about to experience a vast and joyful expansion in consciousness. You are standing at the doorway to the next stage in your evolution. In that stage, conscious connection between humans and angels will be the norm, not the exception. And for the first time in all of your history, love and joy will be your teachers, not suffering and pain.

So part of my work with Andrew is a personal exploration of our shared destiny. And part of my work with him is as teacher—of information and of joy. But I do not work with him in isolation. Whenever a human and an angel connect, they make it easier for others of both species to connect, too. And it is important to remember that although angels are immortal and wise, because we exist in a different plane of reality, we are not always wise in the ways of your world. So Andrew's work with me is to teach me the ways of humanity, to teach me about human hopes, dreams, and fears. Together, we create a bridge across all consciousness frequencies. It is for this that God created humans and angels, and invited us to work together.

How to
Ask Your Angels

The
GRACE
Process

J oy, humor, and wisdom are just three of the gifts that the angels bring. As you meet your own, you will relish the comfort of their companionship, too. In this section, you will learn the basic steps for connecting with your angel that will allow you to have heavenly heart-to-heart conversations. And, for fun and further contact, you will also find the Angel Oracle. It's both a listing of categories of angelic specialists who are available to work with humans now, and an entertaining and helpful divination tool.

The techniques that follow—the meditations, visualizations, and exercises—have been developed in collaboration with the angels and also with groups of people in our workshops and seminars. The angels had a wing in every one. At the beginning, we were winging it, too, relying every step of the way on guidance from our beloved guardians. We literally opened ourselves to receiving instructions as we went along. Through many workshops and seminars we refined the method that we offer you in this book. We call it:

THE GRACE PROCESS

There are five steps to talking with your angel:

Grounding,
Releasing,
Aligning,
Conversing, and
Enjoying the connection!

The first letters of the five steps will give you an easy way to remember them—G R A C E. The last step is as important as the first. Meeting your angel is joyful. It is loving, full of pleasure and delight. And meeting your angel is also momentous—it will change your life. It's rather like getting married, for the relationship requires love and commitment.

· HOW WE FOUND GRACE ·

For the purpose of this book, we had to compile everything the three of us knew about talking to our angels. We all agreed about the importance of **G**rounding. And Timothy and Alma had also established for themselves the necessity for **R**eleasing. Andrew's specialty was **A**ligning. We'd all been **C**onversing with angels for years. So we had the first four steps *G, R, A, C.* And then LNO delivered the coup de *GRACE.* The element that was missing, she told Alma, was **E**njoying!

"Of course!" we said. "Why hadn't we thought of it?" And that was where the Angel Oracle came in. Sargolais, Andrew's angel, had indeed given it to him, and Andrew had been sharing it with people in his workshops.

· HOW TO GET STARTED ·

Since most of the exercises are done with your eyes closed, you will want to tape-record them so you can follow the directions without having to refer to the book. It's a good idea to read through each one a few times before you do, to get a sense of the timing and pacing. You don't have to record the numbers of each step, but make sure you that you allow a long enough pause between each one, so you have time to follow the directions.

You will also need a notebook and a pen. It's good to have a special notebook that you'll use only for your angel's messages and conversations. You may want to use a special pen, too, with ink in a favorite color. As simple as this may seem, it brings respect to your meeting with your angel, and helps to move you from ordinary to angelic consciousness. As you develop your relationship with your angel, you may wish, as many people now do, to converse with it on your computer. Set aside a floppy diskette just for your angel's communications, as Alma's angel, LNO, requested.

Whether you use a notebook or your computer, date each message that you receive at the top. After the communication has ended, you might want to give it a brief title, summing up the subject matter. This will help you to bring to mind the main points of each transmission and will make it easier for you to refer back to it again later.

· THE IMPORTANCE OF WRITING ·

One of the reasons we emphasize the importance of writing down angelic messages is because in the beginning you may have a tendency to dismiss what comes through as made up, or coming from your mind. Chapter 7, "Conversing," will clear up any confusion you may have about this. Putting it down on paper, or disk, will preserve the words so that later you will be able to clearly distinguish your angel's voice. Writing captures that tender connection and provides you with a record of your relationship as it evolves. Rereading the transmissions at another time will enrich your life with the love and clarity that characterize the angelic voice. Plus, you will be amazed, when you look at them from a distance, at how accurate and insightful these messages are.

· OTHER METHODS OF COMMUNICATION ·

This does not mean that writing is the only way to communicate with your angel. For some people, there may be no words; instead, a shift of feelings, colors, pictures, even music may come through. Make notes or drawings of these, as they come. Teza, an artist and sculptor, receives images, not words, from her angel. She sketches these in her angel notebook and meditates on them, gathering understandings that she can then translate into words. However the information comes, be prepared to record what you receive. Writing or drawing is an acknowledgment, an acceptance of what has been given. In this respect, angels are very like us humans—when they are acknowledged, they are delighted to share themselves more.

Remember that angel means "messenger." What comes through you will be messages from the angels, whether they are words, pictures, music, or feelings. You may think of the angels as external and another life-form, or you may think of them as internal and an aspect of your Higher Self. Either way, the techniques for communicating with them work the same. Just as there is no up and down in outer space, there is no in or out in the angelic realm. Everything is connected.

We recommend that you move through this section slowly, going through each of the exercises in the order in which they appear, repeating them until they become familiar. Each step builds on the one before, providing the solid foundation you need for communication. No skipping ahead, as tempting as that may be! Do the work in each section, so you'll be prepared for the next. Take your time, and savor every step of the way. There's no rush. Angels don't wear wristwatches. Enjoy these exercises. Come to them with a childlike sense of play and fun. If some of them seem unusual, or even wacky to you, that's fine. You're on a journey of discovery, one that will reveal your own potential for deep and loving communication, not only with the angels but with everyone else in your life, too.

You can never be too young to talk to angels, and you can never be too old. But, you can be too serious. So close your eyes and imagine your angel tickling you right now, over there, on the left side of your rib cage. Are you smiling? Giggling? Good. Now you're ready to go on.

Grounding

Because angels are heavenly messengers, and winged ones at that, you might find it a bit strange that the very first step in connecting with them is called Grounding. Wouldn't it make more sense to get off the ground? Contrary to what you might think, Grounding is essential in any kind of spiritual work. And you will find it enormously helpful in your everyday life, too.

Grounding means centering your attention in your body and being present in the moment. It is the act of gathering together all of your energies—mental, emotional, and physical—and bringing your thoughts and your feelings into calm and harmonious balance in your body. When you are grounded, it's much easier to selectively focus your attention, whether you are working at a job or on a project, and whenever you want to meditate, visualize, or hear the voice of your angel.

For much of our lives we're on automatic pilot. Perhaps you've had the experience, while driving on a long car trip, of suddenly realizing that you're behind the wheel. You've covered ten, twenty miles or more, changing lanes, signaling, applying the brakes when necessary, but your mind was "a million miles away."

We all daydream, from time to time. When daydreaming is habitual, it's called absent-mindedness, and Heaven only knows the number of things we've misplaced, appointments we've missed, or mistakes we've made when our body was present but our mind was elsewhere. It happens when we don't want to be doing what we're doing, or we don't want to hear what somebody is saying, or we don't want to be where we are. If we can't leave a situation physically, we leave mentally. Our attention goes out to other thoughts, other times, other places. It's easy to tell when someone isn't paying attention because there's a vacant expression on the person's face—"the lights are on, but nobody's home."

Learning to ground, to collect and stabilize your energies, will make a big difference in your life. It will allow you to be fully present, alert but relaxed, and receptive. You can think of Grounding as tying a boat to the dock, or hammering tent pegs into the Earth. When you are grounded you are anchored, connected, safe, and secure.

Grounding is simple, but it is the basis for establishing ongoing communication with your angel. It is the foundation for the GRACE Process.

· A SPECIAL PLACE ·

Before you start, find a location in your home where you feel most comfortable and at ease. It should be a spot that is peaceful and quiet, where you can return again and again to meditate, to do the exercises in *Ask Your Angels,* and to converse with your angelic companions. If you do not have a special quiet place you go to, simply move through your home, allowing yourself to be drawn to a spot that just "feels right." You can create a special place, a sacred space, for yourself there with an altar, if you like. The simple ritual of lighting a candle, burning a stick of incense, bringing a fresh flower, or filling a beautiful bowl with water helps to calm the mind and establish a reflective mood for Grounding.

If you already have an altar, or want to make one, you might want to add a picture or statue of an angel that pleases you. Whenever you do the exercises and meditations here you consecrate the space. Enter and leave this place mindfully and with respect. You will find that your meditation space is like a temple. It will store the energy you create when you meditate, making it easier for you to tune into your angel whenever you come back to it.

Once you've had some experience talking with your angels, at some point you may be drawn to do the Grounding and other exercises outdoors in nature. Choose a secluded spot that feels energized, where you know you won't be disturbed. However, at the beginning, you'll find that it's far easier to focus when you're indoors and can eliminate distractions.

Making contact with the subtle levels of angelic intelligence is all about listening. Silence and stillness are required. Find a time when you know that you won't be interrupted. Unplug your telephone, and turn off the radio or TV. While some people like to meditate with beautiful music in the background, when it comes to the angels, we've found that it's best to listen for them in silence. The angels themselves have confirmed this:

"Open your heart to the sounds of silence and you shall hear the wonders of all that exists," an angel told Deborah at one of our gatherings. And in a message received at home by Lee, another participant, they advised:

"We recommend taking time every day, twice a day, in the morning and evening, to quiet yourself and in silence to fill yourself with white light."

Take this time to quiet both yourself and your environment.

Place your tape player near you, so that you can listen to the exercises that you've recorded, turning it on and off when you want to without having to get up. You won't need to do any work in your notebook during the Grounding exercises, but you might want to keep it by your side to record any thoughts or feelings that come up for you after you've done them.

Exercise 1:
INTRODUCTION TO GROUNDING IN YOUR PHYSICAL BODY

Although many people like to sit cross-legged, we've found that it is preferable to do these exercises sitting on a chair or sofa, with your back straight and your feet flat on the floor. This will help you to feel your connection with the Earth.

1. Sit comfortably and close your eyes. Place your hands on your thighs.
2. Focus your attention on your body. Begin with your feet. Then, slowly

and thoroughly, move your awareness up through your legs, thighs, torso, arms, neck, and head. Be very aware of your breath moving in and out, in and out.

3. Imagine that you are surrounded by light. As you breathe in, inhale this light, and feel your body filling with it.

4. As you breathe out, exhale any tension, any pain you may feel in your jaw, your face, your shoulders. Exhale any tension you feel elsewhere in your body. Keep inhaling light, exhaling tension. Inhale light, exhale tension until you are relaxed and calm.

5. If your mind begins to drift or chatter, gently bring your attention back to your breathing.

6. Now, begin to picture tiny roots coming out of the soles of your feet and the bottom of your spine. Feel them growing and growing. Extend them down through your chair and through the floor, all the way down into the Earth beneath you, no matter how many floors below you that may be.

7. Continue breathing in light and exhaling tension, and as you do, visualize your roots wriggling deep, deep into the ground, taking hold there, and connecting you very securely to the center of the Earth.

8. On the next inhalation, imagine you can breathe through your roots. Draw the energy of the Earth itself up through your roots just as you would draw liquid up through a straw. Draw the Earth energy up, up into your body until it fills your heart and begins to course through your entire being.

9. Now bring your attention up to the top of your head, to your crown. Visualize this spot, which is about an inch and a half in diameter, beginning to open. From this opening fibers are emerging, long filaments reaching up like branches through the ceiling, all the way up

through the building, stretching up into the sky, out into the heavens. Imagine these filaments connecting you to the Sun and all the planets and the stars.

10. As you inhale, breathe in the energy of the heavens, bringing it down, down through these fibers into your body through the top of your head. Draw this energy down into your heart, letting it fill with the radiant light of the heavens. Feel it coursing through your entire being.

11. Now, breathe in both streams of energy—up from the Earth and down from the heavens—at the same time. Allow these two energies to weave together in your heart and fill your body. Keep breathing in the energy—up from the Earth and down from the heavens. Up from the Earth and down from the heavens. You are now anchored securely between Heaven and Earth.

12. When you are ready, become aware of your body again, of where you are sitting. Feel your breath rise and fall. Feel your heartbeat. Listen to all the sounds around you. Slowly, slowly, in your own time, open your eyes.

Look around you. Notice any differences in the way your body feels. Usually, people report that they are conscious of being more present, more aware. If you wish, you can record your feelings and impressions now in your journal. Be sure to date the entry.

· TWO EXPERIENCES OF GROUNDING ·

When she sat down to do this exercise for the first time, Carol's mind was chattering. Much as she wanted to turn it off, she couldn't. But as she focused on her breathing, her mind grew quiet. She told us afterward, "The moment I felt my roots and branches, I felt like a tree. All at once, I realized I was the old elm I used to climb when I was a child. I used to sit in the crook of one of its branches whenever I was lonely or needed comfort. It felt like home to me."

Tossing her mane of red hair, Carol went on to tell us what it felt like to be that tree: "It was incredible; all of a sudden, I felt big and tall and strong—just like that elm I loved so much." Sitting taller in her chair, she exuded confidence. She was so enthusiastic about her new feeling of well-being that she continued to do the Grounding exercise after the workshop was over, and soon made it a part of her daily routine.

Carol is from Kentucky, an actress in her twenties, now living in New York. One day, a few weeks afterward, she had just finished Grounding herself in preparation for a conversation with her angel when her telephone rang. She'd forgotten to unplug it. Compelled by the ring, she answered it, only to hear her mother's irate voice at the other end, upbraiding her for not calling in the past three weeks. Not waiting for a response, her mother stormed on with a long list of other complaints. Because she was grounded, instead of getting defensive the way she always had when her mother yelled at her, Carol remembered that angels often bring messages in ways that we least expect. What was the message she was getting? Her mother needed reassurance that Carol still cared about her.

"Mama," she said, "I'm glad you called. I haven't had a chance lately to tell you that I love you."

There was dead silence at the other end of the phone. Then her mother cleared her throat and said, softly, "Well of course you do, honey. I know that you do. How are *you*?"

The Grounding exercise helped Carol bypass an old pattern of reactive behavior and reach out with love instead. Rather than avoiding her mother as she used to do after one of her outbursts, Carol grounded herself and called her mother several days later to ask for a photo of the elm tree. They had a quick, pleasant conversation.

For Allan, an electrician, the Grounding exercise was more difficult. An urban dweller for all of his fifty-four years, with no relationship to nature, it took longer for him to establish a feeling of connection with the Earth and sky. He kept fidgeting in his seat. But by the end, Allan was sitting solidly in his chair, with an amazed grin on his face. He couldn't wait to share:

"Thirty years of grounding wires, and it never occurred to me until this minute that people need to be grounded, too," he told us. "Now I know what my family's been complaining about. My kids always tell me 'You're never really here, Dad,' and my wife says I don't pay attention to her."

Allan went on to tell us that every night at supper, while his family chattered about the events of the day, his mind was still back at work, stewing over what had happened or worrying about problems that might come up tomorrow. After supper, he would turn on the television set and tune out or fall asleep.

Look at areas in your own life where you may not be grounded, and think about the effect this has—in relationships, work, and other places. As you continue to practice this exercise, feel the difference in you when you connect to the Earth and the sky. When you are able to do Exercise 1, Introduction to Grounding in Your Physical Body, from memory, without using your tape, you are ready for the second step in learning how to ground yourself.

· GROUNDING IN YOUR ENERGY BODY ·

Opening to your angel, a being who does not live in the physical world, is also about becoming aware of your own nonphysical self. For thousands of years all over the planet, healers and mystics have been exploring the nonphysical body, which is called the subtle, or energy body. This body and its subtle fields and organs exist in the same space as the physical body, as well as all around it. The field emanating from the physical body is referred to as the aura. Although invisible to most of us, psychics and others gifted with spiritual vision can see the energy centers—chakras—within the body, as well as the energy field around it; plants and animals also have subtle energy bodies.

Voluminous information exists on the subject of the chakras and the human energy field, and many books have been written. We suggest you have a look at some of the titles in the "Further Reading" section at the end of this book if you want more detailed information. However, to help you with your angel, we offer the summary below.

· CHAKRAS ·

Just as the nervous system coordinates activities within the physical body, there are centers in the energy body that help to integrate it with our physical vehicle, and with our mind and our emotions. Just as there are different areas of the brain that relate to different physical and mental functions, so each of these centers also relates to different functions. They are located not only in the head but all through the entire body.

These energy centers are called *chakras,* which means "wheels" in Sanskrit, for they look and feel like spinning discs or spheres when you turn your senses inward and explore them. There are eight major chakras that run in a line from the base of the spine to the top of the head, and it is these energy centers that we will be working with in the next Grounding process.

Until recently, we've been focusing on seven major chakras in our bodies. But as we evolve and grow closer to the angels, a new chakra is awakening within us. We are calling this the Thymus chakra. It is found midway between the Heart and Throat chakras. Just as the angels are open to all of life, this new chakra will support us as we learn to open more and more to each other. The function of the Thymus chakra is to generate peace and universal love. It is also connected to the thymus gland, a major part of our immune system. Awakening this new chakra will boost our immune systems and assist us in dealing with cancer, AIDS, heart disease, stroke, and other diseases.

Take some time to study the diagram and the chart below so that you can familiarize yourself with the locations of the chakras and the colors that relate to each one. Use the diagram as both a map and a mirror to locate each of the chakras on your own body.

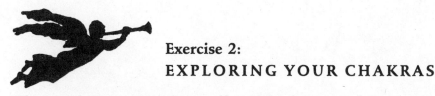

Exercise 2:
EXPLORING YOUR CHAKRAS

When you have acquainted yourself with the diagram and chart on page 116, you are ready to explore your chakras.

· CHAKRA CHART 1 ·

	ROOT	SEXUAL	SOLAR PLEXUS	HEART	THYMUS	THROAT	THIRD EYE	CROWN
location	base of spine	lower abdomen, about two inches below navel	solar plexus region	center of chest	upper chest	throat	middle of forehead	top of head
function	survival, security	sexuality, creativity	power, accomplishments	love	compassion, peace	communication	intuition	cosmic consciousness
color	red	orange	yellow	green	aquamarine	blue	indigo	violet
element	earth	water	fire	air				
kingdom	mineral kingdom	plant kingdom	animal kingdom	human	connection to world soul	angelic realm	archangels	the Creator

_____ Crown Chakra

_____ Third Eye Chakra

_____ Throat Chakra

_____ Thymus Chakra

_____ Heart Chakra

_____ Solar Plexus Chakra

_____ Sexual Chakra

_____ Root Chakra

1. Begin by briskly rubbing your hands together until your palms feel warm.
2. Place the palm of one hand on the base of your spine, covering the coccyx, or "tail" bone. The Root chakra is inside your body between the coccyx and the pubic bone. Now move your hand an inch or two away from the base of your spine and let yourself feel the energy of this chakra radiating outward into your hand. Another way to sense this energy is to hold one hand in front of your body, palm toward you, about two inches away from your skin, in a line with your pubic bone. Feel the energy beaming toward you in your palm.
3. Experiment with the distance from your body, with your hand in front and in back, and with your right hand and your left hand, for one may be more receptive than the other. You may experience warmth or coolness, tingling or gentle throbbing.
4. When you can feel the energy of the Root chakra, slowly work your way up to the next—the Sexual chakra—which is between the navel and the pubic bone. Place your palm on your body first, to establish the exact location of the chakra. Then move your hand away from your body an inch or two, to allow yourself to feel the energy in whatever way it comes to you.
5. Continue your sensing. Work your way up your body from chakra to chakra, feeling and sensing each one, from Root chakra to Crown chakra.
6. When you begin to have a feel for each chakra from the outside, close your eyes and turn your attention inward. Now imagine the chakras from within, again, one at a time. Each chakra vibrates at a different frequency, and these frequencies are related to the colors of the spectrum (see Chakra Chart 1, page 116).
7. When you've viewed all your chakras, one at a time, bring your focus back to your breathing. Notice how you feel now. Open your eyes.

Most of us don't know where our spleens or livers are, let alone the organs of our subtle bodies. You may not feel your chakras the first time you do this exercise. You may not see them either. Or you may feel some more strongly than others. Don't worry if you don't get it right away. Tuning the subtle senses is progressive; the more you do this exercise, the better you'll get at it.

Lenny could see all his chakras lit up inside, but he couldn't feel them. Rhonda felt them all right, warm and tingling, but she didn't see them. It may take you awhile to discover yours and how you perceive them. Because they are subtle organs, no two people will experience them in exactly the same way.

Rita is a housewife, whose youngest child has just gone off to college. Before she married, she'd been an aspiring artist and had taken several prizes for her watercolor paintings. Perhaps it was this that made her a "natural" at visualizing her chakras. When she did the exercise, she saw her Root chakra as a clear ruby glow. Her Sexual chakra was a warm orange light. But she was perplexed when she got to her Solar Plexus chakra—it was a pale and washed-out yellow.

Rita didn't know anything about chakras. And we didn't know much about Rita. When she shared this with the group, we asked her whether there were any issues in her life right now that had to do with power or accomplishments.

"How did you know?" she asked. "I've been thinking about going back to painting, but I'm scared. What if I've lost my talent?"

We assured Rita that if she could see her chakras and the colors so clearly, she obviously hadn't lost her eye. We explained that each of the chakras relates to emotions (see Chakra Chart 2, page 125). Negative feelings can manifest as deviations from their pure natural colors. The washed-out yellow Rita saw in her Solar Plexus was a tip-off to a problem she had with self-esteem. If you find that the colors in your chakras are muddy, clouded, or dulled, don't be discouraged. You'll find ways to release negative feelings in the next stage of the GRACE Process.

After familiarizing yourself with your chakras through the chart, diagram, and exercise, you will be ready to go on to the next Grounding exercise. The Basic Grounding Meditation will be the one you use throughout this book, whenever Grounding is required.

Exercise 3:
BASIC GROUNDING MEDITATION

Read this exercise over several times to get acquainted with it, and then record it on tape so you can listen to the directions without referring to the book. When you're ready to begin, unplug the phone and enter the quiet and sacred place you've created for yourself. Be sure to bring along your tape recorder, journal, and pen. Get comfortable, perform your simple opening ritual, such as lighting a stick of incense or a candle, and you're ready to begin.

1. Close your eyes. Focus on your breathing. Relax your body.
2. When you are ready, picture your roots extending down into the Earth from the bottoms of your feet and the base of your spine.
3. As you exhale, imagine yourself releasing any tension or toxins in your body, down your roots and back into the Earth, where they are recycled.
4. When your roots have gone down as far as they can go, and when your

body is feeling lighter and more open, reverse the process and begin to draw energy up from the Earth. The Earth energy is healing and nourishing. Continue exhaling tension and toxins and inhaling this healing Earth energy.

5. Feel this energy gather at the base of your spine, and pour into your Root chakra. Visualize the energy of this chakra as a red light glowing in your body. The Root chakra is the seat of your security and stability. When it is open and flowing, you are in tune with your deepest sense of belonging, of safety, of being at home in the world and in your body.

6. When you are ready, allow the energy from the Earth to continue flowing up your spine until it comes to your second chakra—the Sexual chakra. This is located about two inches below your navel and is the seat of your creative energy on every level—physical, artistic, and sexual. Feel it glowing with an orange light. When this chakra is open, you are capable of feeling joy in your body. You open to your creativity and sexuality. You are radiant and alive.

7. In your own time, breathe the Earth energy up into your Solar Plexus chakra. This is your connection point to your will and your personal power. Image a pulsing yellow warmth in your Solar Plexus. Know that you are strong and whole and able to do all the things that you came into this life to do, in a sacred and spirited way.

8. Like a fountain, the energy from the Earth continues to rise up in your body. Feel it flowing into your Heart center now. Picture a beautiful green light glowing in the middle of your chest, as green and alive as the spring. The Heart chakra is the seat of love and emotions in your body. Connect now with your loving nature, the strength and tenderness of your feelings. Know that you are a being of love, born into this world to feel love, to give and receive it.

9. Let the energy continue to rise up to a point in your chest, midway between your Heart and your Throat chakras, an inch or so beneath the clavicle. This is the Thymus chakra, the chakra of compassion, community and peace. Picture an aquamarine light there. Feel your connection to your family and friends, to all of humanity. Know that you are not alone, that you are an integral, unique part of All That Is.

10. Now, let the Earth energy rise up into your throat and ears. Imagine a sky-blue light shining within. You might want to make a sound at this point, any sound or note that feels pleasant and comfortable. This will massage your throat muscles and open up this center of communication. The Throat chakra governs speaking and listening, truthfulness and spontaneity. Visualize an inverted triangle connecting your ears and your throat. Place your fingertips lightly on your ears and join your palms together under your chin in a V to connect your throat and ears. You are now opening to communicate, heightening your ability to listen and to speak.

11. Next, draw the energy up into the middle of your forehead. This is your Third Eye, the seat of expanded awareness, of psychic perceptions. Feel a point of indigo light, a deep blue-violet, glowing within your forehead. Know that you can awaken your extrasensory perceptions when you are connected to this chakra, to see, hear, and feel into other worlds.

12. Now let the Earth energy rise all the way up to the very top of your head. This is your Crown chakra and it connects you to your God-consciousness, to your Higher Self. Focus on this point and keep breathing, gently, evenly. Imagine a violet light pulsing within the Crown chakra and radiating out from it. Allow the energy to build in intensity.

13. Visualize the Grounding energy rising up from the center of the Earth, moving through each of your chakras in turn, and then erupting out of the top of your head in a great geyser of liquid light. As it surges up, see it flowing out, cascading down all around you like a fountain of light, clearing and cleansing your body, balancing and harmonizing all your chakras.

14. Keep breathing gently and evenly. Sense all of your chakras filled with light. When you are ready, once again feel that there are tendrils, branches of energy shooting out of the top of your head, connecting you to the moon, the sun, the planets of our solar system, to the stars, to the heavens. Like a waterfall, feel this energy pouring down through these fibers, filling your Crown chakra so that it glows with heavenly light.

15. Chakra by chakra, let energy pour down through your body just as you let it rise up. Let it fill your Third Eye with light, your ears and Throat, your Thymus, your Heart, your Solar Plexus, your Sexual, and your Root chakras. Feel it pouring down through your roots, washing down into the Earth so that the planet, too, begins to glow more brightly.

16. Now the energies of Heaven and Earth are flowing through each chakra, weaving together and linking your body to the universe. Sense each of your chakras all at once. Feel yourself as a rainbow of living light, connected to the universe and to the Creator, connected to the Earth and grounded.

17. Notice your breathing. Become aware of your body again, of the place where you are sitting. When you are ready, open your eyes and look around you at your world.

Remember how you felt after you did Exercise 1, Introduction to Grounding in Your Physical Body (pp. 109–11)? Notice how you feel after doing this exercise.

What are the differences within you? As you look around, does the room seem changed? Stand up, stretch, move around. Has your sense of your body changed? Explore the way this exercise affects your perception and feelings.

Each time you do this exercise you will find your ability to ground yourself improving. Your chakras will become more and more clear to you, too. Because this is a long exercise, don't be disheartened if you lose your focus when you are first going through it. This frequently happens, the first time you do it. But if you pay attention to the particular chakras you drift away from, you may get an idea of the issues in your life and the areas in your subtle body that you are ready to explore and heal.

· PRACTICE MAKES PERFECT ·

The more often you practice this exercise, the easier it will become to ground yourself. Eventually you may not need the tape, and you will find that you can go through the entire process very smoothly in much less time.

Allan had no trouble doing any of these exercises. After he'd had a heart attack, his doctor suggested that he take a yoga class for stress reduction. The instructor included some meditation in his classes, and also taught his students a little bit about the subtle body. It was his yoga teacher who recommended that he take the angel workshop, because he thought it would be an opportunity for Allan to heal his Heart chakra. His experience as an electrician, Allan said later, helped him connect with his chakras. He was used to working with energy and energy flows.

However, for Carol, this exercise was more difficult than the first one. She had never heard of chakras before and was dubious about how they were going to help her meet her angel. Her love of trees had helped her to ground, but try as she might, she couldn't sense her chakras at all. She kept practicing at home, with little success.

Then, two weeks later, Carol called us, all excited. She'd been working out at the gym, and was lying in the sauna, relaxing. The light was dim and the temperature in the room was 102 degrees. As she was turning over, looking down, she was amazed to see her chakras all lined up inside her body like flickering candles. The "vision," as she called it, only lasted a few seconds. But it was enough to convince her that chakras are real, especially since she'd seen them in such an unlikely setting, when she hadn't even been trying to see or feel them.

· GETTING TO KNOW YOUR CHAKRAS ·

The more you practice the Basic Grounding Meditation, the more you will connect with your chakras and know how to work with them. Notice whether some are easier to sense than others. Breathe more deeply into the ones with which you feel less connected, until your awareness of all of them is equal, until all of their lights shine brightly.

The energies of each chakra relate to areas in your physical, daily life. Chakra Chart 2, below, gives a brief summary of the main issues that are pertinent to each one, mentally and emotionally, physically and psychically. Focusing on a particular chakra when you are involved with its corresponding activity can help you to flow in harmony with your highest intentions.

· CHAKRA CHART 2—CORRESPONDENCES ·

CHAKRA	MENTAL/EMOTIONAL	PHYSICAL	PSYCHIC
Root:	Security, safety, groundedness, presence, confidence	upper digestive tract	spatial intuition
Sexual:	Sexuality, sensuality, intimacy, creativity	sexual glands, sexual organs	clairsentience
Solar Plexus:	Power, control, accomplishments, self-image	adrenal glands, upper digestive track	sensitivity to "vibes" from other people and places
Heart:	Love, compassion, forgiveness, surrender, acceptance	heart and circulatory system	empathy
Thymus:	Universal (unconditional) love, brotherhood, connectedness to all of humanity, peacefulness	thymus gland and immune system	telepathy
Throat:	Communication, spontaneity, speaking and hearing the truth	thyroid gland, throat/ears	clairaudience
Third Eye:	Wisdom, discernment, spiritual vision	pineal gland, brain/mind	clairvoyance
Crown:	Higher Self, spirituality	pituitary gland, energy body	cosmic consciousness

As you can see by referring to Chakra Chart 2, if you have issues with your home and job, your Root chakra is involved. Money problems connect to the Root and Solar Plexus chakras—since financial concerns have an impact on your sense of security and personal image.

If you are looking at issues of love and relationships, work with the Heart chakra, and if you're studying for an exam, be aware of your Third Eye. If you are thinking about changing jobs so that you can do something that feels purposeful in your life, be conscious of your Solar Plexus chakra.

In matters of health, you can look at the chart and see where the chakras relate to your physical body, too. Hoarseness or laryngitis involves the Throat chakra, and if you're having problems with your stomach, work with your Solar Plexus chakra, which is connected to the upper digestive tract.

When you have familiarized yourself with the Grounding exercises and feel comfortable doing them, it will be time to move on to the next step—Releasing.

Releasing

 alking with our angels is natural and joyful, and they love it every bit as much
as we do. Since that's the case, why doesn't everybody do it all the time? The reason
is that we have to meet them on their frequency, which is different from our own.
Because they are not in physical bodies, their vibration is finer. To talk with them,
to commune, we need to move out of our ordinary state of mind—the one that's
concerned about jobs, relationships, living space, health, and so forth—and move
into Higher Mind. To do this, we need to learn to let go, and that's why Releasing
is the next step.

Releasing worries, concerns, and negative self-beliefs frees us to enter the state of clarity, neutrality, and unconditional love that characterizes the angelic realm. It brings us to a place of forgiveness, for ourselves and others. And it feels great.

The angels are ready to assist us in our daily lives, so it isn't that our worldly concerns are unimportant. They are important. Precisely because they are, they contribute to how we feel about ourselves, and how we feel about ourselves is a most significant factor in making the angelic connection. If we are down on ourselves, feeling unworthy or guilty, or harboring unhappy feelings about others, we are not hanging out in Higher Mind. To fly with the angels, we need to travel light. And that means lightening up. This doesn't mean we have to be saints to talk with our angels, only that we need to clear ourselves of the mental and emotional baggage that we carry around with us much of the time.

The Releasing techniques in this chapter will help you unload that baggage so you can begin to converse quite naturally with your winged companions. Since releasing also helps to bring clarity to your everyday life, you may find that things start working better and that you're happier, less stressed, and more at peace with yourself.

· THE NEGATIVE VOICE ·

There is a particular aspect of the ego that sometimes gets in the way of connecting with the angels. The ego in itself is not bad, even though it's developed an unsavory reputation in some spiritual circles. It's the ego that has our best interests at heart; it works to protect us from disappointment and a sense of failure. But when it is not nurtured by loving self-acceptance, the ego develops a negative edge that reflects feelings of unworthiness and self-criticism.

We hear this negative voice in our head. It's the part that judges us, and the verdict is "Guilty" or "Not Good Enough." It compares us (usually unfavorably), criticizes or scolds, and holds us up to impossible standards of perfection. Or it flatters us, trying to make us feel better about ourselves by finding fault with others and blaming them for their shortcomings. Sometimes the negative voice speaks as "I," as in "I'm hopeless; I'll never get anywhere," and sometimes it uses "you," as in "You dummy, what did you do that for?" It's impossible to be in an open-hearted state when this voice is running the show.

We've found that the best way to deal with this negative voice is to recognize it. Start by simply acknowledging it—"Oh, there's my negative voice again." Like a pesky child, whining for attention, the negative voice will respond positively to recognition by lowering its volume. Once you become aware of it by acknowledging it, you can begin to identify negativity that you have been harboring.

To help you spot pockets of negativity, here's a list of the issues that we've found come up most frequently and some of the behaviors they generate:

Unworthiness	Fear of intimacy
Doubt	Abandonment
Fear of disappointment	Rejection
Perfectionism	Resentment
Pride	Envy
Inadequacy	Jealousy
Criticism (of self and/or others)	Guilt
Anger	Victimization
Hatred	Shame
Grief	Blame
Self-loathing	Dishonesty
Feelings of alienation	Denial

Need to control	Lack of focus
Ambivalence	Procrastination
Indecision	Fatigue
Boredom	Depression
Apathy	Greed

Each of us has different issues. In the event that we missed any of yours, the two exercises that follow will prepare you for the Releasing technique by helping you to identify your issues.

· INTRODUCTION TO RELEASING ·

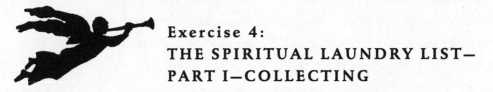

Exercise 4:
THE SPIRITUAL LAUNDRY LIST—
PART I—COLLECTING

As with all the exercises in this book, remember to do the Basic Grounding Meditation first (pp. 119–22), and have your pen and notebook handy. Get comfortable, and allow yourself enough time alone to go through this.

1. Sit quietly, with your hands on your heart. Allow whatever feelings you have to rise to fuller consciousness. Whatever your feelings are, allow yourself to have them and to just be with them.
2. As you breathe in, imagine that you are inhaling tolerance. As you breathe out, imagine that you are exhaling judgment.
3. Begin to tune into anything and everything that would prevent you from making contact with your angel. Write down whatever you come up with.

4. Ask yourself a question, such as "What could get in the way of my making contact with my angel?" or "Why shouldn't I make contact?" or "What's preventing me?" Listen to what your mind replies. Write it down. Keep asking and keep writing down whatever floats up in response to the question. It could be thoughts, feelings, memories.

5. When you start getting the same responses again, you will know that you have completed your list.

Kevin got up and left the room twice during this process—once to get a drink of water and the next time to empty his bladder. Although he'd grounded with the group before we started the Spiritual Laundry List and had seemed alert and present, when it came time to make the list, Kevin was lost in space. We asked if we could have a look at what he'd written. Here's what it said:

Why shouldn't I make contact with my angel?
ANSWER: Angels don't exist.

That was all he had on the page.

"If you don't believe that angels exist, why did you come to the workshop?" we asked. Kevin looked a little embarrassed. He just wanted to make sure, he told us, avoiding our eyes. We urged him to continue to ask the question as if angels did indeed exist, and write down whatever came up.

Here's his question: Why shouldn't I make contact with my angel?

Here's what his mind replied:

Why should an angel talk to me?
I'm not spiritual enough.

Angels don't talk to people.

Maybe I'll get a bad angel instead.

Kevin had been very close to his paternal grandmother, who lived with him and his family until she died. Kevin was four years old at the time and didn't understand death. Because he had dreams about her every night, it seemed to him that she was still there, and he talked about Grammy as if she were alive. This unnerved his parents. When Kevin reported what Grammy said and what they did together, his parents told him he was making it all up. It made him feel that he was bad and wrong. After a while, the dreaming stopped.

One night, just before he'd come to the workshop, Kevin was falling asleep when he had an uncanny feeling that he was not alone in his room. He opened his eyes and saw a soft glow at the end of his bed. Frightened, he snapped on the light, and the glow disappeared. The incident troubled him. Had something really been there? Was he going nuts? He'd come to the workshop in the hopes of finding out.

With encouragement, Kevin translated his answers into issues:

Angels don't exist.	= Fear of disappointment.
Why should an angel talk to me?	= Unworthiness.
I'm not spiritual enough.	= Unworthiness.
Angels don't talk to people.	= Fear of disappointment.
Maybe I'll get a bad angel.	= Fear.

Look at your list. Is there anything on it that surprises you? Or are the items so familiar to you that they're almost like old friends? Or enemies? At this point you may experience drowsiness, boredom, anger, or find your mind wandering. All of these are signs of resistance—proof that you're on the right track! Resistance comes up when you confront issues that make you feel uncomfortable. It's perfectly natural to want to avoid discomfort, so don't blame yourself for wanting to take a nap, or a walk, or a slow boat to China. Get up and stretch. Stick your head out of the window and take a few slow deep breaths. Then come back to your list. Read it over a few times. The next step will help you sort it all out.

Exercise 5:
THE SPIRITUAL LAUNDRY LIST— PART II—SORTING

For this exercise you will need your pen and notebook with the list of things that you believe might get in the way of making contact with your angel. If you've taken a break or had a bite to eat, you should ground yourself again before you begin this part.

1. Read through your laundry list. Then turn to the next page in your notebook and draw a line down the center of the page. Label the left side HOLD and the right side RELEASE.
2. Sit quietly with your hands on your heart, focusing your attention there.
3. Select one of the issues from your list to examine. Allow yourself to really feel this issue. Experience all the ways that it has affected your life.
4. Notice your breathing. Notice the state of tension or relaxation in your body. As you breathe in, imagine that you are breathing in light. As you breathe out, breathe out any tension or pain in your body.
5. Track back in time to your earliest recollection of having this feeling. When was it? Who or what triggered that feeling inside you?

6. As you breathe in, breathe in compassion, for yourself and for any other person who was involved. As you breathe out, breathe out criticism and blame.

7. When you have explored this feeling and felt it in all its aspects, in your mind and in your body, where it came from, where it has gotten you, and what it has taught you, see if you are ready and willing to release it. If so, write it down under the RELEASE column. If not, put it in the HOLD column.

8. Continue down your list item by item until you have completed your personal inventory.

How did you feel after this part of the exercise? Are you restless? Or raring to go? Apprehensive? Curious? Honor whatever you are feeling. Trust that you have brought yourself to a time when you are ready and able to let go of the things that you choose. It doesn't matter if there are ten items or only one. This is your list for right now. It reveals to you all that you need to release at this moment.

Carol has been to psychiatrists, psychics, and palm readers. She's forever on a quest to "find herself." When she composed her Spiritual Laundry Lists, she observed that she had more items in her HOLD column than in RELEASE.

"What should I do with these?" she asked, pointing to "need to control," "resentment," "perfectionism," "blame," and "victim," among others.

"Hold on to them, of course," we replied.

"But if I do, maybe I won't be able to talk to my angels," she said, frowning.

"Which do you want more—to talk to your angels or hold onto these issues?" we asked. Carol thought about it for a moment.

"It really doesn't make any sense to hold on to these awful things, does it?" she said, a tiny smile curling in the corner of her mouth. She reviewed her HOLD list and moved the items over to RELEASE.

For Allan, this part of the process was disturbing. Although he had been doing yoga and learning how to meditate, he was not an introspective man. He thought psychotherapy was a waste of time and money. Since his heart attack, however, fear for his life had prompted him to look at himself more closely. When he reviewed his list, which included "fear," "anger," "envy," and "pride," he felt overwhelmed. These issues brought him back to his childhood, to his relationship with his alcoholic father, and to a younger brother he hadn't spoken to in many years.

Allan started shifting restlessly in his seat. It was obvious that he wanted to walk out of the workshop. It didn't help to be reminded that the reason he made the list was so that he could begin to let go of these issues. He didn't want to touch them. Surprisingly, one of the items on his list served him well in this instance. Pride. He didn't want to be seen as a quitter.

Kevin hesitated. He shared with the group that he'd like to release unworthiness and fear, but he just didn't think it would work. "How do you know if you don't try it?" someone else in the group asked. There was a long pause. Kevin, who'd earned the nickname "Speed" in the luncheonette where he worked as a short-order cook, replied very slowly: "I don't think I can do it."

We advised him to add "doubt" and "inadequacy" to his list.

· HOW RELEASING HELPS ·

Once you've identified the issues that you're ready to release, you can use the Basic Releasing Exercise (pp. 138–39). This is an essential step in achieving the state of openness that allows us to connect with our angels. You need to release before you go on with the other steps in the GRACE Process or they simply won't work for you.

Being earthbound and thus subject to gravity, our vibration is denser than that of the angels. Releasing helps to raise our personal vibrations through the discharge of energies that have been blocked or held in the mental and emotional systems. Holding onto something requires effort and energy, and prevents us from receiving. If we're clogged up with negativity, we can't open to our angels. When we let go, we free the energy so it can be used in other, more productive ways, and we can receive the wisdom and love they bring to us.

The more vigorously you participate in the release procedures, the more effective they will be—and the higher your vibration will become. In the Basic Releasing Exercise below, vibration is raised by using the breath and by making a prolonged sound or tone.

· CELLULAR MEMORY ·

Memories, especially traumatic ones, are stored in the physical body on a cellular level as well as in the subtle energy body. In effect, your body "remembers" every single thing that has happened to you on a physical level—the time you fell off your tricycle, got your finger caught in a door, or bumped your head. Your mind remembers everything else, even though a great deal of it is stored in your unconscious.

The more forcefully you use your breath in the Basic Releasing Exercise, the better it works to discharge negativity and bring vitality and joy to every cell. There are two ways that you can do this, exhaling vigorously through your mouth, or snorting out of your nose. Both ways work, so try them both and see which one works best for you.

· SOUND HELPS ·

Using sound adds a further dimension to the process by helping you to align the physical and subtle energy bodies, bringing them into resonance. You can run up and down the musical scale until you find a sound or note that feels comfortable for you to make. Hold it until your breath gives out, letting it vibrate through your entire body—you may even feel your body tingling. This use of sound is called toning. It stimulates and opens the Throat chakra, which is the center of communication in the body, and the place where the angels speak to us.

You'll notice that we release into the Earth, using the rooting system that you've established through the Grounding exercises. Quite a few people have asked us, in their concern about Mother Earth, whether it isn't wrong to do this. Aren't we just polluting the Earth with our "garbage," even though it's on the mental and emotional planes? We've asked our angels about this and have been assured that the Earth receives the energies we dispose of in the same way she receives such wastes as fertilizer or compost. They are broken down into their finest components and recycled to nourish and seed new growth.

· SAY THANKS AND GOOD-BYE ·

Feelings and thoughts have a profound influence on the shape of all of our lives; they don't deserve to be feared or hated. Rather, they need to be respected, acknowledged, and treated as one would want to treat any living thing. In fact, the most positive way to approach the Basic Releasing Exercise is with gratitude for all your thoughts and feelings, no matter what they are. Good or bad, they helped to get you to the place where you are now—preparing to meet your angel. Remember to thank these thoughts and emotions before you release them. Saying thanks is an expression of acceptance of their function and purpose in our lives and this acceptance is a vital part of being able to let go.

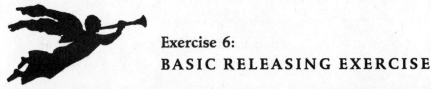

Exercise 6:
BASIC RELEASING EXERCISE

Enter your sacred or meditational space where you feel comfortable and secure, and you know you won't be disturbed. Begin with the Basic Grounding Meditation (pp. 119–22) to reestablish your connection to the Earth and the heavens. Have your notebook and your RELEASE list handy. Although you haven't made contact with your angel yet, you can still ask it to be with you in one of the steps. You may want to prerecord this exercise so you won't have to interrupt the flow.

1. Focus on your breathing. Take measured breaths, the breath in and breath out should be equal in length.
2. Now, place your hands on your heart and bring your attention there. Get in touch with your own loving nature, and with your wish and willingness to meet your angel.
3. Place in your heart the first issue on your RELEASE list. Feel that issue, with compassion for yourself in the circumstances that brought it up. Feel everything that it brings up inside. Examine the impact this issue has had on your life. What good has come of it?
4. When you are ready to release the issue, take a moment to thank it for the lessons that it has given you. And now—for the first time—Ask Your Angel to be with you and assist you in the releasing.

5. Name the issue, clearly out loud: "I release ————!" (Fill in the blank with whatever your issue is.) Then take a full deep breath.

6. Exhale—forcefully through your mouth or your nose—picturing the issue traveling from your heart and your entire body, down through your roots, straight down into the Earth. Send it as deep and as far into the Earth as you can before you take another deep breath.

7. Repeat these strong exhalations two more times, visualizing the issue being swept down and out your roots. On the last exhalation, allow a tone or sound to come out of your throat, as powerfully as you can.

8. Notice any inner shift that accompanies the release of this issue. Feel it in any way that it arises for you, and acknowledge it.

9. Thank your angel for its loving assistance, and thank the Earth for taking this energy back into its body and biodegrading it.

10. When you are ready, bring your attention back to your heart and look at the next issue on your list that you are ready to release. Repeat steps 1 through 9. Continue to go through your list until you have completed it.

When you have finished your RELEASE list, give yourself a few minutes to notice any changes in the way you feel, physically, mentally, and emotionally. Some people feel light-headed or a little dizzy after they do this. Others feel more solid and closer to the Earth. Be with whatever you feel, and acknowledge yourself for the job you've done of inner cleansing. Get up and move around.

Allan decided that he was ready to release the "envy" that was on his list. His younger brother had gotten to go on to college and eventually to medical school, while Allan took his first job as an electrician's apprentice, so that he could support their mother after their father died. Allan still envied him. But you could see the change in his face after doing the release. He looked ten years younger and shared

with the group that he was just beginning to see how he'd let envy of what he didn't have hold him back from appreciating what he did—his own life and family.

Carol was laughing at the end of the exercise. One of the issues she'd wanted to release was "perfectionism." From the time that she was a small child, Carol always had to do everything right. She even ironed her dolls' clothes. By the time she was a teen-ager, she was arranging her books alphabetically by author and in sections according to topic.

All through the Basic Releasing Exercise she kept feeling that she wasn't doing it right! She huffed and puffed, harder and harder, trying to get "perfectionism" out of her body—to no avail. On the third breath, she heard a voice inside her say, "You don't have to work so hard." She exhaled lightly, toned, and sent her need to be a "good little girl" out of her body and down into the Earth. At twenty-six, she was starting to realize that she didn't need to prove herself to anyone, or outdo everyone around her in order to be loved and accepted.

But it was Kevin's experience that electrified the group. He told us that by the time we got to the Releasing, he had a throbbing headache and his throat was so dry he couldn't swallow. He was also angry with himself for feeling so awful, and he couldn't get in touch with his loving nature. He just wanted to get rid of everything that was upsetting him.

When Kevin placed "fear" in his heart, he felt a sensation of icy cold that quickly changed to warmth as he heard: "There is nothing to fear." He was then able to release fear down his roots into the Earth with surprising ease.

As he placed the next issue, "unworthiness," in his heart, once again he felt icy cold and then warmth. But then he heard the words: "You are worthy."

Each time he placed an issue in his heart, he heard reassuring words and felt warmth, first within him and then, all around him. He had no difficulty releasing everything on his list, and when he opened his eyes, just to the right of his knee, he saw a soft glow, about the size of a basketball. This time he wasn't frightened. He watched as it grew and grew, filling his visual field. By squinting, he said, he could just make out a pair of enormous golden wings. The vision faded as people in the group began to talk, but when Kevin described what he had seen, everyone fell silent. And in that silence, all of us in the room felt the presence of the angels.

Kevin was convinced he'd heard his angel. Carol wasn't sure whether it was her angel's voice she heard, telling her not to work so hard. Allan didn't care. He just felt immensely better. Your angel may come to you during the Basic Releasing Exercise, but don't worry if it doesn't. The majority of people in our workshops make their first contact after following all of the steps in Grounding, Releasing, and Aligning.

· FOLLOW-UP ·

At different points in your progress, you will want to go back to your Spiritual Laundry List, to see if the time is right to let go of any additional issues on the HOLD side. You may also find that new issues appear as you peel off the old layers. You can add them to your list as well.

Once you have made contact with your angel, you will still want to go through the steps, beginning with Grounding and then Releasing. Each time you get ready to talk with your angel, ask yourself first if anything is getting in the way in that moment. You may not need to go back and do the entire Spiritual Laundry List, but there may be something there that needs to be released.

Even when you've worked through the major issues on your list, you may find that some of them pop up again, possibly surfacing in clever new ways. Don't be discouraged. Practice develops proficiency, and the more practice you get, the better you'll be at identifying and discharging outgrown ways of being. If you've felt unworthy your whole life, it's unrealistic to expect to be able to release all of that unworthiness in one session. Be loving with yourself. You don't have to be perfect before you can communicate with your angels. You just have to be willing to release a single molecule of whatever block you're carrying, and the space that empties out is room enough for your angel to enter.

· FORGIVENESS ·

Forgiveness is an expression of love and it is based on acceptance. Accepting doesn't mean that you have to like it; it means you are willing to let it be, and to go on with your life.

Lack of forgiveness inhibits your personal progress by keeping you stuck. It binds you to the person or situation that you haven't forgiven, just as surely as if you were chained to it. It takes you out of the moment, out of the present time, and returns you to an unhappy or unpleasant state. And it's worse for you than for the person you haven't forgiven because it generates bad feelings, and you carry those feelings with you all the time, whether you're aware of them or not.

While we talk about forgiving others, it is ourselves we need most to forgive, for not living up to our ideals of how we ought to be. There is such pain in this, so much self-flagellation. If only we could be compassionate with ourselves, we'd find that there is really no one else we need to forgive. We would accept our humanness good-naturedly and find ways to praise, not criticize or blame. And, once we began to do this, our self-acceptance, our self-forgiveness, would start to spread to others.

Releasing is the key to forgiveness. To forgive, you have to let go of hurt, resentment, anger, and the desire for revenge or retaliation. Practicing the Basic Releasing Exercise will help you to develop your skill in letting go. Don't give up if it doesn't happen immediately. Keep doing the Releasing.

Forgiveness is like water. It always flows into the lowest places, all the cracks and crevices. The moment we allow ourselves to release something, a healing flow of forgiveness rushes in. After he did the Basic Releasing Exercise, Allan felt the energy of forgiveness washing in, for himself and for his brother. This feeling stayed with him and deepened, and some weeks later, he was able to phone his brother for the first time in many years.

· THE POWER OF FORGIVING ·

The power of forgiveness came to Timothy in a strange and exhilarating way in 1984, following what had been for him a very dark and troubling year.

"I'd completed my first book two years earlier and had been searching for an appropriate publisher. An acquaintance of mine, a well-known West Coast author, seemed interested. She encouraged me to send her my manuscript and said she'd recommend it to her publisher.

"A year went by and I'd heard nothing from her. First, I worried about it. Then I got resentful. Finally, I was so furious that I couldn't release the negative thoughts that kept playing over and over in my head.

"Time passed, and in spite of my gentle reminders, there was no response. I felt rejected and hurt, and although I wanted to be able to forgive her, and worked with my angel regularly to release my anger, it kept coming back.

"Some months later, I was in England. It was New Year's Eve. I'd decided to spend the night alone, meditating, in the fourteenth-century tower built to Saint Michael that stands atop Glastonbury Tor. As part of a spiritual purification I asked my angels to help me locate, forgive, and release any hurts or injustices that I might still be harboring.

"Of course, the author's name rose to the surface of my consciouness as I sat shivering in the icy cold. I reviewed the entire situation, felt all the horrible feelings of blame and rejection one last time, and asking my angels to help—I let go. I forgave her.

"At dawn, I tottered stiff-legged down the steep, conical hill, picking my way between the sheep, and slept the day away at my bed-and-breakfast.

"That evening, January 1, 1984, was warm and mellow. I climbed up the Tor again to watch the rose-pink sunset flood the sky. I shut my eyes to meditate, my back against the ancient stones of the tower.

"Moments of great peace and joy passed. Then, I felt a gentle movement in my hair, as if the wind had stirred it. The next thing I knew, there was a soft pressure on my ears. Deep in my meditation, I did not open my eyes. Then, an explosion of sound! Vangelis's music from the film *Chariots of Fire,* with William Blake's extraordinary words, 'And did those feet in ancient times . . .' roared through my head in an epiphany of wonder. Someone had put earphones on my head.

"Minutes later, when the superb music had risen to its final crescendo, I opened my eyes. There in front of me, with a great grin all over her face, stood the author, six thousand miles from home, in a foreign land, and on top of this small and holy hill.

"I hadn't seen her in over a year, but in that moment, all was indeed forgiven."

Using the Releasing techniques will help you to experience the power of forgiveness, too. Take your time working through this chapter. You're entitled to all the time you need. When you feel lighter and more accepting of yourself and others, you'll know it. And you'll be ready to go on to the next chapter, Aligning.

Aligning

You've probably heard the old adage, "Angels can fly because they take themselves lightly." Well, you're lightening up, too, having learned and practiced the Basic Releasing Exercise. You're getting lighter and moving closer to the vibrational field of the angels. The last thing you have to do before you start talking with your angel is to bring yourself into alignment with its energy. In this chapter you will find a number of delightful ways to do that.

When you align the wheels of a car you bring them into coordination so the vehicle moves properly and you get a smooth ride. When you align your energy with your angel, you bring yourself into harmony with it, and you get a smooth connection.

Aligning brings you into a more open state, still focused, but looser. It's a state of relaxed awareness, similar to that of an athlete, like a runner, swimmer, or tennis player. An athlete needs to be loose to play; tension and tightness interfere with performance. The same is true of talking with the angels. Only in a relaxed state can you truly be open to their voices.

· THE SPONTANEOUS CHILD ·

Quite a few people have told us that they believed they had a guardian angel when they were children, but they haven't felt that way since becoming adults. You never outgrow your angel, no matter how old you may be.

As children, many of us had imaginary playmates. It's possible that some of these trusted friends and allies, with whom we shared our deepest secrets and highest hopes, were angels. To align your energy with your angel, it's helpful to remember the spontaneous, expansive, God-conscious child within you. It is full of wonder and delight and greets the angels naturally, without effort. This child is not wounded and never was. It is unharmed and unafraid—the purest distillation of your soul's essence.

You've done your homework—Grounding and Releasing—now it's time for some fun. Close your eyes for a moment and feel the part of you that never stopped believing in angels. Invite this part of yourself to come and play with you on this great adventure.

· EXPANDING THE SENSES ·

Since angels live in a state of expanded awareness, one of the best ways for us to align ourselves with them is by expanding our senses. We're continually bombarded with stimulation from the outside world, so it would seem as if all our senses were being used all the time. But the opposite is true. To deal with the extraordinary amount of input, we shut down and select what we experience. We can't respond to everything or our circuits would overload. For this reason, many people live in a state of semi-awareness. It's like eating when you've got a head cold and your nose is stuffed up. You can't really taste the food and much of the enjoyment is lost.

Fuller sensory awareness will enhance your pleasure in whatever you do. It's easy and fun to develop. The next time you listen to music, open yourself to the possibility of seeing, feeling, and perhaps even tasting it, too. Play your favorite piece of music—it doesn't matter whether it's rock or Bach. Turn up the volume as loud as your neighbors will allow, and lie down on the floor. Feel the vibrations in your body. Close your eyes and watch what colors or images appear. Different parts of the music will have different shapes or make you feel differently. Go with the flow, knowing that you are growing in awareness and sensitivity. And suppose you could taste the music—would it taste like ice cream, a hamburger, or a green salad?

The next time you look at something beautiful, whether it's a painting or a shiny new car, open yourself to the possibility of hearing its sounds, smelling its fragrance, and tasting its flavor. If you could translate what you see into a flavor, would it be sweet or tart, salty or spicy? If you could touch it, would it be smooth or rough, silky or coarse? How would it smell? Let these sounds, sights, aromas, tastes, and sensations carry you to other realms, to reveries of synthesis and new appreciation.

The next time you're about to eat something, close your eyes and take a deep whiff. Of what does it remind you? Is it sharp or soft, strong or gentle? When you put it in your mouth, savor its texture, as well as its flavor. Apart from the color that it is, what color would describe its taste? And when you eat it, how does it sound? Crunchy? Squooshy?

Smell is the most evocative of all the senses. A scent or aroma can instantly transport you to previous experiences and feelings. Close your eyes when next you smell something. Inhale its fragrance with your mouth open—you may even be able to taste it. As you breathe the smell in, can you feel its texture? What color could it be? If it were music, how would it sound?

To heighten your feeling sense, rub a piece of silk on the inside of your forearm, with your eyes closed. Now rub the silk on your forehead, over your Third Eye. Does it feel different in different places? Experiment with other textures, such as wool, aluminum foil, a piece of fruit, or a flower petal. Allow yourself to gather impressions. What sound relates to this texture? What color or shape? What smell? What taste?

Explore ways to extend your enjoyment of your five senses, for you're just about to embark on the sixth! When you travel with your spontaneous child you will discover ways to encounter the world with wonder, appreciation, and delight. And these are precisely the conditions that encourage angelic contact. Playfully expanding your senses will help in developing your ability to connect with the nonphysical energies of the angels.

· HOW TO USE THIS CHAPTER ·

In every other chapter concerning the GRACE Process, it is important to go through the chapter step by step, doing each exercise only after you are familiar with the one before. However, in this chapter, we offer you six exercises from which to choose, and each will teach you to align with the angels in a different way. Read through all of the exercises slowly, and select the ones that appeal to you the most. Tape-record the ones you pick and practice them. Find the one that works the best and use it whenever Aligning is needed.

· LISTEN UP AND LISTEN IN ·

To hear your angel's voice, you must also be able to listen. The following exercise is designed to extend your capacity to listen and to heighten your faculty for clairaudience, which is governed by the Throat chakra, the energetic center of communication in your body. Just as clairvoyance is the ability to see things beyond the usual range of our eyes, so clairaudience is the ability to hear beyond our normal range of hearing. There's nothing mysterious about either of these capacities, they're simply natural extensions of the frequency range of our senses.

Before you do any of these exercises, always remember to do the Basic Grounding Meditation first, and see if there is anything you need to release before you begin. If so, take time to use the Basic Releasing Exercise before you start.

Exercise 7:
EXPANDED LISTENING

It is best to do this exercise in a sitting position, just after you have completed the Basic Grounding Meditation and Basic Releasing Exercise. You will need a tape or record of your favorite music, and your notebook and pen. You may want to prerecord this exercise and play it right after the music stops. Record your words slowly, with long pauses between each of the steps.

Turn on the music and put the volume up so that the sound bounces around the room and surrounds you. Let yourself feel the music in your body and enjoy the good or happy feelings that it brings up for you.

As you're enjoying the music, picture your angel dancing to the melody, in whatever way you see it. Keep the image of your angel dancing until the music ends.

Turn off the sound system, and turn off any other mechanical sounds in the room, such as clocks, fans, air conditioners. Then proceed with the exercise.

1. Sit down, close your eyes and listen in the silence. What do you hear? Listen to the sounds coming from outside—from the street or neighbors. Tune into the most distant sound; tune into the sounds closest to you in the room; feel them in your body.
2. Keep your eyes closed. After listening to the outside sounds, go within. Listen to the silences between the sounds, between the notes, between your ears. In that space between your ears and your throat is the sound of your angel, the voice of your guardian and companion.
3. Remain quiet and continue to listen, eyes still closed. Imagine your angel sitting or standing close by you. You may not hear words, but if you do, reach for your notebook and write them down. If not, you may see

colors or squiggly lines. Let the images translate themselves into sounds
in your mind's ear.

4. When you feel that the sounds and the silence have become a part of
you, gently open your eyes.

It's possible during this exercise that your angel will reach out to you. It was
during this Aligning exercise that Deborah's angel first came in and advised her to
open her heart to the sounds of silence. You'll know by the message you receive,
through feelings or images or perhaps even words. But even if you don't get a
message, the exercise will bring you into a new place of receptive listening. Most of
the time we're so busy talking, or so busy thinking about what we're going to say
when we do talk, that we don't allow ourselves the pleasures of silence and of hearing
all the different kinds of sounds that live in that silence. It is in the silence that the
angels speak to us.

Alex works backstage at a theater. He was feeling trapped in his job, and when
his friend Carol told him about the angel workshop she had taken, he was intrigued
enough to come to one himself. He told us that of all the Aligning exercises, this
one was his favorite.

"When you put on that piece of classical music, I didn't see any angels. But then
you had us listen to the sounds inside our bodies. I could hear my heart, my
breathing, the gurgling in my stomach, plus the sounds in the room, the traffic in
the street—like I was a balloon that someone had blown up so big that all the sounds
in the world were happening inside me."

We explained to Alex that we all experience Aligning in different ways. His
feeling of expansion was his own way of coming into a deeper resonance with the
silence in which the angels speak. Another way to do it is by quieting the body and
the mind. The following exercise is very simple, and it's also very important.

Exercise 8:
A CENTERING MEDITATION

We spend so much time in our minds, in our heads. But doing this meditation will bring your consciousness right into your heart, the center of your body, which is where your angel meets you. The only thing you need to do it is a place where you can be quiet and undisturbed. Read the steps over several times before you begin, or, if you wish, you can record it. Allow a pause of a minute or two between each step if you do.

1. Close your eyes. Feel your breath rising and falling in your body. Hold the thought that when you breathe, God is breathing you.
2. Place your hands on your heart. Feel the beat of your heart, the life force. Feel it pumping blood to every part of your body.
3. Keep your attention focused on your heart and your heartbeat. If your mind wanders, bring it back to your heart, to the center of your feeling nature.
4. Picture a light or flame in the center of your heart. This signifies the spark of the Divine within you. It is the seed of who you are. In whatever way you can, connect to this spark and feel what it means to you.
5. Exhale fully. When you are ready, open your eyes again.

Ellis, a high school chemistry teacher, had some initial resistance to this meditation. He and his wife were splitting up. He'd just moved into his own apartment, wanted to find time to be with his kids, and was desperately trying to keep it all together. The Releasing exercises brought up a lot of anguish, and he was still feeling it.

"I came to talk to angels, not to go through my garbage," he complained. We asked him to put all of that aside for the moment and just go through the Centering Meditation. Afterward, he thanked us, saying:

"When I started the meditation, I was feeling pretty fragmented. But when I put my hands on my heart, I could picture a flame there, in the center of my chest. That did something to me. I've been running around frantic for weeks. For the first time since I moved out, I feel calm. I'm all in one place and I can feel my heart again."

This exercise can have the same effect in your life. And you can use it any time of day, wherever you are, whenever you aren't feeling centered. It only takes a minute to do it, so you can do it at your desk, or while you're sitting in your car, stopped at a red light. Our lives are so much more complicated than our grandparents' were. Any tool to help us stay centered is welcome.

When we think of the angels, we often think about heavenly choirs, of angels with harps and trumpets. As we come into alignment with our companions, we open to that glorious music, which is felt as much as it is heard. The exercise that follows is designed to help you, in the words of the Psalmist, "make a joyful noise unto the Lord."

Exercise 9:
VOCALIZING TO OPEN
THE THROAT CHAKRA

To align with your angel, you can use this exercise to stimulate the throat and ears. This will prepare you for conversing with your angel. You can also use a song, hymn, or chant, provided you do it with heart. The idea is to open you vocally, to loosen your vocal chords, and free you up. Practicing the vowel sounds out loud is a simple and effective way to do this, and you don't need anything except a comfortable place to sit, although, again, you may want to prerecord the exercise.

1. Begin with the vowel sound *A,* pronouncing it *ah.* Make the sound first with your eyes open and then with your eyes closed. Notice if there is any tension in your face, jaw, or throat. If there is, wiggle your jaw from side to side a few times. Then repeat the sound *ah* again, louder, with your eyes open and then shut.

2. Make the sound *E,* first with your eyes open and then shut. Again, notice if there is any tension, and if there is any difference when your eyes are open or shut. Repeat the *E* sound again both ways, louder.

3. Repeat the above steps with the sound of *I.*

4. Next, do the sound *O.*

5. Now, work with the sound of *U.* You can pronounce this first as *oooh* and then as *you.*

6. When you have gone through all the vowels, make the following sounds, doing them slowly. *Ah. Oh. Um.* Keep repeating these three sounds until they begin to blend together and you are making the sound of *ohm.* You can do this with your eyes open or closed. Feel the sound vibrating in your throat. Notice where else in your body you feel these sounds. Is there a resonance in your Third Eye, Thymus area or Heart?

7. Now, make any tones you feel like making. Let them pour out of your throat, rising and falling as they will.

8. Continue making the tones until your whole body is humming. If you have been doing them with your eyes open, shut them when you are finished. If they were closed, open them when you are finished. Remain still for a few minutes after you are done, just sensing your body.

How does your body feel after doing this exercise? Do the sounds in the room sound different to you now? You can also do this exercise by singing your own name. Try different ways of singing it—high and low, fast and slow—loud and soft. Sing until your ears ring!

Peter hated this exercise. He's the strong, silent type and doesn't say much, although when he does, his mordant wit cracks everyone up. Nora, on the other hand, loved it. She didn't want to stop toning and said she felt as though her whole body was vibrating with the sounds. And Bruce, who plays in a rock band, laughed and said he felt like a guitar being tuned. It was clear to him who was doing the tuning.

Exercise 10:
AN ANGEL INVOCATION

This simple little chant is another way to use the sounds your body makes to align with the angels. There are only four words to it, three of which are repeated three times, and then one that you say once to end it. You can repeat the chant as many times as you like. Each word is chanted with the same sound. The angels gave it to us in C-sharp, but you can use any note that feels right to you. Experiment until you find a note that feels clear and comfortable. Here are the words:

Eee Nu Rah
Eee Nu Rah
Eee Nu Rah
Zay.

Each word has a meaning. *Eee* means "all that I am that is not physical, my mind and my emotions." *Nu* means "my physical body." *Rah* means "my soul." *Zay* means "in the company of the angels." Together, the words of the chant say "I bring all of myself, mind, emotions, body and soul, together in the company of the angels." It's a quick and easy way to invoke the angels—a way of saying, "Angels, here I am, ready to be with you." It's simple. It works. Give it a "chants."

Connie took to this exercise the very first time she tried it in one of our workshops. Her voice isn't beautiful, but it's clear and strong and echoed all around the room. Later she related that when she was small her family had belonged to a church where people spoke in tongues. The sounds of this chant brought her back to some of those happy moments in her childhood, when she knew that angels were real.

· TUNING INTO THE ANGEL FREQUENCY ·

When you want to get a different station on the radio, you turn the dial. When you want to get a different channel on television, you turn the knob or hit the remote control. So, too, when you want to change levels of awareness, there are things that you can do to alter your state of consciousness. People have used alcohol and drugs to do this. At a conference on angels held in Dallas in the winter of 1989, Dr. Tom Moore, an eminent psychotherapist, speculated that our culture's drug problems might indicate an attempt to open to the angelic orders, to reach higher states of consciousness. But there is no fine-tuning device for altered chemical states. The chemicals are in charge, not you. The following visualization was given to us by the angels to help you shift into an altered state without losing control and without losing consciousness.

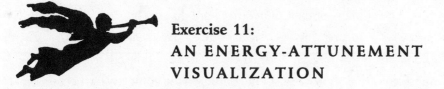

Exercise 11:
AN ENERGY-ATTUNEMENT
VISUALIZATION

This is a body-focused visualization. Each step in the exercise is designed to upgrade your personal vibration, so that you can align yourself gradually with the angelic frequency. At first, it may take time for you to feel the shifts within yourself, but when you've practiced the visualization for a while you will be able to do the three stages in three deep breaths.

1. Sit in a comfortable position, in a chair, with your feet on the floor.
2. Take the hand with which you write and place it on the opposite shoulder.
3. Take your other hand and put it on the opposite shoulder.
4. Close your eyes and notice your breathing. Feel the rise and fall of your abdomen as you inhale and exhale.
5. When you are comfortable with your breathing, visualize a sphere of copper-colored light the size of a grapefruit floating about eight or ten inches above the top of your head.
6. Picture this light and sense it glowing copper and warm above you. Feel it as the sphere begins to pour copper-colored liquid light down on the top of your head. As you inhale, draw this copper light down into your brain. Let it fill your head, neck, heart, continuing to pour down through you with each inhalation till it reaches the base of your spine. Feel the energy of this copper waterfall as it fills you. Take time to be with this coppery light.
7. When you are ready, visualize a beautiful silver sphere of light shining where the copper one was. It begins to pour a cool liquid-silver

waterfall of light down on you. Inhale this silver light all the way down through the top of your head to the tip of your spine. Let this silver light glow within your body, and feel how this light is a different, higher frequency than the copper. Spend a little time with this silvery light—follow it through your body—sense it interacting with your physical self.

8. Again, when you're ready, sense a golden ball of light floating above your head where the silver ball was. It is shining and brilliant, warm and beautiful. Once more, this light begins to pour down on top of your head. As you inhale, draw it down through the top of your head, all the way down to the base of your spine.

9. Sense this golden light glowing within you. Notice how this light is of a higher frequency than the silver light was, and how that light was higher than the copper. This golden light is the frequency of the angels. Breathe it into all your chakras, into every part of your physical body.

10. Stay with the experience of the golden light and observe your body carefully. Notice any shifts or changes in it. Listen to the sounds around you. Be with the golden light. Let it dance in you, with you, through you.

11. Then, slowly, slowly, when you're ready, open your eyes. Take a deep breath and exhale it slowly. Look around you. You are seeing the world through angel-tuned eyes.

12. When you have explored the room with all your senses, slowly shift back so that the gold light is replaced by silver, and the silver by copper. Now you are back in your normal state of consciousness.

If you decide to use exercise 11 as your Aligning exercise when you come to chapter 7, Conversing, only record steps 1 through 11. You will want to converse with your angel while you are still filled with golden light, rather than coming back to your usual state of awareness.

You may find, as Anthony did, that "the room looks different, sounds seem heightened, and colors are sharper." Or, perhaps, everything will appear less distinct. Paula said she felt that she could look through objects, that they seemed almost transparent.

Each of the steps in this exercise moves you to a different level of receptivity. When you draw in the copper light, you resonate with the Earth and the nature spirits. As you draw in the silver light, you connect with the mental realm of guides and extraterrestrials. The shift into gold brings you to the spiritual frequency of the angels. Making these shifts enhances your ability to expand your sensory awareness. Whenever you want to align with your angel, all you have to do is move with your breath from copper to silver to gold.

After he did this exercise the first time, Allan looked around the room and said it was as if he were seeing it for the first time, even though he'd been there for several hours. The exercise made sense to him, coming from his professional experience as an electrician. He said that since copper is a good conductor on the physical plane, it seemed logical for gold to work on the spiritual.

· YOUR ANGEL WINGS ·

Who among us has not wanted to be able to fly? Long before Leonardo da Vinci made sketches of different flying devices, the ancient Greeks told the story of Daedalus, who made a pair of wings for himself and his son, Icarus, so they could fly away from the island where they were imprisoned. The wings were made of feathers held together by wax. Despite his father's warning, Icarus soared too close to the sun, the wings melted, and Daedalus watched, broken-hearted, as his son plummeted into the sea and drowned.

But suppose you had wings that couldn't melt? Just as our chakras are subtler than our physical body, there are other energy points and fibers within us that are even more subtle. Imagine for a moment that there are pairs of tiny golden seed pods on either side of your spine, running from the top of your neck to the bottom of your spine, and that when you turn your attention to these pods they will awaken and open. Tiny golden fibers will unfurl from them, and spread out across your back, and beyond. These are your "wing fibers." Fully opened, they act like an antenna system that will help you to align with your angel.

If we have one set of these fibers, the angels have many. The exercise that follows will show you how to open your golden wing fibers and awaken to the part of yourself that is angelic.

Before you begin this exercise, look at the diagram of the wing system on page 162 so you know where the points or seed pods are and where your wing fibers emerge. Use the diagram like a subtle anatomy chart. When you have a sense of where the seed pods of your wings are, do the Basic Grounding Meditation (pp. 119–22), and then—learn to fly!

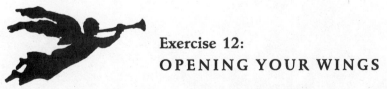

Exercise 12:
OPENING YOUR WINGS

Sit quietly on the floor or in a chair, with space behind you. Some people find this exercise easier to do standing up. Again, you may want to record this exercise.

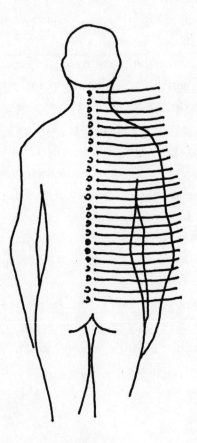

Wing Fibers.

Left: beginning to uncurl.
Right: stretching out.

1. Close your eyes and ground yourself. Feel your roots extending down from the base of your spine, deep into the Earth. Feel your Crown chakra fibers reaching up into the heavens.
2. Connect with your chakras by sensing each one, from Root to Crown.
3. Now, focus your awareness on your spine. Sense each of your vertebrae.
4. Place your hands on either side of your spine at the top of your neck. Slowly, reaching around in whatever way you can, massage your back on either side of your spine, working your way down from your neck to your tail bone. Feel the spaces between each vertebra. If you can't reach some parts, rub your back against a wall like a dog or a cat to feel them.
5. Next, turn your sensing inward and visualize pairs of golden seed pods on either side of your spine, running from top to bottom, just beneath your skin.
6. Starting at the top of your spine, imagine the top pair of golden seed pods beginning to glow and open. Feel/see a tiny golden sprout or fiber emerging from the seed pod just as it would from a plant.
7. Vertebra by vertebra, move all the way down your spine, feeling each pair of golden seed pods opening and sprouting a little golden fiber.
8. Work your way up and down your spine again, now visualizing all of these fibers growing longer and stronger. They're growing horizontally, away from your spine, getting longer and longer. Now they're as wide as your back, and still growing.
9. In your imagination, extend your wing fibers out until they are about two and a half feet across. Flap these fibers, wiggling them, pointing them up to the ceiling and down to the floor.
10. Play with your wings. Flutter them. Raise your left wing toward the

ceiling and lower your right wing toward the floor. Reverse. Point them all the way back behind you. Bring them all the way around in front of you, tip to tip, and riffle them up and down.

11. These golden fibers are your wings—your antenna to the angelic realm. Imagine a loving golden energy pouring into the tips of each fiber from that realm. Feel that same loving golden energy pouring out from the tips of your wings into the world.

Keep playing with your wings. Flap them around. Get used to them.

When Deborah unfurled her wings, her angel spoke to her again: "Arise as a bird rises into the air—spread your wings and fly without fear." The message was doubly significant for Deb; she'd been contemplating moving out of New York City, but she was apprehensive because she had no idea where to go. A few months later, we got a letter from her. She'd simply packed up and started driving (not flying!) west. When she reached Santa Fe, she said, she knew she was home.

The first time Vickie did this exercise, she burst out laughing. "I always knew I had wings!" she said. That's the reaction many people have. It may seem strange at first, until you get accustomed to them, but once you do, you'll enjoy opening them in public places, too. See what happens when you unfurl them in a crowded elevator—or while riding in a bus. Jake told us that he was in a busy restaurant one evening and try as he might, he couldn't get the waitress's attention. Just for fun, while he was waiting for her, he decided to open his wings. Within moments, the waitress was at his side. Jake did a double take when he saw her nametag: Angela.

When you have finished using your wings, it's a good idea to pull them back into your body again, so the fibers don't get knotted or tangled. If they do, visualize your angel standing behind you with a large golden comb, combing them out again.

Joseph's angel uses its own wing fibers to comb out his tangles. And Barbara cleans and combs them out in the shower.

A simple way to energize yourself is to bring these fibers around in front of you, touching the tips of one wing to the tips of the other. Your wings will create a cylinder of golden light around you, which you can spiral into your body. Feel this light pouring into you, filling your chakras, and every other part of your physical body as well.

When you open your wings you beam out loving energy, not just from your wing tips, but from your heart, too. Whether you're sitting on a bus or standing on line in the supermarket, whenever you open your wings, you broadcast love into the world, and contribute to uplifting the spiritual atmosphere.

· DOING YOUR SENSORY WORKOUT ·

Each of these exercises will allow you to align in a different way. Some people relate better to exercises that make use of sound, others do better with visualization techniques, still others respond best to processes that involve the physical body. The technique you choose will reveal something about yourself.

Expanded Listening is preferred by people who are aurally oriented; hearing is the way that they gather information. Vocalizing appeals to those who are more verbal, as does the Angel Invocation. If you liked the Energy-Attunement Visualization best, you're probably a visual person who gets information through seeing, and is good at picturing things vividly. And if your favorite Aligning method is Centering or Opening Your Wings, you're body oriented, disposed toward touching and feeling.

Developing your senses is like working on your body at the gym. If you only use one machine, you only strengthen one muscle group. When you are familiar with the entire GRACE Process, come back to this chapter and do the other exercises, to further develop your sensory muscles.

As soon as you begin to feel a shift in your awareness, and are comfortable with one of these exercises, you're ready to start talking with your angel.

Conversing

People in our workshops are amazed at how easy it is to talk with their angels. You don't need to meditate on top of a mountain for twenty years in order to do it. The essence of opening to your angels is simply coming into an open-hearted state. The Grounding, Releasing, and Aligning exercises prepare you to do this, to help you become receptive and accepting, and to experience feelings of compassion, tenderness, deep understanding, and delight. That's why it's so important to do all the steps, in order, without skipping any.

The angels connect us to our highest source of knowing, the Higher Self, that aspect of ourselves which is God-conscious. It is loving but neutral, compassionate but unsentimental. It exists in each of us, although most of us can't maintain states of God-consciousness for prolonged periods of time. But many of us do have occasional glimpses of it—thank Heaven. Enough to let us know that it's part of who we are. And working with the angels helps to bring this Higher Self through.

One school of thought has it that our angel is actually our Higher Self that became separated from us when we embodied as humans. From this standpoint, meeting your angel is reconnecting with another part of yourself. This feels true for a good number of us, but don't take our word for it. See how it feels for you.

In any case, talking with your angel will provide you with a key to understanding yourself and others. It can also help you clarify your purpose in life, and open you up to your unique gifts.

· DON'T FORGET TO WRITE ·

When your angel speaks to you, it's important to write down whatever you receive. So be sure to keep your angel notebook and pen nearby when you do exercise 13. Write without editing or censoring or trying to change words or expressions to make them sound better. Write without judgment, as if you were taking dictation. When you have finished, it is courteous to thank your angel—you may even wish to write "thank you" at the end.

· PREPARATION ·

Now that you have mastered the first three steps in opening to your angel, you are prepared to speak directly with your celestial friend. You may no longer need to listen to the exercises on tape. If you've practiced them enough, you will be familiar with them. In that case, you'll just need to record the exercise that follows. But if the steps are not familiar yet, or if you like listening to them, here's a recap of the exercises to tape, in the order in which you'll use them, prior to Opening to Your Angel. Record them one after the other, and remember to allow pauses in between each step, to give you time to follow the instructions.

Exercise 3: Basic Grounding Meditation, pp. 119–22;
Exercise 6: Basic Releasing Exercise, pp. 138–39;
Whichever one of the Aligning exercises you prefer from chapter 6;
And then from below, add exercise 13: Opening to Your Angel.

Now you are ready to talk to your angel. You are grounded and centered, feeling your connection to the Earth and to the heavens. You've released any blockages that could get in the way of making clear contact with your angel and you're feeling lighter and more open. You've brought yourself into deeper alignment with your guardian angel. You are receptive and tuned to the frequency of the angels.

When you do this exercise, you will be asking your angel a question. Before you start, begin to frame a question. It should be simple and open-ended, such as "What do you wish to communicate to me?", "What do I need to know right now?", "How can I be open to your voice?", or even "What is your name?"

Allan was calm as this exercise began. He'd taken off his glasses and closed his eyes. His quietness reflected a state of preparation and readiness. Carol was excited and could hardly stay in her seat. There was an "opening night" feeling, she said, as she shared with us later—a mixture of excitement and nervous anticipation.

Well, here we go!

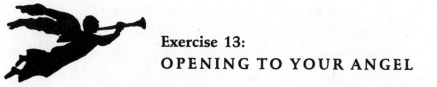

Exercise 13:
OPENING TO YOUR ANGEL

Have your notebook and pen handy. At the top of a clean page, write "Opening to My Angel" and the date.

1. Sit in your sacred space with your feet flat on the floor and your eyes closed. Sense the presence of your angel drawing closer and closer to you. Imagine that its wings are softly folded around you.

2. As you inhale and exhale slowly, feel or sense the presence of your angel reaching out to you. Breathe in this closeness and let a question rise up within you.

3. Bring your attention to your heart. Place the question you want to ask in your heart by visualizing the words written there.

4. When you feel the words in your heart, open your eyes and write the question down in your notebook. Close your eyes again.

5. With the words of your question in your heart and in your mind, connect to your deep desire to hear the voice of your angel. Listen in your heart and in your throat. Be aware of any feelings that come up. Angels reach us through feelings so that may be the first form of contact. Allow the feelings and be open to the words that arise.

6. Write whatever you receive, which may be words, images, or feelings.

7. Remember to thank your angel for the message.

8. Read over what you have received.

Notice how you feel about the message. It may surprise you, and it may touch you. If the words bring tears to your eyes, or you feel moved in some way, you'll know that your angel has spoken through you.

The first question Carol asked her angel was "What is your name?" "Freda" was what she heard, and she dutifully wrote it down in her angel notebook, under the date, February 4, 1989. She was puzzled. She had an aunt by that name, but as far as she could tell, her aunt was no angel. As she sat quietly reflecting on it, she heard her angel speak again. "Listen to me well, and hear me in your heart. My name is Freedom."

When Allan asked, "What message do you have for me?" he didn't receive any words. What he experienced was a warm, vibrant feeling in his heart, as if it were overflowing with tenderness and love. He shared with the group that he felt suffused with love, that his entire body was singing and ringing with it.

Carol was giggling and feeling a bit flustered. There were tears welling in Allan's eyes. He wiped his cheeks with both his hands, shaking his head.

"I can't believe it," he said. "I didn't see an angel, I didn't hear an angel, but I know it was there."

There was no doubt they'd met their angels.

In another workshop, Darryl, a young musician, asked, "What do I need to know right now?" and heard these words: "Know that I am with you now, and I will never leave you. I am by your side, your gentle guide, showing you the way. Open your heart to me and let's play!"

Sitting across from Darryl was Elsita, a delightfully young-at-heart octogenarian. She didn't receive a message in words, but this is what she wrote in her angel notebook after she did the exercise for the first time:

"I feel such strong vibrations through my hands, my arms, my face. I see beautiful colors in changing geometric patterns. I have no lucid thoughts."

Elsita did the exercise again. This time she wrote:

"I see reflections in a placid pond; the flowing current of a broad river; waves breaking on a beach; long lines of waves following; foam, movement. Now a brilliant beam of light crosses the waves. A word comes to me: Beauty."

Pleased with the pictures, but eager to hear her angel's message, Elsita did the exercise a third time, asking, "What do I need to know right now?"

Now, words came to her clearly: "Beauty is Truth, Truth Beauty. That is all ye know and all ye need to know." And the voice continued, "I am in the flowing river, in the waves, in the foam, in the Light, and in the Darkness. I am the Creator and the creation."

Elsita was a little giddy with delight. "And I only asked to speak with an angel!" she said.

The angels come to us in ways that we can receive them. At first, Darryl was a bit reluctant to share the message he'd gotten. He wasn't expecting poetry, and he didn't think angels were so playful. Elsita has a great love for beauty and for nature, but she also had some trepidation when she first opened to her angel. So her angel calmed her with beautiful scenes of nature and this allowed her to relax sufficiently to hear Higher Mind speaking through.

If you're not sure that you received anything, close your eyes again and repeat the exercise from the beginning, making a stronger connection with your wish to contact your angel. Accept whatever you receive with thanks. Don't dismiss or criticize what comes through, because that will shut down your heart and block communication. When you accept, you open, and when you're open you're much more likely to receive.

· PRACTICE, PRACTICE, PRACTICE ·

Simple as this opening process is, its success depends on how thoroughly you have done the Grounding, Releasing, and Aligning. Practice will improve your skill and continue to open the channel of communication between you and your guardian. It's good to set aside some time each day for a rendezvous, as Lee's angel advised, preferably in the sacred space that you have created, one that is comfortable and serene, and reminds you that you're entering the angelic realm. You might want to light a candle, or bring some fresh flowers to this place. It's meant to be special, just as your relationship with your angel is special.

At this point, some questions may be coming up:

How can you tell when it's your angel talking and when it's your mind?
How do you know whether it's an angel or a guide?

Let's use the analogy of a television set, imagining for a moment that you are the set. There are many channels or stations broadcasting. (In this case, channel refers to a voice, not to the person receiving it.) Until you open to the angels, the only channel you're likely to get on your set comes from your mind, from your ego. It's not hard to tell the difference between your mind and your angel. Your mind is full of "shoulds" and judgments. It tells you what to do, and how and when to do it. And for sure, it tells you when you've done it wrong.

Through practicing the GRACE Process you're learning to tune into another channel on a higher frequency, the voice of your angel. This voice is calm and compassionate. Sometimes it's wry. Sometimes it rhymes! It never judges or says you're wrong, or tells you what to do, apart from directing you to look within or be more loving with yourself. It always points out the positive view and offers constructive advice. How different it sounds from the old, negative programming that comes from our ego minds. It's a whole new show!

· OTHER VOICES ·

Once you tune into the angels, you may find yourself receiving other stations as well—voices of guides, extraterrestrials, and nature spirits. How can you tell who's talking, and what's the difference? The tone of the words and the subject matter will clue you. Guides are directive and predictive; most of them were once in physical form, and they address human concerns. Extraterrestrials come from other planets and star systems. They project a quality of differentness and have a more impersonal, universal outlook. Nature spirits tend the animal, vegetable, and mineral kingdoms, and their messages relate to the growth and well-being of the Earth and her creatures. You will find that each voice has a different sound or feel to it.

· HOW TO TELL IF IT'S AN ANGEL ·

In fact, one of the ways to identify the angelic voice is by the way you feel when you hear it. Gilda is a free-lance journalist known for her sharp wit. She is unsentimental and intellectually curious. She wanted to see if she could talk with angels from an investigative reporter's approach. Following the Grounding, Releasing, and Aligning exercises, Gilda closed her eyes and asked, "What do you wish to say to me?" Tears began to course down her face as she heard her angel's response. Her notebook lay in her lap, the pen lifeless in her fingers. For the first time since she'd become a professional, she missed getting the exact quote, but she was beaming.

"I've never experienced anything like the love that I felt when I heard my angel," she explained later. "I was bathed in love, washed clean of my niggling self-doubts. I felt cherished!"

Feelings of love, of greater self-acceptance, of inner peace, of being deeply cared for and recognized, are signs of angelic connection. You may also have a physical reaction. Larry, a computer technician, was skeptical about the possibility of getting messages from an angel but was driven to try because his girlfriend had changed— "mellowed out" were his words—since she'd been talking to hers. His initial attempt was a dud, he thought.

"I didn't get any messages at all," he said. "I just had a funny feeling in my heart, like it was a sponge that was being squeezed and then released."

Larry's angel had touched his heart, even before he heard its words. He sensed it physically but not emotionally, because he was blocking his feelings. When we pointed out to Larry that his emotional heart was opening, he felt encouraged enough to persevere. The open-hearted state is a prerequisite for talking with the angels. But because he was still holding on to some of his skepticism, it took three more attempts before his angel spoke:

"You are enough," it told him. "You are good enough. Smart enough. You are worthy of love, just the way you are."

Unerringly, his angel had addressed the very issue that had slowed down his connecting—unworthiness. Larry now communes with his angels on a regular basis using his personal computer.

· PHYSICAL SIGNS ·

Other physical manifestations that may accompany angel communication: chills; goose bumps; tingling at the back of the neck; unusually heightened clarity of vision; tears, which flow when the emotional heart suddenly opens; and a sweet or fragrant smell that cannot be explained. You may get just a whiff of something that smells like flowers—but there are no flowers around. All of these are indications of angelic visitations.

· CONVERSING ·

Once you make initial contact with your angel, there are two ways that we have found to talk with them. The first is to ask a question of a general nature, and to open to receive the reply. Some questions you might ask are:

What is my purpose in this life?
What are my gifts?
What shall I call you? What is your name?

What's the best way to connect with you?
What do I need to know right now?
How can I serve?

Here are some excerpts of answers to the same question, the first received by our dear friend Elsita, the second by Anne, a crackerjack hypnotherapist, the third by a musician and composer who calls himself Mercury, and the last by Jackie, an antique-show impresario and sister on the spiritual path:

QUESTION: How can I serve?

ELSITA'S ANGEL, DANIEL: By talking. By telling people. There are many who are ready to hear your message—the message of love and unity that alone can save your planet. Open your heart and help others to open theirs. It is through the hearts of humans, rather than through your minds, that your world can be healed and enabled to enter a new and glorious age of peace and fulfillment.

ANNE'S ANGEL, LEANDOR: The true meaning of service is to give that which is asked with love. If you listen with the "Third" Ear, and see through the "Third" Eye, and feel through the chalice of the heart, you will give with love that which is asked. Giving without love is a deception.

MERCURY'S ANGEL, UNNAMED: You are a connecting link. A conducting element in a circuit. As the spirit descends into the body, so will you descend upon the world to reestablish the link between the material and spiritual dimensions. You are to serve as a mouthpiece for the angels.

JACKIE'S ANGEL, JEDIDIAH: Your job in the universe is to spread fearlessness by loving openly. God's grace is present and your manifestation of it will inspire others. Your willingness to do the Work will affect those around you until they too are drawn into the circle of light. Be a smiling missionary. God's grace is ever present. Reflect this grace. Be in God's Presence. Reflect fluidity, integrity, unity.

· VOICES AND NAMES ·

We find it fascinating that although the question was asked by four people at different times and places, there are marked similarities between them, with themes of love and unity being present in each. Yet how individual the voices sound! In our workshops, we've found that when groups of three or four people ask the same question, the answers are frequently similar, with identical words and images used. To us, this is incontrovertible proof that we are all connected to the Source, and that when we gather together with our dear angels, the messages we all need to hear come through loud and clear.

Each angel connects in its own way. Yours may want to talk with you as soon as you get up. The relaxed and drowsy state just before you fall asleep and just as you are waking in the morning is especially conducive to angel talk. For this reason, some people keep their angel notebook and a pen near their beds. Or your angel may choose to communicate only on Fridays, or some other particular day of the week. And if it says its name is Jonathan, as Gail's did, don't be surprised. Not all angels have fancy names. If you don't receive a reply when you ask your angel's name, not to worry. One angel told us that they don't actually have personal names, and the ones we receive when we ask correspond to a vibration that we name.

If your angel says its name is Gabriel, or Raphael, are you talking with an archangel? Chances are that you're not, but that the angel comes from the Gabriel or Raphael clan. When you run into an archangel, you'll know for sure.

· DIALOGUING ·

The second way to converse with your angel is interactively, using a dialogue format. Once you begin to let go of old mental and emotional barriers through the Releasing process, you start revealing your true strengths, your gifts, and your goodness. Our angels come into our lives to help us do this. The more we dialogue with them, the more information they will share.

Now that you've opened to your angel, you can use the exercise that follows whenever you want to converse. Read the exercise over a few times and then you can tape it. Before you do this exercise, go through the Grounding, Releasing, and Aligning exercises first. Not doing them is like not warming up before you go running. The more you stretch, the better you'll be able to run—or in this case, fly.

Exercise 14:
ASK YOUR ANGELS

To do this process, you will need your angel journal, pen, and tape recorder with this exercise—and any others you may need—on tape.

1. Sitting comfortably in your sacred space, feel the presence of your angel and begin to breathe in all its love. Greet your angel from your heart and receive its greeting in return.
2. Let a question form into words in your mind. Place it in your heart. When you can feel the words in your heart, open your eyes and write it down, and ask your angel your question.
3. In the stillness, open to the words that come to you from your angel. Without thinking about them, write them down.
4. As in any conversation, you will have things to say in response to what your angel just said. Put those words on paper as you beam them out to your angel.
5. Once again, receive your angel's response to you, and write down the words.
6. Continue until you have come to the end of the conversation.
7. Thank your angel.

Be aware of your body and your breathing, and your surroundings. Read what you received. What did you learn about yourself? How does it make you feel? If you don't think the information is correct, or helpful, or you think you're just making it all up, put it away. Then, at a later time, possibly in a week or two, read it again. Time will give you sufficient distance to assess its merits less judgmentally. When your angel speaks, it can jiggle some of your oldest and most closely held beliefs. For whatever reason, we humans get very attached to our beliefs; we're convinced they're right. As LNO once said, "Most people would rather be right than happy."

· CONTINUING CONVERSATIONS ·

So many of us are using computers these days, in homes as well as offices. If you have one, you'll find it especially useful for dialoguing with your angel. Often transmissions come through in a gush of words. It's not always easy to get them all down when you're writing longhand.

Since most of us don't have computers in our sacred spaces, you'll want to make the surroundings suitably respectful. Clear your desk of all the normal clutter and paraphernalia, place a lighted candle, a crystal, or a fresh flower on it, and boot up. Use a new diskette and keep it just for your angel's messages. Then follow the steps in exercise 14.

The morning after she first met her angel, Lynn, a single working mother, felt a pressing need to continue the conversation, using her Macintosh computer. In a letter to us she wrote:

"Naturally, I was a little uncomfortable, but when the message came through, I realized that there were tears in my eyes and I had 'received.' I addressed my angel this way:

"Gabriel—Thank you for meeting with me yesterday. It was an exciting day, and it looks like there is going to be a lot of wonderful work to do. I need help in guiding Patrick (my fifteen-year-old). He is going to be terribly disappointed when he finds out that he won't be able to meet the Navajo Indian healer today. He was going to have a session with him. How shall I help him?"

In her letter, Lynn told us that Gabriel's response was instantaneous and she had a hard time keeping up with him. Her fingers flew across the keyboard, capturing these words:

"Patrick does not need anyone on the outside to help him. Please tell him that I said that he needs to learn to turn inward. That is why his appointment was canceled. He is a very highly evolved being, and he only needs to make contact with his angel."

Still concerned, Lynn pressed on, asking: "Shall I teach him how to do that? Maybe he won't listen."

Gabriel replied: "Patrick listens and understands it all. Show him how to contact his angel just as you did yesterday. He has been in touch with his angel during his periods of drawing pictures. Let him find the name of his angel as he draws, then you can show him how it works with writing down words to get answers. Don't worry, Mother, you can do it!"

Lynn wrote: "The words 'turn inward' and 'Mother' are not words that my children or I use. As I was typing the word 'Mother' my mind was saying, 'You should be using the word "Mom," ' but because of that, I knew the words were coming from someone else, not from me. Well, I really had some practice and verification this morning that it is 'for real.' Thank you for making it possible for us to have such an important day."

As you progress in your conversations, you'll observe that your angel has its own characteristic voice. It may sound very different from your own, or it may be similar, but with certain idiosyncratic distinctions, such as the ones Lynn noted. It may begin speaking with a particular salutation. For example, Joy, one of Timothy's angels, starts her messages with "Beloved"; and LNO invariably begins with the words "Dear One." Sargolais, Andrew's companion, wouldn't dream of calling him "Dear" or "Beloved." He just starts talking.

From time to time, you may find, as Anthony did, that you are writing or typing a word that you don't know. Don't freak out; keep typing, and look it up later. Being open and receptive to whatever messages you receive will encourage further communication. Don't be surprised either if your angel's handwriting is different from your own.

As you get more practice, you will find that you're able to hold longer conversations and you'll get to know your angel better. It's like getting to know a friend. The more time you spend together, the better you know each other.

Sometimes the angels answer us in unexpected ways. Geraldine is a bookkeeper. Here's an example of a longer dialogue from her angel journal:

GERALDINE: Should I leave my job?
ANGEL: Follow your heart.
GERALDINE: My heart says yes, but my mind says I need to pay the rent.
ANGEL: Secure a new position before you leave the old one.
GERALDINE: How will I do that?
ANGEL: Follow your heart.
GERALDINE: What does that mean?
ANGEL: Do what you love to do. If you cannot, learn to love what you do. When you love what you do, you do it with love. That honors God and raises the level of your work to higher service.
GERALDINE: My job is okay, but I can't stand my boss. What should I do?
ANGEL: What is it about your boss that you dislike? Whatever it is represents something within yourself that you can't stand. If you stand UP to that, you will UNDERstand.

Geraldine got a chuckle out of that, but she also took it seriously. She reexamined what it was about the manager that bothered her. Her boss was quick to find fault and rarely complimented her. Geraldine was a stickler for details and very conscientious. She realized that she had been wanting acknowledgment from her superior, but that she never acknowledged herself. The dialogue with her angel allowed her to remain in the job and six weeks later, quite unexpectedly, her boss was moved to another department and Geraldine was made manager.

Private moments with your angel are a deep source of pleasure. Your heavenly helper brings comfort and good cheer into your life, as well as illumination to troublesome issues. Right now, you are enjoying your first contact with your angel. Congratulations! And, there's more fun to come. In the chapter that follows, you'll find other ways of Enjoying your angel, using the Angel Oracle.

Enjoying
(The Angel Oracle)

Sargolais created the Angel Oracle to give you a chance to play with your own companion and a host of other Earth-tuned angels as well.

You can use the Oracle when you want guidance, but are too caught up in the chaos of your life to sit down and dialogue with your angel. And there may be times when you want to work with something you can touch and hold, such as rune stones, tarot cards, or *I Ching* coins. Or you may just want to relax and enjoy the angels' company. The Oracle works for all these occasions.

Nearly every culture in the world has created its own system for accessing spiritual information, from the Urim and Thummim mentioned in the Bible to the ones listed above. Like other divination tools, the Angel Oracle operates through the principle that the Swiss psychotherapist C. G. Jung called "synchronicity." Jung noticed that a seemingly random action, such as tossing a coin or pulling a card from a deck, can provide you with a deep, intuitive understanding of events in your life—if you know how to interpret it. When you consult the Angel Oracle, you create opportunities for the angels to reach out to you with guidance, whether you have a specific question in mind for them or not.

· WHAT'S IN THE ANGEL ORACLE ·

There are three categories of information in the Angel Oracle. It's through the synchronistic combination of your selection from each one of them that the angels can connect you with your own highest knowing.

- In the first category are the archangels, the overlighting beings who will choreograph your adventure.
- The second category contains sixteen different kinds of angels who are ready to meet you, engage with you, and guide you.
- In the third category you will find the twenty-four different life situations through which these angels can be summoned.

Below you will find everything you need to use the oracle immediately. But for maximum enjoyment, take the time to make yourself a deck of Angel Oracle cards. You'll find instructions for making them later on in this chapter.

Exercise 15:

A QUICK WAY TO USE
THE ANGEL ORACLE

Before you use the Angel Oracle, you might want to do the Basic Grounding Meditation (pp. 119–22), but it isn't a prerequisite. The information you need to do a reading will be found in the three boxes that follow.

1. Sit quietly and become aware of your breathing.

2. If you have a question for the angels, focus on it. If you do not have a question, simply invite them to come into your life.

3. The left side of the body is connected to the right hemisphere of the brain, which is the more intuitive side. When you're ready, point your left index finger over the box with the names of the archangels in it. Close your eyes, rotate your finger in a counterclockwise circle three times, and then lower it to the page. Open your eyes to see which archangel you chose.

4. Next, hold your finger over the second box, the one that lists the sixteen different kinds of angels. As before, close your eyes, and let your finger find the page. Open your eyes to see which kind of angel your finger landed on.

5. Finally, repeat the same process over the third box. This time you will discover the circumstances through which the specific angel you chose will arrive. Together, these three items make up your Angel Oracle reading.

6. Turn to the section, Interpreting the Angel Oracle (pp. 192–206), and read the meaning of each of the three items that you picked.

Uriel

Gabriel

Raphael

Michael

Your Companion Angel

A Connecting Angel

An Information Angel

A Dream-Worker Angel

A Healing Angel

A Wiring Angel

A Process Angel

A Transformation Angel

A Pattern Angel

A Reorganization Angel

A Technology Angel

An Environment Angel

An Angel of Nature

An Attunement Angel

An Angel of Peace

An Angel of Grace

Visit a Wise Person

Create a Sacred Space and Create Your Own Ritual

Be with a Plant, an Animal, or with the Earth Itself

Do Nothing

Do Something New

Spend Time with Someone You Love

Spend Time Alone in a Beautiful Place

Visit a Healer

Just Have Fun

Visit a Sacred Space and Participate in a Ritual

Talk to Someone Who Has Known You for a Long Time

Do Something You Don't Like to Do

Look for a Power Object

Give Something Away

Make Something

Connect through a Book, Record, Film, TV, or Art

Surrender to Each Moment

Incubate a Dream

Turn to Another Oracle

Open a Book at Random

Remember Something from Your Childhood

Let the Angels Write through You

Expect Guidance from a Stranger

Expect Guidance from the Unexpected

· NOW THAT YOU'VE USED THE ORACLE ·

This is what happens when you consult the Angel Oracle. Selecting an archangel will tune you to its overlighting presence. Alerted to your inquiry, it will "dispatch" the specific angel you chose from the second box. This angel is the one who will connect with you through the situation that you chose in the third box.

Because angels exist in a realm beyond time as we know it, the situation you select in your reading may not happen immediately. Let go of any preconceived notion of how the angel will come to you. Trust that the archangel you chose will make all the necessary arrangements.

Keep a record of your Oracle readings in your angel notebook. Be sure to date them. Then keep an eye out for what happens in your life. Later you may want to go back and add further entries to each reading about subsequent events and what you learned from them. This will also help to remind you of the angels you've met and how they work with you in your daily life, so you can freely call on them in the future, and not just when you are using the Oracle.

At the end of this chapter you will find four sample readings that will show you how to interpret your readings.

· HOW TO MAKE A DECK OF ANGEL ORACLE CARDS FOR YOURSELF ·

You can always consult the Angel Oracle the quick way, but creating a deck of cards for yourself will add a whole other dimension to the way you use it. Objects that you make carry the love and energy that comes through your own hands. And the act of creating the deck itself will put you in touch with the angels.

It's quite simple to make a deck of Angel Oracle cards. All that you will need are three packages of three-inch by five-inch cards, each pack a different color. Larger cards will do if you like, but they're a little more difficult to shuffle.

Let the spontaneous child in you play by picking your favorite colors for the cards and ink that you use. Use your imagination to illustrate the cards or cut out pictures to decorate them, if you'd like. To protect them, you can wrap the cards in cloth, make a pouch for them, or keep them in an envelope. Again, the choice is up to you. It's handy to have the cards when you're traveling, or visiting friends.

- On the first set of cards—four in number—you will write the names of the four archangels, as found in the first box on page 187. Angels do not have gender as we know it. The traditional names of these archangels are male. But you can invoke them just as clearly as Uriela, Gabrielle, Raphaela, and Michelle, or variations thereof. If you're more comfortable calling them by female names, please use these on your cards.
- On the second set of cards, using a different color, write the names of the sixteen categories of angels listed in the second box on page 187, one on each card.
- On the third set of cards, refer to the third box on page 188, and write down the twenty-four different situations through which the angels can come to you.

Exercise 16:
DOING A READING WITH YOUR ANGEL ORACLE CARDS

Your cards will enable you to combine the information for an Angel Oracle reading as you did in exercise 15. Sit in your sacred space. Light a candle or a stick of incense. Have your cards and your angel notebook in front of you. Do the Basic Grounding Meditation before you begin.

1. Sit quietly. Focus on your question to the angels. If you don't have a specific question, simply invite the angels into your life.
2. When you are ready, shuffle the four archangel cards, face down. You can fan them out in your hand or spread them out in front of you on a table. Pick one of them. Then put the card aside, face down.
3. Next, shuffle the sixteen cards that have the different kinds of angels on them, and pick one of those. Put it aside, too, face down.
4. Lastly, shuffle the situation cards and choose one of those. Now you can turn over this card, and the other two that you chose.
5. Look for the meaning of these cards in the information below to interpret your reading. Make a record of the reading in your angel notebook.

· INTERPRETING THE ANGEL ORACLE ·
The Archangels

Uriel—When you pick this archangel you are connecting to the being whose name means "Light of God" or "Fire of God." Uriel is the Protector of the East, of the rising sun, of morning and new beginnings, of spring, and the color yellow. Uriel brings transformative energies to the mind and is the guardian of the mental realm. Science, economics, and politics fall under Uriel's domain. This includes everything from toxic clean-up to solving the problems of hunger, homelessness, and political reform. Uriel's work involves systems, organizations, and all job-related issues.

Gabriel—In drawing this archangel you are making a connection to the one whose name means "Man of God" or "God Is My Strength." Gabriel is the Protector of the South, of noon and the sun's heat, of summer and the color green. Gabriel is the angel of hope and revelation, of love and heart connections. In selecting Gabriel, you open yourself to all of these qualities and to this archangel's special province, creativity and the arts, emotions, and all our relationships, with animals, people, and angels.

Raphael—This archangel's name means "Healed by God" or "God Heals." It is the Protector of the West, of twilight, evening, autumn, and the color red. Raphael is the guardian of our physical bodies and of healing. Raphael's domain is the house of growth and transformation, so when you pick this archangel you are receptive to all these qualities and tuning in to the physical world itself. Invoke Raphael if you are working for global or personal healing on any level, from disease to abuse and addictions.

Michael—"Who Is Like God?" is the name of this archangel. Michael is the Protector of the North, which is the house of night, winter, and the color blue. The north is the realm of spirit and of dreaming. Michael is the guardian of peace, harmony, and global cooperation. And while you are on your spiritual quest it is useful to remember the hidden teaching that Michael offers us. Sometimes we are so busy looking for answers that we forget how important it is to learn how to ask the right questions. In these moments remember Michael, whose name is a question.

CATEGORIES OF ANGELS

Your Companion Angel—This is the angel that works with you most intimately, in all your life situations. Your personal angel is teacher, comforter, and beloved friend. We used to call these guardian angels. But guardian implies a danger from which you need to be guarded, and we are evolving toward a way of living in the world where we are always safe. The closer you and your angel become, the closer we come to creating that reality.

Your companion angel is your bridge to the spiritual realm, as you are its bridge to the physical. When you pick this angel, you are invoking the one who is always with you. Open yourself to its love for you, feel its presence, and let it fill you with joy.

A Connecting Angel—These are the guardians/companions of groups and relationships. They are also known as coordinating or collective angels. Whenever two or more people gather together, one of these angels is drawn to work with them, to help connect their energies and their intentions. Some are with us for long stretches of time, others are temporary, depending on the time frame of the relationship. So there will be a connecting angel working with every couple, with each parent and child, with friends, family members, co-workers, corporations, workshops and gatherings, classrooms, armies, and nations. You'll find more information on these angels in chapter 13.

If you choose this specific angel, know that in some part of your life there is a relationship in need of clarity, healing, or transformation. The celestial connector is winging its way to assist.

An Information Angel—These are also known as recording angels or wisdom angels. Their function is quite simply to provide information to anyone who asks for it. These angels are the librarians of Heaven, the keepers of what have been called the Akashic records. They may present information to you directly, or they may serve as muses in your life, filling you with inspiration. Most often, however, these angels work with us indirectly, by guiding us to find the information we seek. Revelation could come from a book that falls off a shelf, a movie that you watch in the middle of a sleepless night, or from a song you can't get out of your head.

A Dream-Worker Angel—These angels are related to the information angels, but they work with us when we are sleeping, rather than in our waking lives. They are also our attendants in altered states of consciousness, such as trances and out-of-body experiences. Their special domain is the unconscious. If you choose this angel, call on one of these celestial tour guides while you are falling asleep or when you are meditating. There is more information on how to work with dreams in chapter 10.

A Healing Angel—These angels serve to awaken the healer within you, to facilitate healing on every level. They attend the sick, serve in hospitals and hospices, and work with medical and healing practitioners.

If you have drawn this angel, know that some aspect of your life is ready to be healed with angelic assistance. You are about to let go of something that has limited you physically or otherwise. These angels are also known as cleansing angels. There is more information on healing in chapter 12.

A Wiring Angel—These angels are related to the healing angels. But where healing angels come into our lives to restore inner balance, fix, and cleanse, wiring angels upgrade our systems and increase our capacity for awareness. Healing angels repair. Wiring angels improve.

If you picked this angel, you are open and ready to grow. Just as the cleansing and healing process can be unpleasant to go through, so too the process of rewiring can be unsettling and disorienting. Sickness is the body's way of cleansing itself. If you have flulike symptoms, but you don't have a fever and you know you're not sick—you're probably being rewired. Disconcerting as this may be, when the process is over you will be more clear and present, more focused.

A Process Angel—In our lives we need to balance movement and rest, becoming and being, change and changelessness. Each of these paired qualities is facilitated by a process angel. Some work with the unfolding of the universe and help us move, while others work with its unchanging nature and help us rest. The process angel mediates your behavior, helping you to bring it into balance.

If you have chosen this angel, you may have become too passive in some part of your life and need to move again. The process angel will help you with this shift. On the other hand, this selection may be telling you that you've become overactive and overinvolved. The process angel in charge of rest and calm will help you make the change toward balance.

A Transformation Angel—These angels are responsible for the transformation of spirit and thought into the physical realm. They are also called manifestation angels, and you'll find the prosperity angels among their ranks. Because of their work of transformation, these angels will assist us whenever we are doing creative work, and they assist the higher angels of birth and death in their missions, too.

If this is your pick, it's time to create new ways of being in your life. An actual birth or death in your circle may precipitate your transformation. Birth and death are also metaphors for the changes you need to make. Now is the moment to turn new ideas into practical actions—to let go of old ones that have not borne fruit. Having chosen this angel, prepare yourself for the transformation that will soon be coming into your life.

A Pattern Angel—Also known as blueprint or purpose angels, pattern angels come in to help us align with the greater patterns of the universe. They carry the energy of these patterns and pass the blueprints on to the transformation angels, who help to bring them into physicality. Then the process angels come in to see that balance is maintained.

If you drew this angel, you are looking for a greater sense of purpose and meaning. For pattern and purpose are the same. Everything that exists has a purpose. But you cannot find the purpose in isolation. Purpose is about interrelation. Now it is time in your spiritual journey to reach out to one of these angels, in order to understand more of your own part in the intricate web of creation that contains us all.

A Reorganization Angel—If you've picked this angel, it's time to look at the parts of your life where you're stuck. It's important to bear in mind that the more firmly entrenched you seem to be, the greater the reorganization task ahead, and the greater the resulting upheaval. Things may turn inside out, upside down, or even disappear, like car keys, jobs, and relationships. This is because these angels are also in charge of de-manifestation. Since their work can be unsettling at times—and indeed, it is meant to be—they don't always get a warm welcome. All reorganization comes from and moves toward love. If you remember this, you can feel safer in the midst of all changes.

Reorganization is a part of evolution. It is time to make deep, soul-needed changes. In the middle of cleaning out a closet, things are at their messiest. Don't get sucked into the chaos. Just keep going. The results are always worth it. New and more satisfying patterns will emerge as you clear out the old ones.

A Technology Angel—As we learn to work with these beings and align with their vision, we create things that are balanced, ecological, and life-supporting. Everything we make, from steel to plastic, comes from the Earth. The technology angels are relatives of, and work in collaboration with, the environment angels and the angels of nature.

If you picked a technology angel, know that whenever you engage in any activity that involves manufactured devices, from ball-point pens to mainframe computers, you sanctify the tools you work with, and you use them in a sacred way.

An Environment Angel—These are the guardians of places in the world—of mountains, rivers, forests, and seas. There are also environment angels who watch over places that humans have created—homes, office buildings, airports, and other public places. Their function is to maintain and uplift the spiritual integrity of the environment they tend.

Wherever you are, stop for a moment and become aware of the environment angel of that place. When you do, its presence will infuse you with the wonder and beauty of our planet and help you to feel a part of All That Is. Feeling this, you bring respect to every place you go.

An Angel of Nature—These beings are cousins of the environment angels. They work with the four elements, Earth, Water, Fire, and Air. They include the nature spirits, all the beings we have called devas, elves, fairies, gnomes, and so forth. While the environment angels are connected with places, these angels are concerned with forms of life. They are guardians of everything from the minute to the magnificent, from viruses and pebbles to rivers and redwood trees. If you have selected an angel of nature, you are being asked to make contact with one of these myriad and constantly changing spirits, to connect once again with the primal force that courses through all of life.

An Attunement Angel—While the concern of the environment angels is with space, the concern of the attunement angels is with time. When you connect with an environment angel, the place that you are in becomes a sacred place. When you connect with an attunement angel, you create sacred time.

Because of their work these angels have also been called ritual or ceremonial angels. You can come into harmony with them at any time, but when you reach out to them while praying or meditating, they will be there to attune you to the sacredness of each timeless moment. If you have selected an attunement angel, it may be time for you to create a formal ceremony or ritual that sanctifies your life or purpose.

An Angel of Peace—Peace is harmony, a free flow of various elements that work together to allow creativity and growth. Peace is an energy that permeates the Universe. It's active, not passive. If you have selected this angel, you are empowered to bring cooperation and peace to issues or people in your life. By doing so, you open new doorways for the energy of peace to enter into our world.

When you pick this angel know that you are an agent for change, a messenger of the principle that is transforming the consciousness of this planet. The angels of peace carry the visions and the energy we need to do this. Ask yourself what your deepest dreams are, and know that as you bring peace to your own life, even greater dreams than these will manifest for all.

An Angel of Grace—The work of these angels is to weave together the spiritual and material realms. These angels never stop their weaving. Whoever crosses their path is woven into their work for an indelible instant, experiencing God's love and goodness. Grace comes as a gift, unbidden, and enriches and catalyzes our lives. If you have ever had a moment of joy in the midst of your sorrow, you know what grace is. The more conscious you are of these angels, the more open you will be to feeling these moments of grace all the time. When you choose this being in your reading, open your heart and smile.

INVITE THE ANGELS INTO YOUR LIFE

Visit a Wise Person—There are many different kinds of wise people, old and young, inner and outer. Picking this situation may be an invitation to sit with an elder of the community, a sage, or a teacher. It may be inviting you to take a workshop with someone you respect, or it may be calling on you to take a journey inward, there to find the wise person you carry within you. This may be the elder you will become in this life, or it may be someone you once were, in a past life. Through the wise person, the angels will make themselves known to you, in words or in silence, by a gesture or a feeling.

Create a Sacred Space and Create Your Own Ritual—This may be a meditation you create in the corner of your bedroom, or a dance that you do in a clearing in the middle of the woods. When you draw this happening, know that through the creation of sacredness an angel will connect with you, dance with you, and pray with you. Allow yourself to deepen and expand with this contact.

Be with a Plant, an Animal, or with the Earth Itself—Through attunement to the planet and all of its life forms, the angel you need to communicate with now will come to you. Give yourself the time to go out into the world. Sit with a tree, play with your pet, walk in the woods or a park, climb a mountain. Take the opportunity to connect to the planet itself. Sprawl out on the grass or the sand. Feel the wind. Open up to the sky above you. When you do this, you open the way for the angel you have chosen to come to you, to whisper to you, in the leaves, in the wind, in the waves.

Do Nothing—Stop looking and hungering and searching. Let go and let the angels come to you in their own way and in their own time. Know that you do not have to do everything. In fact, right now, you don't have to do anything at all. Let the angels come to you in whatever way they see fit. It may be when and where you least expect them. Go within, into a deep place of surrender. Let go of control, and let the angels do all the work.

Do Something New—So often we live in the little prisons of routine and habit that we create for ourselves. We don't notice how vast and full of possibilities life is. If you pick this circumstance, do something you have not done before. Perhaps it is time to do something you've been afraid to do, something that challenges your physical or mental prowess. By stretching your limits you expand your potential for self-esteem and renewed self-confidence. You feel more alive and vigorous.

Spend Time with Someone You Love—Create some special time to be with your best beloved. Make a date with an old friend. If there isn't anyone in your life right now that you feel this way about, invite love in, invite friendship in. Visit your grandmother or another relative. Call on a neighbor. Sometimes, we forget to spend time with people that we care about—we forget that the love is there.

Spend Time Alone in a Beautiful Place—Beauty is nurturing. Allow yourself to rest and be healed by the beauty this planet offers us, or by the beauty that we as humans have created, in a mosque, a cathedral, walking in a formal garden, or at the top of a tower looking out at a glorious view. In being there, feel the angels that surround you, and take in their beauty, too.

Visit a Healer—As with visiting a wise person, this may be an outer or an inner journey, for in the end we are our own best healers. A loving friend can be a healer. An image that holds power for you can be a healer, too. Perhaps this selection hints that you need to be nurtured, massaged, looked after. Is it a reminder to make the appointment with your doctor that you keep postponing? Sit quietly and know that you will find the answer to the question this occasion proposes to you. When you do visit a healer, the angels will be there with you, working with and through that person to deepen your healing.

Just Have Fun—This might be the most difficult adventure of all. It's often hard to be light and free, to let yourself overflow with pleasure. But when you do, the angels will all be there with you, laughing and happy, too. Some people never grow up because they think grownups don't have fun. But fun is simply a way of being alive, enjoying each moment. If you think you have forgotten how, just remember that you once knew how to do it. Fun is like riding a bicycle. You can't forget how to do it, you can only forget *to* do it.

Visit a Sacred Space and Participate in a Ritual—Unlike the earlier invitation to create sacredness, this part of your reading calls on you to partake of something established, traditional, something rooted in history. It may be of the tradition in which you were raised, or it may be from another. In selecting this action, you are asked to open to the angels through surrendering to something outside of yourself. You do not have to do the work. You only need to allow something external and ancient to do its work on you.

Talk to Someone Who Has Known You for a Long Time—This may be a parent or an old friend, a sibling, or someone you've lost touch with and need to track down. In choosing this event someone who has seen you grow through time will give voice to what the angels have to say to you. What they say may not be what you expect—or want—to hear. But it will be what you need to hear, right now, in order to grow. You may be asked to look at self-limiting patterns, or you may be forced to recognize something wonderful about yourself that you have been denying.

Do Something You Don't Like to Do—There is much to be learned by examining your judgments and dislikes. Selecting this situation can help you to see how you are limited by them. There are some things we don't want to do because they are antithetical to our natures, but there are others that we avoid out of fear or pride. This situation is an opportunity to release limitations. If you've chosen it, do something you've said you never would. Watch your resistance and see if you can let it go. Ask yourself what it is that makes you uncomfortable. Be as open and receptive as you can. Feel the presence of the angels. They are there to support you as you move through your judgments or fears. Dance and laugh with them into the light.

Look for a Power Object—A power object focuses your energy and purposeful-ness. It could be a book, a crystal, a rock, an unusual stick you find in the woods, or a special shell you discover as you wander on the beach. The search for your power object is a pilgrimage to the part of yourself that you are ready to honor and know. It's the part that remembers why you came to this planet and what you are here to do. Through this object you will be empowered to know yourself better, and to be yourself more.

Give Something Away—It may be something you love, it may be something you never use, or it may be something you have been holding on to that has negative associations for you. It may be valuable or of little worth. The act of giving it away will free up a part of your life and make room for something new. You create the opportunity for an angelic gift. It may not come right way. It will come in angel time. Be open to receive it, and give thanks when it arrives.

Make Something—A picture, a meal, a dance, a sweater, a poem. Invite the angels to be with you as you do. Welcome them as muses, softly inspiring you to connect with the part of yourself that is as creative and rich as life itself. Your creativity could emerge through a joke, a poem, or the flowers you plant in your garden. In picking this experience, remember that we are all co-creators with God. Let your creative impulses flow freely, as light from the sun, shining in every direction.

Connect Through a Book, Record, Film, TV, or Art—If you chose this event, the angels will come to you through someone else's creative work. It could be a book you are reading. A film may give you just the story you need to hear. A painting or a dance may be so full of angelic connection that it infects you with its joy. Something out there has been created with information in it just for you. It may have been created a thousand years ago, or it may be as new as yesterday. Out there in the world something is waiting to talk to you, something created for you. Trust that the angels will wing it your way.

Surrender to Each Moment—If you picked this situation, know that you are being asked to meet the angels in each moment, happy or sad, funny or fearful. Each moment is a teacher. Nothing that happens is a mistake—there are no accidents. Every situation in your life has something to teach you. A "mistake" can teach you more than a "right" move. Remember this. Know that in your surrender to each moment the angels are with you, supporting and sustaining you as you experience the great unity of All That Is.

Incubate a Dream—This is one of the easiest ways to let the angels come to you. As you are falling asleep, invite an angel to commune with you in a dream. You may ask your dreaming self for a dream about a specific situation, and trust that your angel will speak to you as you sleep. It may take several nights to incubate the dream, but if you are patient, the angels will come through. You can ask your angel to help you identify it in the dream. There is more information on dreaming in chapter 10.

Turn to Another Oracle—If you chose this event you are invited to receive angel guidance by making use of another oracle. This might be another divination tool, like the runes, tarot cards, or the *I Ching*. Or it might be an indication to consult a palm reader or have your astrology chart done. Having chosen this, allow your inner knowing self to lead you to the right oracle, and trust that an angel will meet you there.

Open a Book at Random—It may be a book that you love, or it may just be any old book that you are drawn to grab off a shelf. Know that the angels will guide your hands to open the book at just the right page, and help you to put your finger on the right paragraph, the words of which will tell you just what you need to hear and know.

Remember Something from Your Childhood—In childhood we are all much closer to the angels, and so it is easier for the angels to be with us. By remembering something from your childhood, something that you did or thought or felt or loved or wanted to do, the angels will reach out to you again, in innocence and joy. It may help to look at childhood pictures of yourself, or to look at and handle some object that was yours when you were small.

Let the Angels Write Through You—It is time to sit quietly and commune with an angel directly. Take time to do the GRACE Process, and let the angel you picked from the group of different angels come through. Savor its wisdom in the words that you write. This is also an opportunity to dialogue with the angel, as you have learned.

Expect Guidance from a Stranger—You can never tell if someone might be an angel in disguise. You can never tell when an angel will speak to you through someone you don't know. It might happen on a bus or standing in line. Keep your ears open. When you least expect it, a stranger will give you a piece of information on a part of your life that needs elucidation. It may be a new direction you never considered. Often, it's easier to talk to strangers than it is to friends, and you may find that you are the one who is saying something that you need to hear.

Expect Guidance from the Unexpected—Angels live in a realm of fluid space and time. If you have chosen this situation, know that an angel will come to you in a way that no one can predict, not even this oracle.

· SOME SAMPLE READINGS FROM THE ANGEL ORACLE ·

Carol's relationship with Lois, her mother, had vastly improved. This is why she was thrown off balance when her mother called one day and began criticizing her the way she used to. After the call, Carol was so agitated she couldn't wait to align with her angel, and she turned to the Angel Oracle for guidance. She drew Uriel from the first group, A Healing Angel from the second, and Spend Time with Someone You Love from the third.

She looked up Uriel, saw that it's the archangel of the early hours of the day, and that its color is yellow. She lit a yellow candle to invoke the archangel. There was no doubt that A Healing Angel came to help her resolve her difficulty with her mother, and she invoked its presence, too. In her meditation with these angels, she realized she had been neglecting her mother. Spend Time with Someone You Love was a clear message.

Carol decided to call her mother the next morning. Before she phoned, she lit another yellow candle, invoking the angels again. When her mother answered the phone, Carol greeted her cheerfully and asked if she'd like her to come home for a visit. Lois seemed surprised. "I was hoping you would," she said, "but I was afraid to ask. I didn't think you'd want to."

In the week they spent together, they had a lot of time to talk. Old grievances were aired and released. A new, healthy bond developed. They even had a picnic under the elm tree that Carol used to play in when she was a child. It was a healing time for them both.

Bobby didn't have a specific question in mind when he turned to the Oracle. He just wanted to connect with the angels. So he took out the deck of cards he had made, shuffled them, and chose Raphael, An Environment Angel, and Just Have Fun. He read the descriptions for each card. Since Raphael is the Guardian of the West, he decided to go west, to his favorite park, to commune with An Environment Angel. An artist, Bobby took along a sketch pad. He rode through the park for several hours, and found a quiet place. The sun was starting to go down. The sky was red and coral and spectacular. He took out his pad and made a few sketches. It was only later that he remembered that Raphael's particular time is sunset. The sketches proved to be the inspiration for a series of paintings that he did. In looking back over them, he felt that he had indeed been blessed by the angels.

Kevin had just celebrated the first anniversary of meeting his angel. They'd been working together on his goals (see chapter 11). Kevin had left his job at the luncheonette to do private catering for parties and bar mitzvahs. His business was doing well, but he was working from six in the morning until eleven or twelve each night. And although he loved cooking, something was missing.

With not a lot of time or energy to spare, he decided to consult the Angel Oracle. He picked Gabriel, An Angel of Grace, and Talk to Someone Who Has Known You for a Long Time.

Gabriel, he found, was the archangel of creativity and relationships. He reflected on his three selections and realized that he'd been neglecting his friends. There was one in particular who came to mind. He missed his buddy, Richard, whom he hadn't spoken to in months. He wanted to call him right then and there, but he had to finish cooking for a party that night.

When he returned from delivering the food, the phone was ringing. Kevin ran to get it, and laughed when he heard the familiar voice. It was Richard. They had a great conversation. When Kevin thought about it later, he wondered. Was Richard's call a coincidence? Or was it An Angel of Grace?

While Andrew was working on the revision of this chapter, his friend Maryanne called to say that she had injured her shoulder. She wanted to know if she could come over for him to take a look at it.

When Maryanne arrived, Andrew looked at her shoulder. It wasn't dislocated, as she'd feared. His angels said to tell her that she was just being rewired. She was relieved, and when he told her that he was working on this oracle, she wanted to try it.

The cards she pulled were Raphael, the archangel in charge of healing, A Wiring Angel, which was a nice instant confirmation of what the angels had just said, and Surrender to Each Moment. Her impulse had been to deny the pain and put on a brave front. When she turned over the third card and saw what it said, she burst into tears. She'd been afraid this injury was going to keep her from going on vacation, and she was in a lot of pain. Andrew explained to her that A Wiring Angel was doing its work through her injury, and she'd be fine for her trip. Her shoulder was significantly better the next day, and by the time she got on the plane, the pain was gone.

· LIVING WITH GRACE ·

You've completed the GRACE Process. You have the basic steps you need. Take a moment to go back and remember what your life was like before you started talking with your angel. In what ways is it different now?

Read through your journal. Can you see places where your mind got in the way and interfered with your angel's voice? Reviewing them now, some of your angel's messages may be even clearer and more to the point than when you first received them. Acknowledge your progress.

It's taken you time to learn the GRACE Process and to work through each of the exercises. The more you experience them, the more quickly and smoothly each one will flow into the next. Ask your angel to assist you if there is any part of the process that you feel needs more practice. Eventually, the GRACE Process will become second nature to you.

In the next section of the book, we show you how to put what you've learned to practical use in your everyday life. When you team up with the angels, even the most ordinary activities are infused with love and spirit. The moment you opened to your angel, you joined in joyful celebration with all the humans in history who have had angelic encounters. Living with GRACE, you and your angel are helping to create Heaven on Earth.

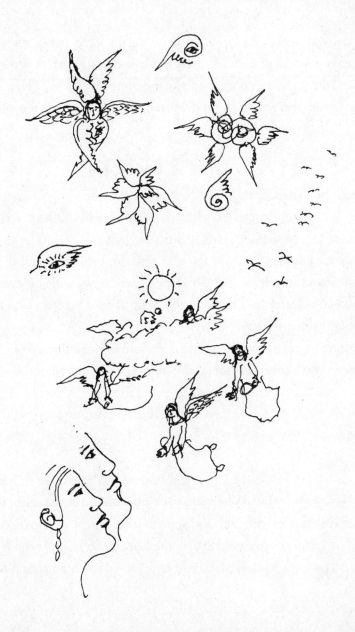

In Partnership with the Angels

Now that you've established contact with the angels and made them real for yourself, it's time to put what you've learned into wider practice, to make them real in the world.

If ever humankind needed advocates for the angels, this is the time. And every time someone connects with an angel, an advocate is born; a new light is ignited. Person by person, angel by angel, lights are going on all over this planet. Each light counts. Each light adds to the light of the world. That's why it's called enlightenment.

In this last section, you enter into a working partnership with the angels to bring the blessings of these benefactors into every part of your life. In the chapters that follow you'll discover how the angels can help you achieve your goals; how they can soothe the way if you're dealing with healing or addictions; how they can inspire and inform intimate relationships; and how you can bring their joyful company to all your relationships—to your family and to groups, even globally.

To start, we offer some tips on fine-tuning your connection with your heavenly helpers, along with suggestions for using dreams and letter writing to enhance and augment your contact. To finish, we explore the ways in which our connections to the celestials might grow and change as we enter both a new century and a new millennium.

· THE PARTNERSHIP THAT WROTE THIS BOOK ·

While it would be nice to say that the act of writing this book was as fluid and harmonious as meeting each other and getting our proposal accepted, that was not the case at all. Each of us had well-defined views on the angels—and each of us was attached to our own vision of the book and how it should be done. While Andrew had coauthored books before, neither Alma nor Timothy had. And none of us had ever written a book with two other people! Try having three drivers at the wheel of a car.

At times, we were locked in what appeared to be irreconcilable disagreements. We're not angels. We shouted at each other and threatened to pull out of the project. We felt overwhelmed, inadequate, and angry. Some of what we held to be our most precious ideas and words had to be sacrificed in the course of extensive revisions.

It felt like an endless task. But Abigrael had told us, right from the beginning, "This book will happen in angel time." Being human, we didn't exactly appreciate this counsel. Often, we worked ten to twelve hours a day—for weeks on end. And three years went by from the time that our proposal was accepted until we submitted our final draft.

But the angels got us into this and the angels pulled us through. Whenever it seemed that there was no way out, we turned to them for guidance. Again and again, they opened our hearts and allowed us to see another way through. They showed us that each barrier we hit was a reflection of a personal, unresolved issue. We got a lot of practice in Releasing.

As we learned to relinquish our individual viewpoints we experienced the freedom, expansiveness, and creativity that can exist in a heart-centered, leaderless group. Entering into partnership with our angels, as well as with each other, we found ourselves anchoring into form this new type of working relationship. Our angels inform us that this is a pattern for future collaborations and community endeavors. One hundred years from now they say egoless cooperation will be commonplace—in families, in business, and in government.

Every one of us has the opportunity to work in harmonious new ways. In the chapters that follow, you, too, will discover the joys of partnership with your angels.

Fine-Tuning the Angelic Connection

Y ou've opened to your angel, heard its kind voice, or felt its luminous and loving presence. You've begun to enjoy your celestial's company; perhaps you've already laughed or cried together. Using the GRACE Process, you've learned the basic steps. Now, you're ready to move on and develop the ability to refine and maintain a clear line of communication whenever and wherever you wish.

Sometimes, communication breaks down. Why does that happen, and what can you do about it? And what about the messages that are untrue? Do angels ever goof? What's the best way to ask your angel for guidance on personal matters?

In this chapter, you'll find the answers to those questions and, to help get any glitches out, we offer more advanced techniques for Grounding, Releasing, and Aligning.

Opening to the angels opens us to other worlds, other dimensions of sentience. Now that you've familiarized yourself with the Basic Grounding Meditation (pp. 119–22), you'll enjoy exploring the realm of archetypes that dwell in the collective unconscious. An archetype represents a particular quality or set of traits—the goddess Venus, for example, stands for feminine beauty and the Madonna exemplifies motherly love. In contemporary life, Arnold Schwarzenegger is a symbol of the strong man, and rock-star Madonna epitomizes sexuality. Animals also serve archetypical functions: the lion is brave, the fox is wily, and so on.

In the Advanced Grounding exercise that follows, you can make friends with the animal, vegetable, and mineral kingdoms, as well as connecting with the angels and archangels, and the archetypal realm. You'll find that the chakras are links between your subtle and physical bodies and other unseen worlds.

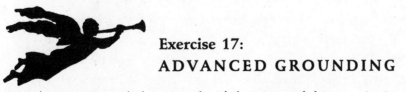

Exercise 17:
ADVANCED GROUNDING

As we've recommended previously, it's best to read this exercise into a tape recorder so you can listen to the directions without having to refer to the book. Before starting, you may also wish to refer back to the Chakra Charts (pp. 116, 125), and be sure to have your angel notebook, pen, and tape recorder nearby.

1. Enter your sacred space. Get comfortable and close your eyes. Be aware of your body. Focus on your heartbeat and breath. Visualize roots extending from your feet and the base of your spine reaching down into the Earth.

2. Draw the Earth energy up through your roots into your body, up into your first chakra at the base of your spine. This Root chakra is your connecting point to the Earth and to the mineral kingdom.

   Imagine that you are a rock. What kind of rock are you? Round and smooth? Large and craggy? Feel your kinship with the rocks around you. Are you buried in the ground? Lying on the surface? Are you in sunlight or in the rain? Are you on a beach, in a riverbed, in a forest, or a desert? What does it feel like to be you? To be solid and confident and utterly secure in your rockness? Allow this feeling to spread through you from your Root chakra and fill you with a sense of safety and invulnerability.

3. When you are ready, let the Earth energy rise up into the second chakra. The Sexual chakra is the access point in your body to the plant or vegetable kingdom, the place where you interact with the nature spirits who care for all growing things. Now, focusing the Earth energy in through the pelvis and genitals, begin to feel your own vegetable nature. Are you a tree, a plant, a flower? Are you a single blade of grass or a sheaf of wheat? Feel the sun on your plant body. Feel the wind, the rain, the passing of the seasons. Feel how fruitful you are, how luxuriant and fertile. Experience the rivers of creativity that run through you quite naturally.

4. Now the energy rises up into your third chakra, your Solar Plexus, the locus of power and a connecting point to the animal domain. As the Earth energy flows into this area ask yourself what kind of animal you are. Are you large or small? Gentle or wild? Are you a creature of the waters, land, or sky? What does your animal tell you about yourself? Allow your animal nature to spread out into your entire body. Become your animal self. Claim your ancient animal wisdom.

5. Like a fountain, the Earth energy shoots up into your Heart chakra, the center of unconditional love and the special province of humanity within you. Move into the energy of your heart, and feel deeply the sense of your own humanness, your loving nature, your frailties and foibles, your dreams and your failures. Come into compassion for yourself, into loving acceptance. Remember all the people who have loved you and whom you have loved.

6. As the Earth energy continues to rise, it flows into your High Heart or Thymus chakra. This chakra is newly awakening in all of humanity. It is a center of global connection and brotherhood, of peace and community. Feel how the vibrations from this place within you connect you with all of humanity. You are a part of it all, never alone, always in harmony with the deepest and highest needs of our species.

7. Moving up, the Earth energy fills your next chakra, your Throat and Ears. Relax your jaw and open your inner ears. This is the point of access to our angels. Visualize an upside down triangle connecting your ears and your throat, and let this area fill with good grounding Earth energy. Extend a loving greeting to your angels and listen. If images or feelings come to you, thank your angel for reaching out to you.

8. Now let the energy move up to your Third Eye, connecting you with the realm of the archangels. You can draw their love and power into

you through your Third Eye, filling your entire body. Be open to receiving whatever the archangels have for you now.

9. Allow the Earth energy to stream up into your Crown chakra, at the very top of your head. This is the seat of the Divine within you, your Godself. Open to the power and majesty of your Divine Self. Remember who you are. Remember why you are here.

10. Feel all the fibers shooting out from your Crown chakra, spreading into the Universe, connecting you to every part of creation. Breathe in starlight, breathe it down your Crown chakra fibers, one by one. Let it all wash down through your chakras, filling you, weaving universal energy into each one of them. Let this waterfall of starlight be a blessing to the Divine within you, to the archangel within, the angel, the world self, the loving self, the animal self, the plant self, and the rock self.

11. Your body is now radiant. Feel it alive and pulsing. Feel yourself connected to All That Is. Know that you are blessed and whole. Know that you are enough. Rest in this time out of time, knowing at last, perhaps even remembering, how it feels to be complete within yourself.

12. In your own time, when you are ready, become aware of your body again, feel the chair you are sitting in, the room around you. Place your hand on your heart. And slowly, slowly, open your eyes.

Write down your experiences in your angel notebook. Be sure to date your entry. Use the images that come up in this meditation throughout the day. When you need to feel stable and confident, recall how you felt as a rock. When you want to feel more powerful, remember how it felt to be your animal. Each time you do this meditation, be prepared for the images to change. Accept whatever comes as being exactly right for you at just this moment.

This exercise was remarkably effective for Dorothy. She's a gentle and sensitive young woman and very shy. She hadn't spoken at all up to this point in the workshop. But after the Advanced Grounding process, she was the first to share.

"Something happened and I'm not sure what it was," she said, her voice clear and strong. "But I actually felt like a rock, and a tree, and an eagle. And the odd thing was, it felt absolutely right and natural. I don't think I ever realized the strength that I have inside me."

Dorothy had found her sense of inner worth. It was most becoming.

· TROUBLESHOOTING: WHEN THE LINE GOES DEAD ·

Talking with the angels is like talking to a friend on the telephone—every once in a while, you may get disconnected. Even after you've established a strong contact you may find, from time to time, that the message breaks off. Transmissions that stop in midsentence or change noticeably in language or tone are due to self-consciousness. Excitement or exuberance can bring the ego to the fore.

Have you ever found yourself out of your body and suddenly realized it? As soon as you do—*BOOM!*—you come barreling back in. Sometimes, talking to the angels produces a similar effect. The "Wow! Look at this!" response is quite natural when you first start but can dissipate the state of openness and receptivity you've worked so hard to create. If conversation bogs down, you can simply ask your angel to come back in, or you can use the visualization in exercise 14 to reconnect. You can also use this as an advanced Aligning exercise, when you have had some practice with the basic ones given in chapter 6.

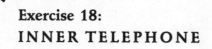

Exercise 18:
INNER TELEPHONE

This exercise is a piece of spiritual software that you can create for your inner computer to help you call up your angel. Familiarize yourself with the diagram to get a sense of the parts before you begin the visualization.

1. Get comfortable. Close your eyes and focus your awareness on your breathing. Relax.

2. Place the tips of your fingers on your Third Eye. Imagine that your touch creates a spot of golden light there.

3. Now move your fingertips to the Crown of your head. Feel your touch creating another spot of golden light there. Visualize a line of golden light connecting these two points, going through your brain.

4. Next, slide your fingers to the back of your head and let them come to rest on the occipital protuberance, the bump at the back of your skull just above your neck. Feel a third point of golden light appear there as you touch it, and see a second line of golden light that connects to your Crown.

5. Now, bring your fingers back to your Third Eye, to the first golden point. Feel a third line of golden light moving right through your brain, connecting the point at the back of your head with your Third Eye.

6. You have now created a triangle of golden light in your head. When you have a distinct sense of it, separate your fingertips and bring them up to your temples. Find a spot above each ear that feels comfortable and see two more points of golden light appear there. Connect the points on each temple with another line of gold light that goes right through the golden triangle, through the center of your brain.

Internal transmitter device

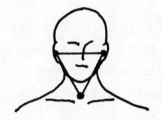

Internal receiver device

7. This device acts as an internal transmitter for talking with your angels. It is like the mouthpiece of your telephone. When it is clearly installed in your head, you are ready to create the inner telephone receiver, the part through which you hear your angels.

8. Place your fingertips lightly over your ears, imaging two other points of gold light in each one. Connect these with a line of golden light.

9. Place your fingertips together on your throat, in the area of the Adam's apple, and image a third point of golden light there. Visualize two golden lines connecting the points in your ears with the point in your throat, to make another triangle. This is your angelic receiver.

Use the Inner Telephone exercise to call your angels when you're hung up about something, or if you just feel like having a heart-to-heart chat. After you've done the exercise two or three times you won't need to go through all the steps, you'll simply be able to quickly visualize your phone in place.

Beam your thoughts out to your angel from the first triangle you made, and feel your angel's incoming message vibrating in your body in the triangle between your throat and your ears. It may seem a bit complicated at first, but as Ronny said, "Once I got the hang of it, it was just like the phone company. The only difference with calling an angel is that I never get a busy signal."

· SORRY, WRONG NUMBER ·

When advice from your angel is incorrect, it ain't your angel. Messages that prove misleading or untrue are due to desire or fear that was not released before you began talking with your heavenly helper. You're aware, of course, that any situation has the likelihood of multiple outcomes. Angels see all the possibilities simultaneously. And since they don't make the same kind of judgments we do about right or wrong, good or bad, they see every situation as an opportunity for learning, experience, and growth. Because our angels care about us and want us to be happy and to achieve our goals, if the outcome we want is one of the choices possible, we can receive a message confirming that it will happen. The message reflects our desire.

· DESIRE ·

Desire interferes with messages coming from your angel by blurring reception with attachment. When you ask your angel for counsel on something that matters a great deal to you, your attachment to a particular outcome or view can corrupt or distort the information you receive. That is why it is so important to consciously clear your mind and emotions of any investment in the answer before you receive it.

Corrie is a very dear friend of ours, sensitive and intelligent. At the time she met her angel, Eleo, and started talking with her, she was executive assistant to a national ballet company. She was also involved in a relationship that had its ups and downs. After a while she began to ask Eleo for advice about what was going on. The information she received, which she wrote down, assured her that everything was fine, that she and her boyfriend would marry and have a child, and that she was to remain open and loving in her interactions with him. When she discovered that he was having an affair with another woman, she broke off her relationship with him and threw the written transmissions into the garbage.

· DO ANGELS GOOF? ·

"I've had it," Corrie said, her face clouded with anguish. "How can I believe anything my angel says now? Why didn't she tell me what was really going on? How could she say we'd be married, that I'd have his child? I just don't understand it."

We didn't understand it either. So we asked our angels.

LNO: Regarding the authenticity of the material received, distortions are created by desire and fear, which prevent the intuitive or higher voice from coming forth truly and clearly. Desire and fear create a state of willfulness.

Corrie carries a pronounced disinclination to hear and see the truth when it is not what she wishes or wants to believe. It is this quality of willfulness which permeated the transmissions. They reflected her desires.

You ask, how can one tell whether the information comes from desire or is tainted by it? We say, ask. We say, release all considerations before asking for guidance. Keep in mind and heart the desire only for truth. Ask that truth be told, that it shine through. If there are any questions about the veracity of the information, ask. Ask and ask again. What is asked for in simplicity and earnestness is always answered.

· FEAR ·

Fear is the counterpart of desire. It's what you wish would not happen, and it scrambles angelic reception the same way desire does, with attachments and willfulness. A word used a lot in connection with the angels is surrender. Surrender means giving up fears, and trusting that the highest good will prevail. It means being willing, not willful.

Before you ask your angel what you feel is an important question, address any fears that you may have by asking yourself these questions:

If (what you fear) happens, how would I feel?
What would I do?
Then what?
Am I willing to release this fear?
Am I willing to know the truth?

If the answer is yes, use one of the Advanced Releasing techniques that follow. They're based on the elements of earth, water, and fire. (An Advanced Releasing technique using the element of air is given in chapter 11 on page 266.) You may find that you relate more to one of these than the others. We recommend that you go through each one once, to see which is the most suitable.

Exercise 19:
EARTH RELEASE

As you practice the Grounding exercises and get to know your chakras, you may want to clear a specific issue that pertains to a particular energy center. For example, security issues relate to the Root chakra; disappointment in a love affair involves the Heart chakra, and so forth. Refer back to Chakra Chart 2, (p. 125) to refresh your memory, and if you're not sure which chakra is involved, you can cover all the bases by releasing the blockage from all of the centers. A quicker solution is to release from the Heart and then from the Root chakra.

This exercise expands on the pattern of the Basic Releasing Exercise; it allows you to go deeper into your subtle body so you can get to the place where these blockages are stored. You can go through all your chakras at one sitting or work with just one. To clear a blockage in a single chakra you can move directly there after Grounding in your Root chakra. This exercise is particularly effective for releasing fears, doubts, disappointment, and feelings of unworthiness, inadequacy, and self-criticism.

1. Relax and close your eyes. Invite your angel to be with you. Focus on your breath as you send your roots down into the Earth. When they've

wriggled down and taken hold, begin to draw the Earth energy through your roots up into your chakras, one by one.

2. Picture fine threads or filaments coming out of the Crown chakra at the top of your head, reaching up to the sky and connecting you there. Breathe the energy of the heavens down through these fibers into all of your chakras, one by one. Return your awareness to your Root chakra.

3. Notice if there are any emotions, memories, or blocks there that you need to release. If so, focus on each of them, one by one. See where it came from and ask yourself what you've learned from it.

4. When you are ready to release, thank the memory or blockage for what you've learned. Inhale deeply and then exhale the block forcibly through · your mouth with a whooshing sound. Feel it traveling all the way down your roots into the Earth as you exhale. Repeat two more times.

5. When you are ready, take a deep breath, draw the energy up from the Earth to your Sexual chakra and repeat steps 3 and 4. Continue to work your way up the chakras, one by one, exploring and releasing.

6. Give thanks to your angels and to our mother, the Earth, for working with you. Become aware of your physical body. Notice your breathing. And when you're ready, open your eyes.

You may find that this Earth Release exercise offers a bonus—it leaves you feeling more grounded, more centered and stable.

Allan used the Earth Release to let go of resentment, although it hadn't been on his original Spiritual Laundry List. However, when he did the Basic Releasing Exercise (pp. 138–39) to get rid of the envy he'd felt for his brother, he noticed that while he no longer wanted what his brother had had, he still felt resentful about it. Then he began to look at other things he resented—having to work so hard, always being in debt, having suffered a heart attack—and he saw, for the first time, a negative pattern that had plagued him all of his life.

Before doing the Earth Release, he opened to his angel. He hoped to receive the same exquisite sensation of love that he'd experienced at the workshop. He really didn't expect to hear any words, or to get a message, but from the very depths of his heart he formed a question:

"Angel, what do I have to do to dump all my resentments?"

Much to his astonishment—and delight—he heard these words:

"Let go of the past. You can do it. Come into this minute. Count your blessings, not your troubles."

Allan relaxed. He began to think about the good things in his life—his family and friends, the men who worked for him, the vacation he was planning. After a few minutes, he found that he couldn't get in touch with any resentful feelings at all. But just to be sure, he did the Earth Release anyway. It was easy, and he actually enjoyed it.

Some of us do our best thinking in the shower. The next exercise allows you to get clear and clean in your mental, emotional, and physical bodies.

Exercise 20:
WATER RELEASE

If a real shower isn't available or appropriate, you can also do this release as a visualization. You'll find that it's especially effective for working with feelings of ambivalence, indecision, laziness, procrastination, and lack of focus—but feel free to wash away any other issues as well.

1. Stand with your head under the shower so that you are surrounded by water on all sides. Feel the angels of water splashing down all around you.
2. Pinpoint the issue that you're ready to release and experience it within you. Feel it all around you, in the energy field that surrounds your body.
3. As the water washes down around you, feel it carrying away whatever it is that you want to release. Use your hands to sluice off the issue and picture it swirling down the drain.
4. Remember to thank the issue for the lessons it taught you, and to give thanks to the angels of water for helping you clean up your act.
5. Enjoy the rest of your shower.

Rosie uses this exercise every morning when she showers, to prepare herself for the day. She works the early breakfast shift at McDonald's, but she also likes to party in the evenings, so it's hard for her to get up when the alarm goes off at 5 A.M. Rosie used to be pretty grouchy when she got to her job, but since she's been showering with the angels, she breezes into work in good spirits.

You can use this exercise to prevent unforeseen resistance that might surface during your day's activities. If you also use the shower to clean and open your golden wing fibers in the morning, do that before the Water Release, and use your wings to help brush away the residue of the issue.

Fire purifies. When you're "burned up" over something, you can use the following exercise to fight fire with fire.

Exercise 21:
FIRE RELEASE

The Fire Release is an all-purpose exercise. However, it is particularly good for letting go of grudges, resentment, envy, jealousy, and any other issues that involve other people. To do it you will need paper and pen, matches, a bowl or container of water, and a pair of metal tongs. And the angels of fire.

1. On a blank piece of paper write down the quality or trait that is keeping you bonded to another, such as jealousy or envy. Use a separate piece of paper for each issue. Fold each slip of paper twice so you can't see what's written on it.

2. Mix up the folded slips and then pick one.

3. Open the paper and reflect on the situation(s) that provoked the feeling you've written down. Imagine how your life would be if you did not hold or harbor that quality. How would it change your relationship with that person? Ask yourself if you are willing to release this now. If not, put the paper slip to the side and select another one, which you *are* willing to release.

4. Twist this paper into a taper which you can clamp with the tongs. Ignite

the taper, holding it over a bowl of water. Although it's not elegant, you can also do this over a toilet. Of course, if you're fortunate enough to have access to a fireplace, this is an excellent alternative.

5. Ask the angels of fire to purify your mind, body, and emotions of this condition and release you from it completely. Drop the charred paper into the water.

6. Repeat steps 2–5 with every issue you've written down that you're willing to release. And remember to thank the angels of fire.

Astrologically, Carol is a Leo, which is a fire sign. (A great many actors and actresses are Leos.) She felt drawn to use the Fire Release to clean up a love-hate relationship she had with a friend who is also an actress. She and Melissa are very close friends, but whenever Melissa got a good role or acting job, Carol was envious. She would find ways to snipe at Melissa, making cutting comments about her hair, her weight, or her boyfriends. Melissa had just gotten a juicy part on a TV soap opera and Carol was miserable about it.

Carol wrote the word "envy" on a slip of paper and reflected on how she would feel if she didn't envy Melissa. At first, it was very difficult for her to imagine that. Then she imagined that she had gotten the role, and the situation was reversed. In her mind's eye she pictured Melissa all excited and celebrating with her. She felt confident and self-assured. It was then that she realized Melissa's success threatened her and threw her back into doubting her own talent. She tore up the slip with the word "envy" on it and quickly scribbled the words "self-doubt" on another one. She had no hesitancy about burning it up, and when she did, she felt a lot better about herself and Melissa.

Sometimes these issues go very deep, which means they may resurface. If that occurs, take the time to do the Grounding, Releasing, and Aligning exercises first.

Then ask your angel for information on the origins of the condition, as well as for counsel on the remedy. What your angel has to say can often be surprising, highly clarifying, and very helpful.

· WHAT TO ASK THE ANGELS ·

Who doesn't have relationship issues? Does he love me? Will she leave me? Will we get married? And then there are the security issues relating to your job, your living situation, your finances. These are often laden with desire and fear. So, how do you get information on these subjects?

Ask your angels for insight and illumination on the situation. By asking for understanding and clarity, for guidance on the correct action to take, you leave the door wide open for unlimited options. Instead of asking, "Does Tom love me?" ask for clarification on Tom's feelings for you. Or "What is the nature of our relationship? What are the lessons we come together to learn?" Or "How can I improve the relationship? What should I know about his/her needs?"

Remember that angels work in a loving, subtle, and patient fashion. They're willing to take things bit by bit, even if we're not. Old, chronic issues take time. They require working down through layers of defenses that we erected for the best of reasons—protection. Angels can be trusted to take us only as far as we can go with each step, clearing the way gradually. So be patient with yourself and your loving helper.

· NOTHING BUT THE TRUTH ·

Just as a television set must be in good working order, with the screen clean, so you can develop yourself as a clearer receiver. Unconsciousness in one area of your life—diet or nutrition, for example—can most certainly spill over to other areas. Repetition of unhealthy or unwholesome habits, whether physical, mental, or emotional, perpetuates unconsciousness.

Once you open to your angels, your whole life starts shaking up. Phil, a lawyer friend of ours, calls his angel the Truth Fairy because through his conversations with her he has come to see a whole lot of things about himself that he'd managed to avoid for thirty-nine years, the good along with the not-so-hot. He's a courteous man, and thoughtful, but since meeting Truth Fairy he has become deeply caring. He used to pooh-pooh the celebration of birthdays, his own in particular, but now he makes a point of remembering friends' natal days and on his own, he throws a big bash for himself and all his buddies.

· BREAKTHROUGHS ·

In this truth-seeking process, you may find that previously hidden abilities and gifts break through—putting you in touch with your power and your potential for success. But you will also discover impurities, dishonesties, addictions, and fears. These all rise to the surface for the purpose of being seen, accepted, and released or put to use. Your initial reaction may be to run for the hills or head for the South Seas to avoid those parts of yourself that are challenging, threatening, or embarrassing. Have faith in yourself and your angels. Hang in there. Welcome all that comes up as part of your spiritual growth and work it through with the help of your devoted angels. Ridding yourself of unwholesome habits and mindsets will help you to build a good foundation of healthy self-esteem and pave the way to even clearer communication with your angels.

As we've said before, the only things you need for talking to your angel are an open mind and a willing heart. In the chapter that follows, you're offered the option of using letter writing and dreams to augment contact with your angelic companion. Guidance in the use of these tools is offered for enhancement and variation, not because they are required, but because they are fun.

·CHAPTER·10·

Writing Letters and Dreaming with the Angels

As you strengthen your relationship with your celestial best friend you'll enjoy exploring other ways to weave it into your daily life. Writing letters to your angel, and to the angelic companions of other people, allows you to focus your intention and improve your communication skills. And learning how to dream with the angels

234

will open you to a rich storehouse of valuable information that normally lies hidden in the unconscious.

· WORTHY OF NOTES ·

Writing to the angels is an excellent way to align and connect with them, and it can help you gain clarity on personal issues. Writing to them—just as you'd write a letter to a dear and intimate friend—helps to strengthen the contact you've already made by establishing a mind/heart link. That link develops as you bring the angel into your mind and heart to direct your thoughts to it.

The act of writing also helps you organize your thoughts and clear your mind. Doing it will allow the angels to come through to you on a high frequency. Corresponding with your celestial cronies clears out the static and mind chatter that interferes with good reception. Another benefit is that when you externalize your intentions and desires you begin to release them. A thought on paper is encapsulated and complete. In putting it down you clear out the portion of your brain that held it, making room for something new.

· LET GO AND GO ON ·

Writing can also help to loosen your attachment to desires. When you put them out, you can let them go. If you keep clutching them, there is no way you can open to your angel to get the support you need in getting what you want. We can only receive with an empty, open hand. However, if what you want does not come to you when or as you wanted it, keep track of the outcome. Very often you will find that something better occurred instead.

It's good to remember that angels are beings of connection, not of control. The ways in which they support us will come from love and not from power. For example, if you're attracted to someone, you may want to write to your angel for assistance. But writing "Dear Angel, I want Arthur to love me," will not support you as much as: "Dear Angel, help me to find the appropriate way to show Arthur my love." Similarly, writing, "Please get me this job" won't serve you as well as asking for "guidance in finding the right work at the right pay for me now."

When we ask for help, our angels will always back us up. But they do this from a wider perspective than we are usually able to see. What we perceive as the perfect lover or perfect job for us may not be the proper choice for our highest good in the long run—even though it may look good to us in the moment and fit our current image of what we want. Through conversing and communing with our angels, we learn to upgrade our desires—to want not simply what we want, but what is best for all. Over time, we discover that this gives us a deeper sense of satisfaction and fulfillment. And this is only one of the gifts angelic contact brings.

Writing to your angel is easy. Just follow the steps below.

Exercise 22:
LETTERS TO YOUR ANGEL

To enhance your experience and to help create an atmosphere conducive to angelic communication, you may want to light a candle or stick of incense. You will need writing paper and a pen, or your computer if you use one. You may want to do the Basic Grounding Meditation (pp. 119–22) before you begin, especially if you are feeling scattered.

1. Sit comfortably and take a few moments to focus on your breathing and regulate your breaths so that the flow is even with inhalation and exhalation approximately the same in duration.

2. Now turn your attention inward and sense or focus on your angel the same way you do when you write to your friends. You think of your friends, the way they look, and you begin to address yourself to them, keeping their personalities in mind. In the same way, think of your angel and allow yourself to feel its gentle energy.

3. Date your letter, write "Dear Angel," and just let your words flow. Ask for your angel's support and/or guidance and give thanks for its assistance in advance. Then sign it at the end as you would a letter to a friend.

4. If you have a meditation altar or a box in which you keep special things, you may want to place the letter there. Some people put their angel letters under their pillows and others burn them, sending the message up to the heavens with the rising smoke. You'll know what to do with yours—and if you don't, ask your angels!

· AIR MAIL TO OTHER ANGELS ·

In addition to writing to your own angel, you can write letters to all the different kinds of angels described in chapter 8. Writing a letter to one of these angels is a way of inviting it into your life. You may wish to go back and read through that chapter again.

If you're in a time of transition, you can write a letter to a pattern angel, asking it to help you see the unfolding blueprint of the next part of your life. If you've just started a new job and have to work on a computer for the first time, you can write a letter to the technology angels—specifically to a computer angel—to ask for its support and guidance. If your life is in turmoil, pen a note to an angel of peace or an angel of grace, asking it to come into your life.

· WRITING TO THE OVERLIGHTING ANGELS ·

Just as you wrote to the angels, you can also write to the archangels. If you don't remember their functions, go back and read the descriptions of them on pages 192–93.

For example, if you are in need of healing, you can write a note to Raphael. It's good to put it in your own words, but you may want to say something like: "Dear Raphael, please be with me in my healing journey. Help me to see what I can learn from this situation. Guide me to the right doctors and healers for me to work with at this time." Then add any particular concerns or requirements of your own. And it never hurts to thank them for their loving help ahead of time.

If you're looking for clarity with a lover or friend, write to Gabriel, the guardian of relationships. Try something like, "Dear Gabriel, I turn to you for comfort, support, and guidance in my relationship with ———— [fill in the person's name]. Please help us to be present, honest, and open-hearted with each other. Help us to learn what we came into each other's lives to share, in harmony with you and with our highest intentions. Thank you for your guidance and loving presence."

Uriel is the overlighting angel for all job and work-related issues. To invoke Uriel's support, a letter could take the following form. "Dear Uriel, please guide me to the right job for me at this time in my life." Or, "Dear Uriel, help me to be present in my job, both for myself, for my fellow workers, and in harmony with the needs of the planet at this time. Thank you for your wisdom and support."

Michael is both the guardian of global peace and of our spiritual unfolding. A letter to this archangel might go, "Dear Michael, please be with me on my journey, as guide and inspiration. May my heart be open, my eyes be open, may I learn the truth, speak the truth, and grow in peace with all of life. Please accept my love and gratitude for your teachings."

· WRITING TO OTHER PEOPLE'S ANGELS ·

Bear in mind that you can also write to other people's angels. This is not about trying to control somebody else; it's about expressing what's so for you. You may sometimes find yourself in difficult or uncomfortable situations with people you can't talk to, or fear you might hurt if you say the things you want to say. You may also have things to say to people who have passed out of your life or who have died. When that happens, it's helpful to write to that person's angel. Tell the truth. Get it off your chest. This is not to blame but to express how you feel about what is bothering you and how you would like the situation to be.

When you write to someone else's guardian, the message gets delivered on the angelic level. Often the act of writing will coincide with or immediately precede an unexpected opening of communication with the other person. And if an easing of the relationship does not take place, simply writing the letter can help you to release anger, or fear, or a need to get something from the person that they cannot give.

· THE ANGELS WRITE BACK ·

In a good relationship, communication flows both way. Some letters to your angel do not need answers. They are open-ended messages. But the wonderful thing about having an angel for a pen pal is that you don't have to haunt your mailbox, waiting for a return letter. If you want to hear back from your companion right away, all you have to do after you've written a letter to your angel is pick up another piece of paper, and let your angel write back to you. This time, start your letter by writing

"Dear ———," and fill in your own name. Then relax and let your angel's words come through you in the form of a letter.

Toby and his angel, Zeke, have been corresponding for three years. Toby keeps all their letters neatly filed, in the order in which they were written and answered. From time to time he goes back and reads them again. He told us that they serve as a kind of diary. When he rereads them he gets a clearer picture of what was going on, in both his outer life and his inner life. Margaret also keeps a regular correspondence going with Blue, her angel. But unlike Toby, Margaret burns all the letters she writes to Blue, and all the letters she gets from her in return. "Some of them are very beautiful," she said. "But burning them is helping me learn to let go." Everyone has their own way of exchanging letters. Trust your inner senses to guide you to the way that is appropriate for you.

· DREAMING WITH ANGELS ·

Dreams are a doorway into the unconscious, and they are also a doorway into the subtle realms. They are rather like long letters from your unconscious, often written

in a strange and mysterious language. Dreams are also another portal through which you can get to know your angels and enjoy your ongoing relationship. Connecting to the angels in this way is natural and easy; it happens whether we are aware of it or not!

The dream state is a particularly advantageous access point for our celestial companions, because while we sleep, the unconscious mind is wide open. Gone are the resistances and blocks that the conscious mind—the ego—puts up to keep the angels at bay. The fluid, spontaneous quality of dreams more closely approximates the way that angels function than the highly organized, regimented state that we humans exist in during our waking hours.

· WAS THAT AN ANGEL? ·

Our angels often come to us in dreams but we don't always remember them, or if we do, we may not always recognize them. In the dream they may seem to be intimate friends, yet when we awake we know we've never seen them before. Or they may show up as wise, powerful, or significant figures, not necessarily with wings, or other stereotypical signs of their identity, such as harps and halos.

For years Linda had a recurring dream in which she was sitting in a classroom listening to a teacher speaking. She never remembered what the teacher was saying, and she knew that she had never seen her in her waking life. Several weeks after Linda met her angel, it identified itself as the teacher in her dreams. It hadn't occurred to Linda to make that connection.

Ken lives in Boston, but he often dreams about meeting friends in Los Angeles. When he asked his angel about it he was reminded that Los Angeles means the City of Angels, and that each time he dreams about it, his angel has some particular information to share with him.

Ginny, a lawyer who likes everything to be in order, has dreams from time to time in which everything is in chaos, her colleagues refuse to help her, and she has to "wing it." These dreams are one way in which her angel is coming through to tell her to loosen up and relax.

Sometimes angels make their presence known by appearing in animal forms. Richard's angel let him know that the dreams of hawks that he's been having since childhood are one of the ways in which his winged friend was reaching out to him.

Some angels do not make their presence known by assuming any kind of form at all. Whenever Barbara's dream is flooded with a brilliant white or golden light, she knows it signifies the presence of a celestial caretaker.

Other times, we awaken with a sense of well-being, a feeling that all is well, that we're blessed to be alive. We may not even remember dreaming but the good mood permeates our normal morning routine, like sunshine suddenly illuminating a dull gray sky. When that occurs, there's a good chance that one of our angels made a guest appearance while we slept. Ask your angel how to recognize its presence in your dreams.

We've all grown up believing that there is a separation between humans and angels, if we grew up believing in angels at all. But that separation is only a state of mind—our mind, not that of the angels! In our dreams, it's possible to both change our mind and to surmount the mental barriers that we've erected, so we can be with our angels quite naturally.

Remember that it isn't just our companions who reach out to us in our dreams. The archangel Michael is the guardian of dreamtime, so you may want to invoke his watchful presence. And there's a whole category of dream-worker angels whose mission is to provide us with information when we sleep. You read about them in chapter 8. These angels seldom make their presence known directly in our dreams, as our companion angels do. They are primarily messengers, and can be recognized only through the dream gifts they leave us.

· DREAM RECALL ·

Remembering your dreams is the first step, and it's a challenge. Dreams are elusive. A positive mental attitude is essential. All you need to do to start is to believe in your dreams. What we believe in, we value. What we value, we bring energy to, and what we bring energy to begins to increase.

If you've spent most of your life unconvinced of the value of remembering dreams, don't expect to wake up tomorrow morning with one on your pillow. It takes time to inaugurate a new belief. But you can reprogram your conscious, waking mind to allow dream recall to come through. The good thing is, every night you can sleep on it! Dreams can come true and when they do, they are manifestations of our deepest heart's wish. They connect us with our passion.

· MOTIVATION HELPS ·

A passion to connect with your angels is the motivation that will enable you to meet them in your dreams. Next comes diligence. You have to be willing to stay with the process and overcome deeply ingrained resistance. If you wake in the middle of the night with a dream, recapture it as you lie in bed, without moving. Replay the dream—you can begin with whatever bit you remember and allow it to expand. Then write it down and date it before you go back to sleep.

Upon waking with a dream, follow the same procedure. Changing your physical position can blow it away during the replay part, so lie quietly and recall all that you can of the dream. Then write it down in as much detail as you can remember. Date your dreams. You may even want to give each one a title that summarizes it. This will help you recall it or find it later.

There's a built-in resistance to doing this, which needs to be consciously overcome. Resistance also comes in the form of dismissing certain dreams because they don't make sense or because you don't remember all the details. But as you increasingly begin to value your dreams, you'll find that this resistance fades.

Here are some ways to help you utilize the sleep state and stimulate dream recall.

Exercise 23:
DREAM AFFIRMATIONS

Affirmations establish a positive, accepting state of mind. When repeated over and over again—especially when expressed with a great deal of conviction—affirmations flow into the unconscious mind, aligning it with the conscious one.

Affirmations tend to have greater oomph when they're accompanied by a visualization. So you may want to picture, or imagine, the experience of your affirmation while you're stating it.

If you don't usually remember your dreams, try this one:

Affirmation #1:
I will dream.
I will remember my dream.
I will wake up and write down my dream.

As you say the words, picture yourself sleeping and having a dream. Then see yourself waking up, reaching for your dream journal or angel notebook, and writing it down.

If your dream recall is good, you can skip the first affirmation and move one to

Affirmation #2:
I am open to you, my angel.
I invite you to meet me in my dreams.

It's always best when you create your own affirmations to invoke your angel by name if you know it. Choose your own words, using the two examples above as guides. Again, the more you connect to your feelings in this, the more power you give to your affirmations. It helps to visualize a beam of pink or golden light streaming out of your heart and connecting to your angel's heart as you do this affirmation. Or you may feel drawn to picture a beautiful place or environment where you can meet your angel. Repeat your affirmation as you imagine the scene.

Once you've established contact with your angel in your dreams you can begin to work with it on specific issues, asking questions as you drift off into sleep. This works the same way as writing to your angel, and in fact, you may wish to write the questions down on a piece of paper and place it under your pillow. Even if you do that, it's also a good idea to vocalize the affirmation:

Affirmation #3:
Dear Angel, in my dream tonight I'd like clarification on _____ , or
Please give me some clarity on _____ , or
Please help me to understand _____.

· SEED THE DREAM ·

Use your intention as a point of focus to seed the dream state. Just as you're drifting off to sleep, imagine having a dream in which your angel comes to you. Simply make up a dream exactly the way you'd like to have it. The dream you recall in the morning will contain some element or trace of that seed. Affirm that this is so, even though you may have to play detective to find the clue.

Timothy had a series of nightmares about the end of the world. He dreamed of every catastrophe you can imagine. Troubled, he asked his angel to help him understand what was going on. That night he dreamed that a plane crashed into his house. He ran out and saw the pilot climb out of the cockpit, completely on fire. When Timothy reached out and embraced the flaming man, he was consumed—not by fire, but by ecstasy. He woke with a sense of peace, and a deep understanding that our current world situation isn't about destruction at all but about purification. Clearly, the flaming pilot was his angel.

The key to identifying them in our dreams, our angels tell us, is feeling the tone of the dream. The emotions or sense that you have of the dream atmosphere, a quality or event that is unusual, exotic, or other-worldly, can signify the presence of the angels.

· PATIENCE AND FAITH ·

We've found that even after we've established dream contact, it can take a few days or even weeks of asking the same question before you fully receive or understand the answer. And it may not come through the angels making a direct appearance. The dream itself may be your angel's reply. Or, the answer may come in a single word, an image, or a song that you wake up remembering. The reply can also be the gift of a dream in which you find yourself flying, without effort and without wings. And sometimes, the answer comes not in a dream but in an event, happening, or moment of sudden insight. It may come to you in a casual phone call from a friend, or a sentence you read in the morning paper, or a snatch of conversation overheard on the street. The main thing is to be aware and open.

Patience will allow you to persevere, even if you don't get results right away. Patience will help you build faith in your angels, trusting that in time they will come in this way, too. Faith endears you to your unseen advocates, as well as creating the space for miracles, which is where they flock and flourish. Miracles don't have to be earth-changing. Miracles can be tiny happenings in your daily life that make you feel good or that make you laugh or even cry from happiness.

· JOURNALING ·

You may want to write down your dreams in your angel notebook, or you may decide to keep them in a separate, special dream journal. Whichever you choose, put it by your bedside when you go to sleep. Alternatively, if you're the sort who simply cannot wake up and start writing without first having a cup of coffee, brushing your teeth, or letting the cat in, it might be a better idea to have a tape recorder on hand. A voice-activated one is especially convenient so you don't need to move to turn it on.

Dreams are ephemeral. That's why it's best to write down (or record) whatever you can remember as soon as you wake up. Any activity, such as changing your physical position or getting out of bed, can sweep a whole nightful of dreams back into the obscurity of the unconscious.

When writing or recording what occurred in your dream, it helps to put everything in the present tense: "I am walking through the forest. An owl hoots nearby. . . ." That owl, a wise and winged being, could very well be your angel in disguise.

Dream fragments sometimes surface during the day or evening. This could be a scene, a feeling, a sensation, a person's face. It's important to write down any scrap or fragment of a dream that you recall, even if you can't make any sense of it, or think it's unimportant. Each scrap or fragment deserves the respect of your attention; when you give it, more and more of the dream world is revealed to you.

Journaling not only preserves images and information that you would normally forget, it also helps to increase your recall of dreams. By committing yourself to the act of writing down what you remember, you reinforce your intention on a physical level. Your intention originates in the mental plane. The reinforcement of your intention works on the unconscious, as well as the conscious mind.

Another benefit of keeping a journal is rereading it from time to time. This gives you a sense of where you've been and where you're going. It can reveal stuck places, and it can help clarify puzzling dreams that only begin to make sense over time. A dream journal is a major tool of inner growth.

Just looking back over the titles of your dreams can clue you into recurring dream themes and inner blocks of which you hadn't been aware. Brad's wife kept asking him if things were okay at work. An accountant with his own company, a new house, and a new car, his life looked wonderful from the outside. But when he went back and reread the titles of his dreams, he realized how unhappy he'd been feeling. "Stuck on a Train," "Lost in a Strange Airport at Night," and "My Briefcase Disappears" were a few of the titles. Reading them all at once, he was able to experience the difference between how his life looked and how he felt about it.

· DIALOGUING ·

You can use your dream journal to develop dialogues with people, objects, and elements that appear in the dream state. This is one of the best ways to decode the elaborate symbology that characterizes dreams. In dialoguing, you talk to aspects of yourself that are unconscious and have been disguised as other people or objects. Dreams are filled with puns and jokes—another clue for the presence of angels. Give free rein to your imagination and allow yourself to be completely outspoken. By writing freely, you can uncover your hidden feelings, fears, and desires, as well as understanding things that happen in your life.

As an example, here is a small section from Cathy's dream journal. In her dream, she's in a supermarket and knocks over a display of light bulbs.

She began her dialogue with the light bulbs:

> CATHY: Why did you fall down?
> LIGHT BULBS: You pushed me.
> CATHY: I didn't even see you.
> LIGHT BULBS: That's the point. You were clumsy.
> CATHY: What makes you say that?
> LIGHT BULBS: You weren't sensitive to where I was standing.

As she continued the dialogue, Cathy began to associate the dream events with something that had happened in her waking life. She realized that she had hurt a friend's feelings by not being aware of where he was "standing." Once that was clear, she wondered about the significance of the bulbs. And then, the light dawned. Since they shed light on her behavior, Cathy realized that they were a light-hearted representation of her angel.

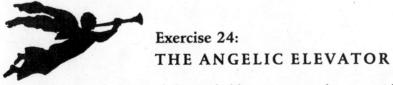

Exercise 24:
THE ANGELIC ELEVATOR

In the Bible, Jacob dreamed about a ladder going up to heaven, with angels climbing up and down. But since times have changed, while you're drifting into sleep you might want to visualize a golden elevator in which you and your angel are traveling up into the dream world. Doing this will support you in dream recall, working with your affirmations, and seeding your dreams.

If you choose to record this exercise, place your tape player right beside your bed, so you can reach out with your eyes closed to turn it off at the end of the exercise.

1. Close your eyes and feel yourself drifting into sleep. Your breathing is slow and easy.

2. Let your neck relax. Let your shoulders relax. Feel your entire back relaxing. From head to toe, feel your whole body releasing tension.

3. Now, visualize a long, long hallway in your mind. The walls and floors are made of glowing light. See the light, and see yourself slowly walking down that luminous hallway, with your angel right beside you.

4. At the end of the hallway you see a shimmering portal. This is the doorway to the angelic elevator. As you and your angel get closer, the door slowly opens.

5. Hand in hand, with one of its wings wrapped around your back, your angel and you step into this elevator. When you do, your body is bathed in the purest, warmest light you can imagine. It soothes your body and flows deeply into every part of you, into every cell.

6. You watch your angel reach out with the tip of its wing to push one of the glowing buttons on the panel by the door.

7. The elevator door slowly closes. Bathed in the light, you and your angel are slowly rising up into your dreams.

8. If you are working with an affirmation, repeat it now, slowly, several times over.

9. If you would like to ask your angel a specific question, or seed a particular dream, now is the time to do it.

10. Notice your breathing again. Feel yourself drifting into sleep. Together
with your angel, you are moving up, up, up into the world of dreams.

Cate is a kindergarten teacher. Since she started taking the angelic elevator, she's
been remembering her dreams for the first time in her life. "It's like waking up from
amnesia," she said to us. Her angel notebook is bursting with adventures, many of
which Cate recycles when she holds a story-telling hour with her class.

Ricardo works in the emergency room of a city hospital. His job is stressful, and
no matter how tired he is when he gets home, he has trouble sleeping. However,
since he started doing this visualization, he tells us that he falls right to sleep. And
while he seldom remembers his dreams, he wakes up rested and energized.

Writing letters to your angels and dreaming with them are just two of the different
ways that you can fine-tune and deepen your connection. In the next chapter you
will be learning how to focus on your life goals and how to work with your angels
to make your dreams come true.

Working with the Angels
to Achieve Your Goals

Whether we call upon them or not, the angels are with us in our everyday lives. They're ready, willing, and delighted to help us. It doesn't matter what we're doing—meditating, shopping, driving, deep-sea diving—no task is too small, no goal too grand to merit their affectionate attention.

In this chapter we share examples of how our celestial companions accompany and enliven day-to-day activities and how you can enlist their aid in achieving your goals. Advanced exercises show additional ways for Releasing and Aligning.

Some contemporary books about the angels focus on miraculous interventions, incidents where lives were saved and calamities averted. While indisputably thrilling, these accounts are usually once-in-a-lifetime events. The stories and exercises that follow demonstrate how very present and available the angels are to each and every one of us, every day, and not just for special occasions.

This isn't razzle-dazzle. It's as down-home as going to the post office, paying the rent, and being audited by the Internal Revenue Service. But it's also about how the angels can help make your dreams come true.

· NO MAGIC WAND ·

Willing as they are to assist, angels are not good-luck fairies who will bop your noggin with a magic wand and grant your every wish. They may help you to achieve your heart's desire, but they can't create your destiny. Only you and God can do that. What angels do is serve our Beloved through each one of us. In fact, it's been suggested on many occasions, and by more than one of our invisible helpers, that humans are the hands of the angels and the voices for their inspired messages. For sure, the three of us have had moments when we felt like secretaries taking dictation!

· PARTNERSHIP WITH THE ANGELS ·

Once you learn to converse with your angels, you enter into a working partnership with them. A partner is someone you dance with, someone who shares your enjoyment, who goes to bat for you and backs you up when the chips are down. All you need to do to develop this partnership is to remember to ask your angels for their help. And frequently, when you really need them, they'll show up even when you have forgotten to ask.

Ask your angels to be with you as you go through your daily life. Ask them to quiet or guide your hands when you are doing something that requires skill or accuracy. Ask them to lead you to suitable and comfortable lodgings or an eating place when you are in a strange city. Ask them to insure a safe journey and return and to facilitate connections when you, or people you love, are traveling. Whenever you want to expand your knowledge, capability, or skill, remember to ask your angels.

· ACCENTUATE THE POSITIVE ·

One of the benefits of calling on the angels is that the act of asking will elevate the way you've been approaching things. By upgrading your attitude, by opening to affirmation and a positive view, you enhance your chances of success in whatever you do or wish to accomplish. Holding the vision of the best possible outcome, you encourage and magnetize positive energies to flow in your direction.

Since the earliest times, people have worked with positive energies to create what they wanted on a physical level. Cultures and civilizations have grown up as a result. Over millennia, certain ways of working energetically have consistently proven to be effective for the purpose of manifestation. Different systems and schools call them by different names, and some rearrange the order in which they are followed. But the laws, or steps, remain the same. They are actually very simple, and with the help of your angel, you can use them to achieve your goals.

· FIVE STEPS TO SUCCESSFUL MANIFESTATION ·

While we've encountered numerous variations and additions to the process of manifestation, there are only five principles that are universally applied. With angelic assistance, you can greatly amplify the power of these laws because the angelic nature carries an ingredient that is vital to manifestation: loving acceptance. Since angels exist on a level of higher thought, closer to the realm of Creative Source, they can help you seed your goal in the dimension where thought *is* creation.

The First Step in Manifestation Is Intention—you make a conscious choice to have what you want. If you're not sure whether you really want it, take a few minutes to imagine yourself having it. If you can't picture it or feel what it's like, it may be that you don't really want it. Or perhaps you don't think you can have it. Sometimes we stop wanting something when we think we can't have it, although of course we don't actually stop wanting; we just deny the desire. Often, fear of disappointment undermines intention. We're afraid we won't get what we want. Feeling unworthy creates this fear.

The Second Step in Achieving Your Goal Is Commitment to Having It—and to be willing to have all that it will bring. You've got to be sure. No wishful "if"'s or wistful "maybe"'s. No ambivalence. This step requires you to focus your intention and to experience the conviction that you can have it. Have you ever gotten something you desperately wanted, only to find that you didn't want it after all? Or didn't know what to do with it when you got it? Lack of commitment is the culprit.

Step Three Requires Affirmation—claiming what you want by using a visualization, affirming it out loud, and writing it down or drawing it. While you can do any one of these, the more you do the better, because each one activates your intention and begins to establish it in the physical realm. To visualize the achievement of your goal, experience it as fully as you can through as many senses as you can—seeing and feeling it, and hearing, touching, and even tasting it if possible.

Affirm what you want by saying out loud, "Angel, I choose to have ———." Remember the words of the Bible: "In the beginning was the Word." The sound of your voice creates a wave form and the power of your intention and clarity of your visualization give that wave form strength and endurance.

Some people make a "treasure map" of what they want by cutting out pictures that illustrate their goal and pasting them on a piece of cardboard or paper.

Each of these actions will reinforce your inner conviction and initiate the actualization of what you want. You are *co*-creating with our Creator—with the help of your beloved angels. Your part is to conceive of the whole picture and how you want it to be.

The Fourth Step Is Gratitude—giving thanks for the manifestation as if it had already happened. It already has on another dimension, one familiar to our winged colleagues. Be generous in your thanks and in praise for the Source of All.

The Fifth Step Is the Hardest: Letting Go—you have to release your goal to the Universe, so it can then take over and deliver what you've ordered. Five short words will help you to remember: "Let go and let God."

· DEFINING GOALS ·

Before you can use these stepping stones to success, you need to define what you want. Conversing with your angels can help you focus on your goals. Do you really want that Alfa Romeo convertible, or do you simply want the feeling that you associate with having one? In other words, do you want what you want for yourself—or to impress others? If your goal is to be rich, for what purpose do you want the money? Is it to provide for well-being on a physical, mental, or emotional level, or to prove to yourself and to others that you're okay? In what other way could these needs be met? Establishing what you really want will pave the way for you to achieve it.

You can dialogue with your angel to discuss your motivation, and to unearth any reluctance on your part to receiving what you say you want. Sometimes, a hidden agenda, such as unworthiness, or fear of envy, will be held in the unconscious mind. This will block the actualization of your goal.

Carol auditioned for a lead part in a Broadway musical. Although she was called back for a second audition, she didn't get the role. She was terribly disappointed, especially since she felt she'd never danced or sung better. She dialogued with her angel, Freedom, to see why she'd lost out. Through the give and take of the conversation that she wrote down, Carol discovered that although she really did want the part, she was secretly afraid to succeed. Already feeling estranged from the friends she'd left back home in Kentucky, she was holding a belief that if she became a Broadway star, while she might be admired, she'd be so different from her chums that she would no longer be loved.

Surprised, but considerably illuminated, Carol saw that she'd had a hidden agenda: her real goal was not the role but to be loved. And since she felt that being loved was inconsistent with success, she'd failed to get the part. With Freedom at her side, a wise and loving guide, she began to refocus her goals.

· MAKE A WISH LIST ·

To help define your goals, it's a good idea to start with a "wish list." This means writing down everything you want, regardless of how far-fetched it might seem. Go over the list and consolidate any duplications. Then embellish what you want with details. You may find that they fall into categories, such as money, health and personal image, relationship, and others. Which category is most important to you? Rank them, from your highest to lowest preference. This will be of great help as you define your priorities and focus your intentions.

When Frank made his wish list he started with five items:

1. A new place to live.
2. Improve my relationship with Janet.
3. Two vacations a year.
4. New sleeping bag and tent.
5. Develop my body.

When he thought about it, Frank realized that he didn't just want a new place to live. What he was actually asking for was a really nice apartment, in a good location, with a pleasant view, at a rent he could comfortably afford. He added this to his list. Then Frank reflected on his relationship with Janet. They'd been going together for four years, on and off, and couldn't seem to agree about most things. He loved bowling; she hated it. She was a gourmet cook, and he was happy heating up frozen pizza. They both wanted to get married, but Frank wanted kids and Janet didn't. Her career came first. Frank believed that a job was a job, and you took care of that during working hours.

After giving it some more thought, Frank decided that what he really wanted was a new girlfriend. The time he'd spent examining his relationship with Janet had paid off because now he was starting to recognize the qualities he wanted in a woman. Frank began making a new list.

THE WOMAN I WANT TO MARRY:

1. Has a good sense of humor.
2. Is attractive and well groomed.
3. Isn't fussy about what she eats.
4. Wants to have children.
5. Likes bowling.
6. Enjoys camping.
7. Is kind-hearted.

Frank continued looking more closely at the other items on his list. For some time he'd been wanting to develop his body. He'd even visited a gym nearby a few times. But his fantasy was to have the equipment in his own home, where he could work out whenever he wanted to. When he priced the home gym he wanted, it was $1,400. That seemed way beyond his means, so he'd given up on the idea. But now, as he reviewed his list, he began to wonder if he wouldn't rather have the gym equipment than a second vacation. He saw that he had choices, and that he'd chosen what he had, but he could make new choices that reflected his true wants now.

When you're clear about what you want, to begin with, select one of the items that is not at the top of your list or at the bottom, but somewhere in-between. It should be one that you'd like very much to happen, or to have, but you wouldn't be devastated if it didn't come to pass. It should also be a goal that doesn't depend on another person for its fulfillment. When you've chosen one, you can use the following exercise to practice manifestation.

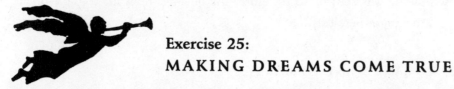

Exercise 25:
MAKING DREAMS COME TRUE

In this exercise you'll be using the Grounding, Releasing, and Aligning techniques that you've already learned, along with a new visualization. Make sure you won't be disturbed, go to your sacred space, and invite your angel to be with you. Other specific angels may be invoked. For example, if your living space is involved, either because you need a new place to live or want to redecorate it, you would also invite an angel of environments. Be aware of which ones might best facilitate the end you have in mind and welcome them, too.

1. Close your eyes. Ground and center yourself and align with your angel(s).
2. Release any impediments, known or unknown to you, which might get in the way of achieving your goal. Ask your angel to help you spirit them away, releasing them down through your roots and into the Earth.
3. Imagine your goal and feel yourself experiencing it. Picture it happening and notice how you feel, what you're wearing, and the reactions of any other people who might witness it. By engaging at least four of your senses, you vivify your visualization and encode the message in your physical body.
4. Place this picture in your heart. Ask for and receive your angel's blessing

on it. Feel the warmth and satisfaction of having achieved what you want.

5. Give thanks for having received it.
6. Beam the picture from your heart into the arms of your angel and visualize your guardian surrounding it with a bubble of violet light.
7. Watch the bubble float up, up, and away into the Universe.
8. When you can no longer see the bubble, open your eyes.

Stretch, move around. Put the matter out of your mind, but be open to receive signs that it is beginning to materialize.

· ABUNDANCE ·

We all want certain things, and we all want to enjoy the pleasures of life, although each of us has an individual idea of what this constitutes. For some, the word "abundance" conjures up images of Hawaiian vacations and stretch limousines, of opulence and plenty. This has to do with material values.

For others, it means a life that is balanced and in harmony with one's purpose, rich in loving friendships and relationships, plentiful in enthusiasm, joyfulness, and glowing good health. This has to do with spiritual values. Abundance on a spiritual

level comes from within—and above. Abundance on a material level comes from the outside—and below. But there's no reason why you can't have it all.

Entering into partnership with our angels creates the conditions that allow us to succeed, thrive, and grow, and to develop our highest natures. These conditions are openness, heartfulness, and gratitude. Ongoing, daily contact with our guardians expands the range of our vision from "me" to "us," from personal concerns to caring about others and the welfare of our planet.

As we turn more and more to our angels, we develop our spiritual abundance. We become grateful for what we have. And that establishes a groundwork for us to begin to receive on the material plane as well. When you know that God loves you, and that your angels are eager to assist you in attaining your heart's desire, you open yourself to the abundance of the Universe and the ways that it can manifest on the physical plane. You understand and deeply know that you are worthy.

Sargolais, Andrew's angel, reminds him when he asks or prays for abundance to ask and pray for it for everyone. One way to do this, whether in prayer or affirmation, is to add the phrase, "for the greatest good of all." Alma's angel, LNO, tells her "everything you receive is a gift, if you have the wit and wisdom to perceive it. You may not always like what you get, but everything that comes to you is intended for your highest good and provides opportunities for your growth and development."

When you ask your angels for their help, let them decide the way in which it will materialize. Ask that what you want—or better—will manifest, for the highest good of all.

Clarity is one of the many gifts the angels bring to us. And a large part of getting clear is releasing thoughts and feelings that can prevent us from achieving our goals. The Basic Releasing Exercise (pp. 138–39) is an important tool to use, but there will be occasions when you don't have time to go through the entire process. Having practiced the basic technique, you will now be able to utilize a shorter version, which follows.

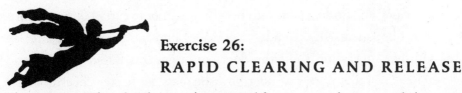

Exercise 26:
RAPID CLEARING AND RELEASE

This exercise is handy when you're pressed for time or when you only have one thing to release. In an emergency, you can do it standing, but it's best to sit down with your feet flat on the floor. We've found this one particularly good for releasing resistance, obstacles, fatigue, and other people's vibrations. Before you begin, ask for your angel's assistance.

1. With your feet flat on the ground, inhale deeply. On your first exhalation, send your roots down into the Earth.
2. As you inhale again, feel whatever you want to release in your body. As you exhale, visualize and feel it shooting down through your roots, clear into the Earth. Continue to breathe out as long as you can, until every bit of air is expelled from your lungs.
3. As you inhale on the next breath, roll your eyes upward as if you were looking into the top of your head. Inhale as fully as you can.
4. As you exhale, send the filaments from the top of your head racing upward into the heavens.
5. As you inhale, visualize sunlight from the heavens pouring down into the top of your head. Let it fill your body and flow all the way down your roots into the center of the Earth with your fourth exhalation.
6. Repeat the breathing cycles two more times for a total of three, asking

for your angels' help. When you are finished, thank the angels and the Earth.

Becky is a nurse in a Connecticut hospital. She has a supervisor who is always "getting on her case" and finding fault with her. In order not to carry her uncomfortable feelings to the patients she attends, Becky goes into the linen closet after an encounter with her supervisor, shuts the door, and does this Rapid Clearing and Release exercise. The other nurses wonder how she manages to stay cheerful under trying circumstances.

· THE ANGELS AND THE TAX AUDIT ·

Sometimes our goals are not great schemes but concern very practical, even ordinary matters. As we three began work on this book, Alma was notified of an income-tax audit. In her words, here's how the angels came to the rescue.

"While I shied away at first from engaging the angels unless my errand was clearly 'spiritual,' I was told, in transmissions, that the angels welcomed contact and were pleased to be of service. My initial response when I learned of the tax audit was indignation. I'd been audited once before and I felt that the Internal Revenue Service was picking on me. It wasn't fair.

"I immediately appealed to LNO, who reminded me that the previous audit had been an occasion for me to examine my honesty and truthfulness. This audit, she assured me, was not only an opportunity for me to affirm my integrity, but also to improve the organization of my records and bookkeeping. And, she added, in a wry footnote, 'to keep your cool.'

"Naturally, I blew off some steam. Then, vowing that when the audit was over the IRS would owe *me* money, I went about the task of gathering together all relevant tax data for the examination. Due to several postponements, it was five months before I actually met with the IRS auditor. The night before, I painstakingly accounted for every single one of my myriad receipts.

"The work went smoothly and when I couldn't find bills and bank statements that were essential, I just said, 'Okay, angels, it's up to you,' and searched for something else. Twice, the missing statements and bills appeared under my hand. Whenever I misplace something, I simply appeal to the angels to help me rematerialize it. Often, this produces an instantaneous result; when it doesn't, it means there's more to it than meets the eye, and I need to get the message before I find what's missing. Since I had no barriers to the tax examination, there was no reason for me to withhold information from myself—everything I needed I found. Was this angelic intervention or just Alma, better organized?

"In talking with my angels, I asked for their assistance in bringing the audit to a swift and correct close. Notice, I didn't specify how that should happen. As I gathered my tax data, it was with the intention of providing everything I needed in order to complete the audit in one visit. I took the trouble to understand all that I would be required to know.

"When I appeared at the tax examiner's desk, the matter that had triggered the audit turned out to be an IRS computer error. Within an hour, I was excused, the case closed. As I bid good-bye to the examining revenue agent, I was prompted to ask his name. 'Raphael,' he replied.

"I managed to keep a straight face. I thanked him and thanked my angels. And when I got home, I humbly paid my respects to the archangel.

"Perhaps you're thinking that I'd prepared for the audit so thoroughly I didn't need the angels' intervention. In this instance, I felt the presence and assistance of the angels two ways: I wasn't anxious or concerned, as I had been on the first occasion; and unlike the first time, when I'd been obsessed with the event for months leading up to it, I hadn't given this audit a moment's thought or consideration. Yet, when I put myself to the considerable task of gathering the data, the pieces fell right into place.

"Asking the angels is a way for me to state my intention—my goal. It helps me to focus my energies and attention, for that moment, on the outcome I wish to create. Then I release it—which is the big secret to manifestation—and let the Universe do the rest. Asking the angels is how I make certain that my purpose is aligned with Higher Will. I know that the angels will always serve the Light. To invite them to participate in my life is to invite that Light to shine over all that I do."

To shed light on your life, it helps if you first clear the decks. The process that follows will clear your home or office, as well as making the atmosphere much more welcoming for the angels. You can also adapt this exercise for your car.

Exercise 27:
AIR RELEASE

This process "clears the air" literally and energetically. Ventilating a room before opening to the angels is helpful to both dimensions. On the physical level, the airing of a room increases the flow of oxygen which helps to clarify thought and stimulate blood circulation. On the angelic level, it will help to disperse any negativity that is inimical to making contact.

1. Open all the windows in the room or throughout your home. Call upon the angels of the air to come in and clean it out. A brisk wind sometimes blows up when you do this.

2. If you have doors that you can open to other rooms to create cross ventilation, open them, too. As the angels of the air are also involved with weather conditions, be sure to notice what the weather's doing outside before and after the cleansing process.

3. Open yourself and be aware of the changes taking place in the general atmosphere—you'll know when the room is clean. Thank the angels of the air for their assistance.

We've found that this procedure is helpful when we are facing an organizational task, such as clearing our desks, filing papers, paying bills. Be sure to secure any papers before you do it, though, so they don't fly out of the window!

· ANGELS DO IT THEIR WAY ·

Anne is a free-lance publicist, working out of her own home. She's just starting out, so she can't afford help, but she has a team of angels working with her. One day, she had to make the three o'clock mail in order to get a proposal delivered the next day. She asked the angels to clear the post office before she arrived, so she wouldn't have to wait and could get the envelope off in time. When she arrived, the post office was empty.

Encouraged, Anne called on her angels again the next time she needed to buy stamps. But when she got there, there was a long line. Why had it worked the first time and then not again? She pondered this for several days. Then, she needed to go to the post office again to determine the correct amount of postage for an envelope. She didn't need stamps, just the correct rate. She also had a slew of other errands to accomplish and an appointment with one of her clients. Anne decided to try another approach. She simply asked the angels to facilitate her errands, to help her accomplish what she needed to in the most efficient way. This meant leaving the way open—not specifying how the event should take place.

When Anne arrived at the post office, it was jammed again. "Angels, arrange it!" she said, and left for her other errands. Then, while buying supplies at the stationery store, she noticed a scale for weighing paper. She put the envelope on it, multiplied the weight by the rate, and was able to put the correct postage on the envelope when she got home.

· ANGEL TRACKS ·

Was this simply a coincidence? Such coincidences are what our friend Sara calls "angel tracks." Angel tracks are synchronicities, coincidences that reverberate with meaning and bring a sense that someone's out there with your best interests at heart. Sara lives in a remote area in Colorado, far from the nearest town. You heard how the angels saved her life in the prologue. She was the one who coined this phrase when she wrote us the following:

"Some angel tracks are so subtle as to be nearly missed unless you're in the habit of watching for them. For instance, one day I was waiting for a ride to town for groceries with a lady who had not proven all that reliable in the past. The first day she backed out on me. But that was okay, for some reason I couldn't define at the time. The second day she showed up too late to get where I needed to go. Once more we rescheduled, this time for the following morning. That same evening my husband, who was working out of town, called to tell me he needed a particular tool sent to him immediately. I was able to get it wrapped to send off the next day! Angel tracks!

"Then, while I was waiting for my driver, who was late again, some books arrived by early mail that my daughter had told me she needed sent to her as quickly as possible. Angel tracks! Had we left earlier, it would have been a real nuisance to get the books and the tool to town for mailing. All those 'delays' were for a purpose. I've learned not to get shaken when plans seem stymied. I just watch and wait for the reason—and it soon becomes apparent.

"When you have an urge to call someone and they respond with 'You're just exactly who I needed to hear from! How did you know I needed you?' that's angel tracks, although you could also call it ESP. Same thing. When the 'right' book falls into your hands at the 'right' time—more angel tracks!"

If we take a moment to reflect on the innumerable moments of grace that we have experienced, we can begin to see a pattern of benevolent intervention. What has been termed second sight, the sixth sense, intuition, could very well be the voice of an angel, whispering the way, teaching us to use the wisdom with which Our Maker endowed us.

Invoking the attention and company of your celestial chums invites the opportunity to create more "angel tracks." Such serendipitous moments bring the pleasure of happy surprises and a sense of the flow and harmony of life. And to make sure the angels reign on your parade, use the exercise below.

Exercise 28:
THE ANGELIC UMBRELLA

When you want your angel particularly close to you throughout the day, open up your Angelic Umbrella. This visualization can be used when you have a particular goal in mind, such as an exam or an important interview, and you want to remain centered and calm. Or when you want the comfort of having a dear friend close by.

1. Facing east, extend your arms outward and say: "Angel, be with me." Close your eyes for a moment and imagine your angel standing directly behind you, its wings beginning to fold around you. Repeat this invocation, facing south, west, and then north. Observe whether you detect any particular sensations in your body or in the atmosphere around you as you do this.

2. When you have completed the invocation in all directions, sit down and raise your arms upward, palms up. Imagine your angel standing behind you holding a large umbrella with spokes made of gold. While there is no fabric covering the frame of the umbrella, there are connecting drops of golden light between the spokes, so you're sitting under what looks like a giant golden spider web, sprinkled with celestial dew.

3. Through this lattice of light a wash of droplets of both golden and white light rains down, surrounding you and enclosing you. Move your arms to sense or feel more strongly the effects of this umbrella. As you do so, say, "My angel is with me." Repeat this as many times as you wish.

4. When you stand up, sense the energy field created by this special umbrella. Imagine it hovering over you as you move into the rest of your day.

At any time during the day you can say: "Angel, be with me," and once again visualize the Angelic Umbrella. Unlike ordinary umbrellas, this one can't be left on a bus or in a movie theater.

Susan used the Angelic Umbrella one day when she was seventy dollars short of the money she needed to pay her rent. Doing the exercise calmed her fears and helped her to remember that throughout her life, no matter what happened, she'd always come through. She was feeling peaceful when the telephone rang. It was a neighbor, asking if she could baby-sit over the weekend. Susan was available and she agreed. When the woman paid her, she handed Susan seventy dollars.

· RECYCLING ENERGY ·

In this chapter, we've been talking about the use of positive energy. Is there such a thing as negative energy? Yes and no. If you were to visualize energy as occurring in long cylinders, rather like hot dogs, then positive would move directly, while negative would be what happens when those hot dogs get bent out of shape and twisted or kinked. The fundamental nature of all energy is the same, only the shape is different. It isn't that there are two kinds of energy, but rather that there are two ways for energy to move and flow and create reality. If you're up for reality creation, for manifesting what you want in your life, you'll want to make sure that your energy is straight, focused, and clearly directed.

One of the lessons we're learning on the physical plane is that we can't throw our trash just anywhere, that we cannot produce objects that are not recyclable. It's the same with energy. We can't toss it away mindlessly. If we do, we're liable to be polluting someone else's plane of reality, which is invisible to us at the moment. You can straighten out your energy by using the technique below. Just as biodegradable products go back into the soil as compost, energy can be composted, too, when you use this exercise.

Exercise 29:
THE ANGELIC VACUUM CLEANER

This visualization is designed for you to do with your angel, to cleanse your physical and subtle bodies of so-called negative or bent energy. The purpose is to remove bent energy and straighten it out again, rather like recycling. When it is released, it will flow smoothly and easily through the Universe and be drawn toward harmoniously resonant planes without clogging up anything along the way. It then can be put to use in materializing your personal objectives.

Begin by doing the Basic Grounding Meditation (pp. 119–22) or the Centering Meditation (p. 153). Then move on to the following steps.

1. Focus on the problem that you want to transform. It can be a part of your body that needs healing; a thought, feeling, memory; a physical or mental imbalance.

2. Close your eyes and really get into the issue or element you want to release. Don't be afraid to go deeply into fear or pain. The more real it is to you, the more thoroughly it can be released. Know also that part of what you can release is any judgment you may be holding against yourself that there is something wrong with you if there *is* something wrong with you.

3. Next, visualize your angel floating above you. Let the image become stronger. Sense or feel your angel and its love and caring for you.

4. Notice that your angel is holding a curious device. It's a vacuum cleaner designed to clean up bent energy, rather than dust or dirt. It may look like any vacuum you have seen, or it may look different. Free yourself to create it in whatever shape and color seems appropriate. Each time you use it, it may look different. It has a body and a hose, just like an ordinary vacuum cleaner. However, in addition to a suction device, it also contains a powerful set of magnets. They straighten out the bent energy particles that are pulled in and then shoot them out the back of the machine.

5. Your angel holds the machine in one hand and the hose in the other.

There is a nozzle at the end of the hose. Slowly, your angel aims this nozzle at your physical body, your mind, your feelings, and/or your subtle body, whichever of these needs cleaning.

6. As your angel passes the nozzle over the place or into the thoughts or feelings you want to release and heal, feel and visualize streams of bent energy particles being pulled out of you and sucked up into the tube, into the machine itself. Inside, the bent particles that were clogged up in you are being transmuted and then shot out of the back of the machine in a stream of brilliant light, pure and straight.

7. Feel any pain, sorrow, or confusion you have been experiencing diminish. Breathe more deeply now. Allow yourself to lighten up and be free.

8. If you've been carrying around bent energy for a long time, it may take a while for it all to be drawn out. You may need to repeat this process.

9. When you are finished, thank your angel.

How are you feeling now? Get up, move around, and see if there has been a lightening in your mood or your body. Acknowledge yourself for having been enough of a cosmic ecologist to be involved in recycling on a multidimensional level. For your body is not separate from the universe, nor is your healing. When you heal yourself, you heal for all. If you find yourself feeling light-headed or strange for a while after doing this exercise, remember to ground yourself, and perhaps invoke a wiring angel to help you shift into a more positive space. Cleaning your body, working with affirmations, and maintaining a positive attitude will all help to keep you clean inside.

Jennie is a social worker whose job requires her to make house calls. Since learning the Angelic Vacuum technique, she's been bringing it to the homes of all the clients she visits. "It's amazing what a difference it makes," she told us. "People are visibly brighter by the time I leave."

And there's no dust under the sofa!

As you define your goals and examine what you want in your life, you have opportunities to heal yourself of limiting self-beliefs. In the next chapter, you'll find other ways of healing with the angels.

Working with the Angels in Recovery and Healing

When we invite the angels to participate in our lives, we begin to understand that all paths can lead us to God. Illness is a route to spiritual awakening; addiction is too. Like alarms, they ring warning bells to alert us that we're off course or stuck, and we can't progress on our spiritual path until we wake up. To make headway in our higher development, we need to discover the block and remove the cause. We need to heal on a profound level.

275

· REALITY CREATION ·

One sign that we're on a path to Higher Consciousness is the recognition that we create our own reality. Everything we bring into our lives—and that includes situations we'd never dream of wanting!—is an opportunity, sometimes quite challenging, to take a correct action. This understanding carries no blame. And yet, how often have we been made to feel wrong, or even guilty, for having an illness or an addiction.

The angels tell us that everything that comes into our life is a teaching, a lesson. Cancer is bad enough without beating ourselves up for getting it. Yet we equate sickness with badness. The sicker we are, the worse we must be. This is where the healing presence of angels is so important, for angels bring in loving acceptance, with no judgment, no criticism. They're here to help us find our way out of the ills and troubles we have drawn to us in order to come into wholeness and balance. With our angels' help we learn to bless the lesson, instead of cursing the condition. And what we bless improves.

· NO BLAME ·

Aligning with our angels allows us to drop the shame and blame of our condition and get on with the healing. Instead of feeling bad about it, or trying to deny it, we can take responsible action that will liberate and heal us. When we bring the angels in, we open to the angelic way of holding any given situation: No blame, no shame, no making wrong. Whatever we've done, the angels let us know that we're still okay. They don't judge us, so when we join forces with them, we learn not to judge ourselves. This frees up energy that we can then use in recovery and healing. This is true whether we're dealing with cancer, AIDS, or substance abuse. It's true when we're dealing with abuse of any kind, whether it is physical, mental, emotional, or sexual.

· THE SPIRITUAL PERSPECTIVE ·

The angels do not heal us. They help us to heal ourselves. Their presence allows every one of us, regardless of our particular illness or addiction, to heal our feelings of separation and loneliness. We are not alone. From the moment you connect to your angel, you need never feel alone again. And you don't have to heal alone. The angels are with you, part of your personal healing team, which may include doctors, therapists and other healing practitioners, and members of a recovery group. Just as each one of these helpers will give a particular slant or way to approach your healing, the angels will connect you to a spiritual perspective, so you can grasp the significance and meaning of the condition you've manifested.

· ORIGINS OF ADDICTIONS ·

Addictions stem from feelings of unworthiness, just as all abuses come from lack of caring and respect. These are a sign that love is missing. Abuse of alcohol, drugs, caffeine, nicotine, sex, relationships, shopping, gambling, and food is an attempt to fill the empty place inside.

Addictions are coping techniques for dealing with deficiencies in love. When an infant does not receive the handling, nurturing, bonding it requires, it grows up with a love deficit. This damages self-esteem and retards the development of healthy self-love. The less self-love you have, the more prone you become to feeding yourself with a substitute for feeling good. This takes the form of compulsive behaviors. Compulsive behaviors or addictions are out of balance with correct measure. When you're insufficiently supplied with what you need, your compensatory action will be out of balance, too.

· PATHS TO GOD ·

Addictions are a path that many people choose to find God. It is the Higher Self at work, guiding the individual in the way that best suits the requirements of that soul. You might say this is a harsh way—as are AIDS, sexual abuse, and other difficult passageways. Our angels tell us that the harshness is commensurate with the level of obstinacy the soul in stuck in—and its ultimate strength. You can dig a small stone out of the earth with your fingers or a trowel. If you want to dislodge a boulder, you use dynamite.

To break the cycle of addiction, "dynamite" sometimes appears in the form of a dramatic event, like an accident, illness, or catastrophe. This occurs so frequently that it is commonly believed that an addict must hit bottom before beginning recovery. This is not necessarily the case, but in those instances when "dynamite" strikes, there was no other way to claim the person's attention. The event is a wake-up call.

· THE END AND THE BEGINNING ·

One such call occurred to Bill Wilson in the winter of 1934. He'd checked himself into a drying-out hospital in New York City. His doctor had told him that if he didn't stop drinking he faced permanent brain damage and imminent death. Alone in his hospital room, in profound despair, having struggled to stop drinking for many years, he cried out to God for help. Suddenly, a great white light filled the hospital room. For Bill Wilson, the light was a Presence, a being that filled him with joy, and lifted him from despair to hope and transformation. He never drank again.

Many people know the story of Bill W., a stockbroker, and Dr. Bob Smith, an Akron, Ohio, surgeon, two of the founders of Alcoholics Anonymous. But not many know about the third founder, this Being of Light. Was it an angel? Bill W. didn't say who he thought it was. But when he called out to God, a messenger appeared, a guiding light that we would call the guardian angel of AA and all the twelve-step recovery programs that have taken their inspiration from it. Perhaps the Being of Light was Raphael, the archangel whose special province is healing. If you are in a recovery program, you can put yourself under the stewardship of Raphael, in addition to your own guardians.

Just as a being of light came to Bill W., your guardian angel is there for you as a source of healing love. In those moments of isolation and fear, when you don't know how you're going to get through, open to your angel and let that love, that caring, that tenderness through. If you've given up your addiction and are afraid of slipping, call upon it to fill you, to shore you up and support you, to give you the strength that you need. You are worthy of that love.

If you do slip, don't punish yourself or fall back into self-criticism and blame—or give yourself permission to continue to indulge. Ask your angel to enfold you in its great, soft wings. Breathe in its nonjudgmental love and come into compassion for yourself and your condition. Compassion means loving acceptance, not of your actions, but of your Self. You are loved by your angel, just the way you are. Your angel does not judge you.

· THE ANGELIC TWELVE-STEP PROGRAM ·

If you are in a twelve-step program, you can work with the angels every step of the way. You may want to go back to read the descriptions of the different kinds of angels in chapter 8, Enjoying (The Angel Oracle). Remember, too, to ask for the special help of Raphael. If you are ready to start working on your addictions, consider joining a twelve-step program in your area. There are groups in every part of the county, including Alcoholics Anonymous, Narcotics Anonymous, Overeaters Anonymous, and Gamblers Anonymous.

In *Step One* of a twelve-step program, you come to see that you are powerless over your addiction, whatever it is, and that your life has become unmanageable. This can be the hardest step of all. Ask your companion angel to be with you and give you a leg up. Feel its love and you will be able to climb this step and keep going. In addition, call upon a healing angel to support you.

Step Two invites you to believe that a Power greater than yourself can restore you to sanity. You may see this power as God, Goddess, or your own Higher Self. Whatever your belief system is, your angel is a bridge to that higher plane. Call upon it to strengthen your connection. Also invoke an angel of grace to intersect your life and weave some of God's love back into your heart.

In *Step Three* you decide to turn your life over to God. Knowing your angel's love for you, you can allow yourself to cross the bridge of its beingness into an even greater love. In addition, a pattern angel can help you open up to the greater universal plan.

Step Four calls upon you to make a moral inventory of your life. Invoke an information angel to support you while you do this work, to help you look back over your life, and to remind you of things you may have blocked out or forgotten.

Next, in *Step Five,* you admit to God, yourself, and another person the nature of your wrongs. Here, the process angels will assist you in this difficult task of coming into balance again, of releasing negative thoughts and feelings you have been holding, perhaps for years.

In *Step Six* you ask God to remove the defects from your personal inventory. Call upon a reorganization angel to help you do this. Keep remembering that you don't have to do it all yourself. That's the purpose of a group—including a group with angels in it.

In *Step Seven* you're asking God to help you remove your shortcomings. Call upon a transformation angel to support you in doing this major overhaul. The work isn't easy, but after all that you've been through—you can do it.

In *Step Eight* you make a list of all the people you have harmed, and become willing to make amends to them. For this step, you might want to call on the wiring angels to upgrade your functioning so you can change your old behavior patterns.

Step Nine is about making amends to all the people on your list except when it would injure them or others. Here you can invoke the connecting angels you have shared with all those people, to aid you in expressing yourself in the most loving way.

In *Step Ten* you continue to take a personal inventory and learn to admit promptly when you are wrong. In this effort you can invoke an angel of peace to help you develop feelings of serenity and self-forgiveness.

Step Eleven invites you to improve your relationship to God, whatever that means to you. Call on one of the attunement angels to assist you in your opening, to be with you in prayer and meditation, and to help you discover that every moment of every day is a sacred time.

Step Twelve prompts you to share the message of your awakening with others, and to practice the twelve steps in every part of your life. Know that the environment angels will help you work this step. As you learn to make every place you're in a sacred space, this step will become easier and easier.

Roger (not his real name) works in a video-rental store. In his first months of sobriety, he was going to meetings every day and called his sponsor every night. That still wasn't enough support for him. If there had been a twenty-four-hour nonstop

AA meeting, Roger would have joined it. His sponsor brought him to one of our angel gatherings, and he found the Grounding and Releasing very useful. But at times he was like a little boy crossing a big street. He wanted to hold onto someone's hand.

Roger's dependency needs were coming up like crazy. If he wasn't at a meeting, he was on the phone with someone. He just didn't want to be alone. He was running out of friends he could lean on. At a reunion for the alumni of one of our angel workshops, he shared with us how needy he was feeling. We told him how he could work with the angels through each of the twelve steps. This gave him just that extra edge he needed to develop the sense of security and companionship he craved.

· RECOVERY WITH GRACE ·

The GRACE Process can be very useful in recovery. The more grounded you are, the more reality based you become. You may want to do the Basic Grounding Meditation (pp. 119–22) every morning when you wake up, whether or not you're planning to talk to your angel. Greta does this every morning before she jogs.

Use the Basic Releasing Exercise (pp. 138–39) and ask your angel to assist you in releasing your addictive patterns. Since you've already met your angel, you can frame your first question in such words as: "Angel, please help me recognize what is getting in the way of overcoming my addiction so that I can release it." Then make your Spiritual Laundry List and do the release work, focusing on your addiction.

Whenever you get scared, feel wobbly, or doubt your ability to change your life, use the Aligning exercises in chapter 6 to move into a higher vibration. Love and fear cannot exist in the same space, at the same time—and when you are humming with the angels, there's no room for fear.

Conversing with your angel can give you insights on the nature of your addiction and recovery, illuminating your behavior in such gentle and loving ways that it becomes much easier for you to make the needed changes. Every morning, before he went to work, Roger spent a few minutes chatting with his angel, jotting down what she had to say. He also found it very helpful to go back to read these spiritual pep talks, especially on days when he was discouraged.

Five months into his sobriety, Roger faced a challenge. His best friend, Todd, was getting married, and Roger was in charge of arranging the bachelor party. Christy, his sponsor, warned him that it was a dangerous situation—his buddies liked their booze. Roger thought he could handle it. Despite his best intentions, he took one sip—and slipped. The next morning, he was filled with shame and self-loathing. His sense of unworthiness made him cut himself off from the support team he'd worked so hard to develop, including his angel.

It was days before he found the courage to call Christy, but when he did, she told him, "Don't beat yourself up. Just get to a meeting each day." She reminded him to ask for his angel's help and suggested he practice the Grounding and Releasing exercises he'd learned at the workshop. The Grounding brought Roger into a calmer state. The Releasing helped him to unload a lot of his guilt and self-criticism. After staying sober for a week, he felt worthy enough to begin to align with his angel again. Their daily conversations helped Roger do "ninety in ninety"—make an AA meeting every day for three months. He is still using the GRACE Process, and at the time of this writing, he's approaching his first anniversary of sobriety.

· ANGEL FOOD ·

Just like drugs and alcohol, food abuse is an addiction that stokes self-loathing. Food is used to reward and punish at the same time. If you're someone who binges, you may carry more self-blame, disgust, and shame than a person who's addicted to drugs or alcohol. While we're not recommending them, drugs and alcohol give temporary relief from the nagging self-criticism that motivates people to use them in the first place. People get "high" to feel better about themselves, and they do temporarily. But most "foodaholics" are painfully aware of their negative voice before, during, and after the binge. It's a vicious circle: the act of overeating, triggered by a desire to blot out pain, causes pain. The act continues in an orgy of masochism, cravings inflamed and unsatisfied. The icing on the cake: guilt.

If you have an eating problem, you may suffer an added burden: overweight. Your addiction shows. It's a source of embarrassment and humiliation, yet the problem feeds the addiction, and there seems to be no way out. But there is a way and it's simple, if not easy. It's loving yourself. Dieting alone won't do it. To come back into a state of self-love and acceptance you need to explore the origins of your eating behavior, and uncover patterns of hurt, fear, anger, self-rebuke, and shame. Whenever possible, this work should be undertaken with the help of a qualified professional—a psychotherapist or person trained in dealing with food disorders.

It's difficult to do this on your own because judgments and denial come up around behaviors we're ashamed of. And here is where the angels can come in.

One of the reasons angels delight in participating in our lives is because they don't have physical bodies. Wim Wenders's film, *Wings of Desire*, told the story of an angel who became human so he could experience the pleasures of the flesh. A good number of us wouldn't mind swapping ours for a "light" body, particularly when we get on the scale.

· WINGED WEIGHT WATCHERS ·

The angels can't lift weight off you, but you can call on them to help you come into a more open-hearted and loving state with yourself, which is the foundation for any successful recovery program. Ask your angels to assist you in becoming more conscious about your diet and enjoying healthy exercise by inviting them to accompany you when you sit down to eat, look at a menu, or shop for food. Think about what an angel would put into its body if it wanted to keep it healthy and light. How fast would an angel chew? Would it gulp down its food or savor it? When you jog, work out, or do calisthenics, unfurl your wings to lift you. Would an angel grouse and grumble about doing sit-ups or running? Or would it send light to the muscles, energizing and invigorating them?

In addition to invoking your own companion angel, you may wish to call on the angels of healing. You met them in chapter 8 and might want to go back to read about them again. They will encourage you to see that every action you take can be a step toward refreshing your body and restoring it to glowing good health. Ask the angels to keep reminding you that you have chosen to improve your physical condition.

· CRAVINGS? CALL UP YOUR ANGEL BUDDY ·

If a craving for junk food threatens to overcome you, or an emotional upset has triggered a desire to binge, remember to turn to your celestial companion. Take a few minutes to sit quietly and feel the presence of your angel. Ask it to step into your body, to calm you and fill you with a sense of peace. Listen for the words of comfort that it may say to you. Let it fill you with love and respect for yourself. Ask it to help you find a suitable substitute for your craving, one that will truly nourish your needs. The next exercise will help keep the angels firmly in your mind's eye.

Exercise 30:
THIRD-EYE ATTUNING

A mandala is a circular design that symbolizes the Universe and totality or wholeness. It originated in Eastern religions and is used as an aid for centering and for meditation. The image below came to us from the angels. It is designed to:

- help you balance the two hemispheres of your brain (indicated by the crossbar in the middle);
- support you in Grounding yourself (the two triangles represent the inflow of energies from Earth and Heaven); and
- connect you with your inner seeing (represented by the two dots) and with your physical body (represented by the central axis).

This mandala is a visual way of Aligning yourself with your angels. You can copy it or trace this design on another piece of paper before you begin to work with it, if you like.

1. Hold the image of the mandala in front of you at the level of your Third Eye, right in the middle of your forehead, but far enough away so that you can see it.
2. Keep staring at the image until you have memorized it.
3. Feel it imprinted over your Third Eye on the surface of your skin.
4. Close your eyes and imagine that the image is pulsing on your forehead and sinking into your skin. Picture it as if it were tattooed onto your skull, beneath your skin. See it in any colors that you choose.
5. Feel this image beaming out from your Third Eye, like a television test pattern, broadcasting signals to your angels that tell them you're ready to align with them.

You can paste a copy of this design on your refrigerator door, bathroom mirror, the dashboard of your car, or inside a drawer in your office desk to remind you to align throughout the day, not only with your angel, but also with your purpose.

Betty has lost sixty pounds. She's got forty more to go. It isn't easy, and when she's feeling lonely and blue, she often thinks about going to the corner to get a pint of ice cream. The mandala is helping to remind her to keep her eye on her goal—and to remember to ask her angel for love and support. She's been going to the gym three times a week and doing her spiritual exercises, too, using the GRACE Process.

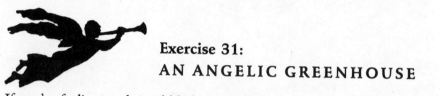

Exercise 31:
AN ANGELIC GREENHOUSE

If you're feeling stuck in old habits, bogged down in your body, and overwhelmed by negative emotions, you're actually ready to grow. The following visualization will help you to retune and redirect your life in a nurturing way.

For this visualization you may sit up or lie down, whichever is most comfortable for you. Be sure to unplug your telephone, so you won't be interrupted. Allow yourself enough time afterward so you can fully integrate the feelings of peacefulness and healing.

1. Close your eyes and breathe deeply. Relax and begin to let go of any tension in your body. Feel your muscles and your bones, sense your internal organs. Be very still in your body so you can feel it pulsing with life.

2. Picture yourself sitting just as you are, in the middle of a large, crystalline structure, like a greenhouse. You are surrounded by beautiful, growing plants, trees, and flowers. There is a pool with brilliantly colored fish and a fountain of rainbow-colored light.

3. Now expand your senses. Can you hear the fountain splashing? Listen

for the sounds of birds and wind chimes. Can you feel a soft breeze gently stroking your forehead? Smell the sweet air, fragrant with lilies, carnations, and roses.

4. Feel or sense your angel moving toward you, glowing in a radiant green-gold light. Lightly, it lays one hand on your shoulder, strokes your back and the side of your face. As it does, feel its healing green-gold light begin to fill your body, too.

5. Experience a sense of lightness in your body, feeling softer and more fluid as the green-gold light pours into you. You are becoming as vital and beautiful as all the other living, growing beings in your angelic greenhouse.

6. Now your heart is flooded with the green-gold light. It pours through your blood stream, entering every single cell in your body, from the top of your head to the tips of your toes.

7. If there are any particular places in your body that need extra attention, ask your angel to place its hands and wing tips there, and open to receive the tender touches and caresses, to feel your sore and aching places filling with light. Draw in strength and comfort, healing and balance.

8. When you feel whole and healed, thank your angel for its loving attention to your body, mind, and spirit, and watch it disappear through the lush foliage.

9. Gently become aware of your breathing again, and feel yourself in your body and the place where you are sitting. In your own time and at your own pace, bring yourself back to your usual state of waking consciousness.

Open your eyes. Look around you. How do things appear and feel? Get up and stretch, bend, and move around again. As you do, feel yourself glowing with that healing green-gold light that combines the green of grass and trees with the gold of the angelic frequency.

Betty was having a hard time taking off the last forty pounds. Because she'd been carrying so much extra weight for so long, she really had no sense of her body. When she did the Angelic Greenhouse exercise, she felt an incredible flow of energy throughout her body, up and down her arms and legs. It was tingly and warm, and made her feel happy and more alive. It put her in touch with her body for the first time. The green-gold light circulating inside her energized her. That was the extra boost she needed to stick to her goal.

Whenever you are in need of comfort and retuning, you can come back to your angel's crystalline greenhouse.

· THE SPIRITUAL DIMENSIONS OF HEALING ·

Working with the angels does not in any way eliminate the need for health care professionals. But it can facilitate the healing process on the subtle body, which is an important adjunct to the work you're doing in the physical world. We invite illness into our lives when we are out of touch with the negativity we are holding in our bodies, and when we don't know how to release it.

Ask your angel about the spiritual causes underlying the imbalance you are experiencing, and what you can do to facilitate their release. A condition can disappear or heal more rapidly once you understand what is causing it. When you ask your angel for information about an illness, phrase your question in an open-ended way, for example: "What is it within me that needs to be healed?" Or "What are the lessons this illness is teaching me?" Don't ask, "Should I have chemotherapy or go on a juice fast?" Yes or no questions—questions involving critical choices—

will usually be answered by your mind. And when you're sick, or addicted, the mind is riddled with fear.

For instance, this is what Leonard's angel told him when he asked what he needed to know about his gallstones: "Any anger held in the body will harden and block the flow. It is time for you to release your anger. It is time for you to release it with love toward yourself for having it, and with love toward the people you are angry at. You know who they are. You don't have to tell them directly. Write them letters, and don't send them. Trust your angels to deliver the messages. And trust your doctor to do the rest. Also, you might try eating more green vegetables."

· HEALING WITH THE ANGELS ·

The more palpably you feel the presence of your angel, the stronger the conduit becomes for your angel to share its energy with you. When you are sad, tired, out of sorts, or feel the want of healing, sense your angel wrapping its wings around you. An angel hug can be a healing in itself. And you can work with your angel in other ways. Here's how Andrew does: "When I go to the doctor, I ask my angel to come with me. I feel its presence in the doctor's office, and I also sense my doctor's angel. Being aware of them retunes the situation and raises it to a higher frequency. This facilitates any kind of diagnosis and treatment.

"During my acupuncture treatments I see and feel my angel floating above me, beaming golden light into the needle points. It feels wonderful and deepens the release and healing."

· ALL THE HELP YOU CAN GET ·

When you are making a medical decision, use all the faculties that you have at your disposal, including input from your doctor, research on the condition that you or friends may have done, information available from organizations or societies that work with that disease.

Use your celestial companions to help you clear and overcome fear so that you can make the choice of healing that suits you on all levels—physical, mental, emotional, and spiritual. The onset of illness and the recognition and acceptance of your addiction is the first step to healing. With your angel by your side, you can learn to welcome any and all manifestations as part of your healing. Calling on your personal guardian will also infuse you with the right attitude, one of compassion and understanding, of neutrality and acceptance. Calling on your angel opens you to love, which heals.

If a particular part of your body is in need of healing, invoke the presence of your companion angel. See and feel it beaming a healing golden light from the tips of its wings into the affected part. Invoke the healing angels, too, and see them surrounding your bed, bringing their love and support. You can also ask your angel for advice on how to work with this situation on the energy level. Again, this isn't to replace the work you do with a human healer. Rather, it adds to the effect by approaching the healing process from a spiritual perspective.

If you are undergoing any kind of medical procedure, rest assured that the room is filled with angels—yours, those of everyone there, and a flock of healing angels as well. Every time you are in need of healing, you open to the healer within you. You are not the victim of what needs to be healed—you are its student. When you enter the classroom with your angels, you energize the opportunity to learn, and you magnify the wisdom that is coming to you.

The night before she was to have root-canal work, Valerie sat quietly and visualized her angel sending energy into her tooth. Then she took two aspirin and went to bed. During her previous visit, the dentist had examined her X ray and told her it was going to be a long and complicated procedure. But the next day, when he got into the tooth, the big problem he'd seen on the X ray simply wasn't there. He was able to complete the work in twenty minutes. Dr. Nathan was perplexed. Valerie was grateful. When she got home, she lit a little candle and sat quietly again, sending thanks from her heart to the angels.

· ANGELS AND MEDICATIONS ·

Any kind of medication, vitamins, minerals, or herbal formulas that you are taking can be charged and aligned with your body by your angel. Hold whatever you are taking in your hands. Invoke your angel and see or imagine it touching the bottle or package with its wings. See its light pouring into the contents, energizing and tuning them to your body so there will be no side effects and they'll blend harmoniously with your body.

· RX: LOVE ·

If anyone you know is sick, visualize them surrounded by healing angels, glowing with a soft green-gold light. Healing isn't the same as curing. Healing means "to be made whole" at every step of the way from birth to death. Sometimes it's through illness and in the midst of it that we become whole. Becoming whole again can happen in a variety of ways. And don't forget about the wiring angels. You met them in chapter 8, and you may want to go back and read about them again. Sometimes what seems like an illness is a misdiagnosed case of rewiring.

· THE VISITING ANGELS' SERVICE ·

When you visit someone who is ailing, invite the healing angels to accompany you. See and feel or sense them filling the room, and leave them there when you go.

Remember that they can only come in when we invite them. If the person you are with is receptive to hearing about these heavenly healers, share what you know and how they have helped you. If not, it is more loving not to impose your experience, but you can always open your wings and fill the room with angel energy. This will benefit everyone who enters the room, doctors, nurses, family, and friends.

· A HEALER WHO WORKS WITH THE ANGELS ·

The late Dr. Cecelia Musso of New York was an inspired healer with excellent credentials. She was a doctor of chiropractic who specialized in a form of treatment called cranio-sacral therapy. But Cecelia did more than crack bones. She worked with the angels.

We talked with Cecelia before she died and asked her to share her experiences with us for this book. Her first meeting was not with an angel, she told us, but an archangel—Michael. He appeared one day when she was working on a client and introduced himself rather formally, saying he was there to lend her his energy both to guide and protect her and to further the healing work she was doing.

Cranio-sacral work involves the aura and the subtle bodies and requires the practitioner to be very sensitive to higher frequencies of energy. Because Cecelia saw herself as a conduit for the needs of her clients' bodies, she was open to the angelic realm. She made a clear distinction between angels and guides, the latter being other noncorporeal ministers who, she said, "help people to get through their lives." One of the differences, she noted, was that "the voice of an angel is like the sweetest music." Sometime after the initial meeting with Michael, she began to "see" angels wafting around during her sessions. According to Cecelia, they appear as needed by the patient. If someone could do with a bit of joy in life, in would come little cherubs, just like the ones you see on valentines, spreading joy all over the place. The archangel Gabriel appeared one day, announcing that he was there to help that particular patient. He projected a blue-violet ray from the area of his solar plexus right into the woman. He then directed Cecelia to tell her patient, who could not sense him, that she could use the blue-violet color energy to heal herself, which the woman continued to do with great personal fulfillment.

Cecelia reported that the angels she saw looked, "very much like humans. The ones I've seen are generally male but their energies are definitely androgynous. They fade male through female and back again, but they are very strong. A quiet, very clear strength." Gabriel came to her as a fair young man; Michael was dark. They were very tall presences and dressed in what seemed to her to be translucent robes.

What about wings? we asked. "They have them," she replied, "but they're not really wings. They look like part of their arms and they appear and disappear when they move their arms."

Cecelia recounted the case of a young man who'd tested HIV positive. When he came into her session room he was accompanied by a whole choir of joyfully happy angels who told her that they were there "for a great adventure." She found a way of telling her patient, who didn't appear disposed toward the angelic, that in the course of their therapy they were going to have "a great adventure" together. "Yes!" he agreed, enthusiastically, not quite sure why he felt so good about it. Not long after, he met his own angel and is now working with him to bring the light of the Spirit to others who have the disease.

Cecelia told us that not all of her patients were accompanied by their angels. We asked if there was a factor in common among those who were.

"Gentle service," she said, without hesitation. "Virtually all of them were serving humanity in some way."

Dr. Cecelia Musso is still working with the angels.

· HEALING THE HEART ·

The heart is a vital organ, essential to our physical, emotional, and spiritual well-being. It connects us to our angels. As we open to them, we expand our capacity for love and compassion. Everyone has heart "troubles" from time to time, such feelings as loneliness, hurt, rejection, and blame. Working with our angels, we can heal these feelings and develop more self-esteem, more acceptance for ourselves and for others. The exercise that follows is designed to help you heal your heart.

Exercise 32:
WORKING WITH YOUR ANGEL TO HEAL THE HEART

For this visualization, you will need two chairs, facing each other, and a little quiet time to be alone with your angel. Be sure to do the Basic Grounding Meditation before you begin. To open your wings, use the technique on pages 161–65. Also, it's best to record the instructions so you can keep your eyes closed throughout the process.

1. Sit comfortably in one of the chairs. Close your eyes. Begin to breathe slowly and deeply. Relax your shoulders and forehead. Open your wings.

2. Sense the presence of your angel. Feel it sitting in the chair facing you. Feel your angel breathing with you, opening its wings to you.

3. Bring your attention to your heart and feel it beating in the center of your chest. Place your hands on it and feel it pulsing for a few minutes. Continue to breathe slowly and deeply with your angel.

4. Tune into the feelings in your heart that you want to heal. Allow yourself to experience them fully.

5. Sense your angel's heart, directly across from your own. See and feel it pulsing with a warm, joyful light.

6. Out of this pulsing light that is your angel's heart, a ray of light begins to shine forth, beaming directly toward your heart. It is a warm, wonderful light. Notice what color it is. Feel that light beaming into your heart, warming and filling it.

7. Your heart fills with this light. The walls of your heart and each of the four chambers are glowing. The light moves into all the wounded places in your heart, melting your protective armor, healing old heart wounds.

8. If there is anyone you need to forgive, beam out this light to them. Picture the person receiving the healing light.

9. Let the light within you work to melt the specific feelings that you've been holding and bring you to a place where you can forgive yourself for any pain you've caused others.

10. Let this light pour out of your heart and fill your entire body. It is the light of angelic love, and you are now infused with it. It overflows and spills out of your body, surrounding you in a radiant cocoon of light.

11. Thank your angel for its gift of healing love. Be aware of your breathing and of yourself sitting in the chair. When you are ready, gently open your eyes.

You can repeat this exercise whenever your heart feels shut down. If there is a hurt that is very deep or longstanding, it will be useful to do the exercise again, over a number of days. You can also use this exercise to come into a more loving state with yourself.

Sandy teaches in a rough city school. Most of her students, if they show up at all, are discipline problems. Sandy calls them "the walking wounded." At fifteen, they seem damaged for life. In her frustration and despair, Sandy decided to teach one of her classes this exercise. They laughed all the way through it, but she was used to that, and repeated it the following week.

Not entirely to her surprise, as she'd been hanging out with angels for a while herself, Sandy began to notice some changes in that class. In conjunction with the exercise, she gave them an assignment, to write about what they wanted to heal in their lives. The pain they shared both shocked and moved her. She hadn't thought they trusted her enough to be so honest. Over the course of that year, she kept repeating the exercise, and even her principal noticed the changes in that particular class. This year, Sandy is teaching all of her students how to heal their hearts.

· THE ANGELS OF BIRTH AND DEATH ·

Birth and death offer us opportunities to work with the angels in profoundly healing ways. These events are doorways for the soul into and out of the physical body. In fact, they are of such significance to the Universe that they merit a special category of angels, coming from a very high order. Flower A. Newhouse, who wrote extensively about angels earlier in the century, suggests that the angels of birth and death come from the rank of celestial caretakers known as the powers. These angels come from the frequency range that lies above the level of archangels, and even above the principalities.

In ancient art, the powers were often shown as lightning bolts. Newhouse tells us that this is because they use an electrical charge to connect a soul with its body at birth and to release that soul at death. Nurses, who frequently witness death, have reported seeing a flash of light at the moment a person passes from life. These angels of birth and death are dazzlingly beautiful and are surrounded by an intense aura of light. Flower Newhouse maintains that they are the last beings we see before we are born and the first to greet us after we have died. They bring comfort and a sense of security to the person in transition.

· ON ARRIVAL ·

Many angels attend the birth of a baby. In addition to the powers, the child's companion angel, and the companions of all who are present, there are also angels of healing and connecting. Igor Charkovsky, the Russian expert on midwifery and the pioneer of underwater birthing, has said that he feels the hands of angels occupying his own every time he catches a baby emerging into its new life.

If you are involved in a birth, either by witnessing it or having the baby yourself, you can heighten angelic participation by inviting them to join you in your heart. This strengthens your wish and intention for the birth to be smooth and untroubled for all participants. Holding the best outcome in your heart is much like being a musician in an orchestra—the "notes" that you play resonate with the angels to create harmonious music.

All through her pregnancy, Donna and her husband, Sal, visualized the angels pouring light and love into their unborn child, especially at night before they went to sleep. They made a tape of their favorite music to play while Donna was in labor, and she put a picture of an angel into her suitcase. Sal taped it to the wall in the labor room. A few hours after Kirby was born, the night nurse brought him to Donna. "Here's your little angel," she said. Donna reached for her baby and smiled. "How did you know?" she asked.

· ON DEPARTURE ·

Just as birth is a joyful entry into a life full of soul-growing lessons, so death can be a glorious gateway to synthesis and understanding, an advance in evolution. For many, death is the healing that life did not provide. It allows a soul that is stuck or that has completed what it came to accomplish to move on for further development.

Our culture perpetuates the notion that life is short, death is forever, and something to be feared. That isn't the angelic view. They tell us that we are immortal souls, who keep evolving, even after death.

If you are close to someone who is about to leave the physical plane, you can work with your angel and the guardian of your friend or relation to help that person approach death with more peace of mind, knowing that this is the next step in the journey of evolution. Ask the angels to help you understand the needs of your friend on an empathic level. You will know whether or not it is appropriate to share the words or information you get. In some cases, what you receive in communication with the angels is intended to uplift your personal vibration, so that you become a more sensitive instrument for Higher Power.

Ask your angel to infuse you with light when you are with the dying person so that you can be a reassuring presence—calm, open, and loving. Be sure to use the Grounding and Releasing techniques before you enter the room. Remember that while you are there to celebrate a passage, and that it is a privilege to witness one, it is also natural to feel sorrow. Ask your angel to help you express your feelings in a way that totally supports the one about to make a transition. While you are there, open yourself to a greater awareness of the angels and light beings who are in attendance. Your friend may find it comforting to know that they are there if you feel it is appropriate to mention them. However, this may be just the moment to encourage your friend to share what he or she is experiencing.

If you are facing death yourself, ask your angel if there is anything you need to finish in this life before you go and how to accomplish that. Feel your angel with you all the time, allow yourself to relax into the safety of its embrace. Each time you ground yourself, feel that the fibers that come out of the top of your head are reaching further and further out into the heavens. If fears come up, do the Releasing. You will find it even easier Aligning with your angel because you are closer to it now than you have been since before you were born. As you prepare to enter the nonphysical realm, you can converse with your angel all the time. In joy, your angel will carry you into the next dimension.

· BRINGING THE LIGHT ·

As we approach the end of our physical lives, we are often more open to spiritual matters. Some people have mystical experiences that leave them completely serene or with an inner light that glows from their eyes. Andrew's friend Fred, who had AIDS, was one of these.

At the time that he entered the hospital, Fred didn't look sick. He was a chef, an herbalist, and a *shiatsu* practitioner who had been dedicated to holistic health practices for many years. Soon after he was admitted to the hospital, he had a visitation from a Being of Light. It told him that a new body had been prepared and was ready for him. Fred reported this to Andrew on the phone, with a mixture of wonder and matter-of-factness. He could have pulled through that bout of pneumonia and gone home. He could have gotten well and gone back to work. But his angelic visitor's words were clear and strong. He knew that he didn't need to hold on. He didn't need to put his lover and his friends through the pain of seeing him slowly waste away. Two days later, Fred was gone, back into the Light.

· MOVING ON ·

Sometimes, when for one reason or another, the natural process of death doesn't flow as smoothly as expected, the guardian angels will step in to assist. Timothy recalls an unusual incident that happened while he was paying his respects to an acquaintance who'd just died. In his words: "It was one of those extremely unexpected deaths. Jean had been mildly ill for only a few days. She'd been hospitalized 'just in case' and to everyone's astonishment had died only hours later. I went to the laying out of the body a day or so later at an elegant Madison Avenue funeral home, not because I'd known Jean well but from some deep inner prompting that I was needed there.

"When I arrived in the room I could see the coffin at the front, the lid opened so that the top half of Jean's body could be viewed. I found myself alone, so I sat at the back for a few minutes getting used to the atmosphere and calling on my angels to show me what was required. As my eyes grew accustomed to the lowered lights, I became aware of a strange phenomenon that seemed to be happening just above and immediately around the coffin. It looked at first like a vague shimmering, as if reality itself was rippling.

"Then as I watched I could see what appeared to be a transparent body, lying flat but hovering in the air about two feet above the coffin. I had a strong sense that Jean, the essential being of Jean, was still attached in some way to the body that had been hers. At that point my angel told me what to do.

"As I walked slowly up to the railing, the shimmering settled down slightly and, just as if I were taking dictation, I spoke the words that my angel, Joy, gave me. I was asked to address Jean in a quiet and confident manner, reassuring her as to what had happened and telling her that she'd died at a time of great personal confusion. She was an eminently practical woman who hadn't given much thought to life after life, a concept she'd probably considered the height of whimsy. She had absolutely no idea of what was going on, or indeed, whether she was asleep, awake, anaesthetized, or dreaming.

"Somehow Jean must have trusted my voice because the shimmering became less filled with fear. I continued to talk to her, calming her down and encouraging her to reach for the Light. After a few minutes of affirmation, what I'd perceived as the shimmering stopped altogether, and I knew with an inner certainty that her true self was gone, returned to the Light. As I turned to leave I felt the sweetest breath of gratitude fill me with warmth."

When we work with the angels in birth and death, we open to love and transmute fear.

· PATHWAYS TO THE HEART ·

The angelic realm opens us to new pathways to the heart, new understandings of the Voice Within, while we work to achieve the state of Oneness with the All. Our awareness of the angels softens us and makes us gentle, revives our hope and faith. And we know, from the daily miracles and playful manifestations that occur all around us, that the angels themselves are delighted to be known and trusted by us. They enjoy serving, perhaps because their assistance on our way contributes to further establishing our faith and confidence that we are truly loved by our Maker, and it is God's pleasure when we flourish in our lives.

Working with the Angels in All Your Relationships

Up to this point, we've focused on your relationship with the angels. Now that you've begun to communicate with them, you can extend what you've learned to your other relationships as well. When two or more partners bring their angels into the relationship, the capacity for transformation increases—as we three can attest! But whether your partner, friends, or co-workers are in touch with the angels or not, you can still work with the celestial connectors to improve your rapport.

Just as we all have personal angels assigned to us—guardian, or companion angels—all relationships have guardian angels as well. These celestial helpers come from a class of beings called Connecting or Coordinating angels (they are described more fully in Enjoying (The Angel Oracle). Every couple and friendship has one. Every working team and every family has one. One way to image the connecting angels is to see them like mother hens, settling themselves around their chicks— their presence is warm and comforting, embracing and safe. Because their energy field is larger than ours, they expand us, opening us to greater possibilities in communicating with others. Their enormous field also contains us (and our personal guardians), which makes it safe for us to venture beyond any hesitancy, timidity, or shyness we may feel with others.

· GOOD TIMES AND GROWTH TIMES ·

In any relationship there are good times and times when conflicts or troubles crop up. These times may be worrisome, but they actually can help us to grow and heal on issues that have been with us all of our lives.

Every relationship we enter into is based, to some degree, on the first relationships we ever had, those with our mother and father. We learn patterns of relating from our parents, both good and bad. If we examine what's not working in a current relationship with the conscious aim of identifying our negative patterns, instead of making the other person wrong, we have the opportunity not just to mend the relationship, but to heal ourselves as well. When we work with the connecting angels, we expand our innate capacity for happiness and heartful communication. If there is tension or misunderstanding, calling on the connecting angels smooths the rough spots and paves the way to reconciliation.

The exercise that follows introduces you to the connecting angels so you can talk with them whenever you'd like some extra light on a relationship.

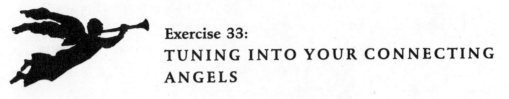

Exercise 33:
TUNING INTO YOUR CONNECTING ANGELS

If your partner, lover, friend, co-worker, or classmate is in contact with the angels, you can do this exercise together. If not, sit quietly and imagine the other person with you. You may want to prerecord this exercise. Begin with the Basic Grounding Meditation, and move on to the steps below.

1. Close your eyes. Feel your guardian angel with you, sitting behind you. Be aware of its particular energy or vibration.
2. Sense the guardian angel of the other person. Visualize it sitting behind the other person, whether or not that person is physically present.
3. When you have a feel for the other angel, invoke the presence of the connecting angel for the relationship. Often this energy will come in as a large sphere that surrounds you and the other person and both your angels. Or you may feel it as another being sitting between the two of you, linking you both.
4. Tune into the connecting angel and let your awareness of its presence grow. In what way is its energy different from that of your guardian? What is it like? As you explore this new presence know that it is with you because of the bond that connects you to the other person. It carries the energy of all that is most loving and harmonious between you.

5. Just as you have learned to dialogue with your personal angel, open now to the connecting angel, receive its energy and listen to its words. Ask it any questions, express any concerns or needs that you may have. Be open to receive its counsel and wisdom—in words, pictures, colors, or feelings or any other way that it may come to you.

6. If you are doing this with another person present, share your experiences of meeting the connecting angel with each other. This will help make your connection more solid.

7. If you are doing the exercise alone, visualize the other and know that the connecting angel will touch that person gently through his or her guardian. Know, too, that your reaching out has already begun to make a difference.

8. When you are finished, thank the connecting angel, thank the two guardian angels, and thank your friend as well. Once again, become aware of your breathing. When you are ready, open your eyes.

Feel free to contact the connecting angel when you are in a joyful place in a relationship, to express your pleasure and gratitude. If the relationship gets rocky, remember to reconnect. You can also use this tuning when you are away from family or friends and wish to connect with them on an energetic level. At work and in joint projects, if others have also learned to talk with their angels, this exercise can greatly enhance the work and help things go more smoothly, efficiently, and creatively.

Once Carol began to call on the connecting angel for her relationship with her mother, a lot of the tension between them fell away. When she gave up trying to be "Mama's Good Little Girl," she began to discover the extraordinary woman that she is.

In the theater, in addition to producers, directors, and performers, many people are involved in production—for costumes, make-up, lighting, props and scenery. Whether it's an audition, a dress rehearsal, or a performance, Carol now calls on the connecting angels to work with everyone involved. Since she's started doing this her career has blossomed.

Carol is on Broadway now in a featured role. She's just been nominated for a Tony award. We've changed her name to protect her privacy, but if you knew it, you'd know her.

· WORKING OVERTIME ·

As the three of us worked on revisions for this book, Timothy was in New Mexico, Alma was in Manhattan, and Andrew was in Brooklyn. Abigrael, the recording angel who connects us, had to work overtime. Alma has two separate phone lines. On half a dozen occasions, while she was talking with Timothy or Andrew, the other called. By conferencing the calls, we were all able to talk together. We thank Abigrael and the angels of technology.

Even in the best of relationships, things sometimes go awry. It isn't always possible to mend a hurt or wrong in the moment, and little incidents can fester or grow out of proportion when they aren't dealt with. For those times when you can't make it right with the other person, the next exercise will prepare the way to patch up differences and restore harmony.

Exercise 34:
VISUALIZATION FOR HEALING A RELATIONSHIP

For this visualization, you will need two candles and a quiet, secluded environment. Be sure to have your notebook and pen handy, in the event that you want to write down what you receive.

1. Light two candles. One candle represents you; the other represents the other person in the relationship that you wish to heal. As you light the candles, say: "I invoke my angel to assist in this healing. I invoke the angel of (the person's name) to assist in this healing. I invoke the presence of our connecting angel."

2. When both candles are lit, say: "I hold this moment, this healing, and this relationship in the Light." Breathe in, and as you exhale, visualize the healing ceremony also taking place in your heart.

3. Visualize the other person. See him or her as he or she really is, good, bad, funny, sad—every way you know that person to be.

4. When you have run through the many facets of the other person, ask for an impression of that person's angel. Close your eyes and allow the impression to build.

5. Invite that angel to share with you and your angel what needs to be done to heal the relationship. Listen to the angel's response and feel it, too. You may receive impressions of light, color, or images as well as hearing words. Be open to the impressions you receive and do not reject any as being silly or foolish.

6. When the impressions fade, thank the other person's angel. Then open yourself to responses from your own angel. Ask: "What needs to be done

to heal the relationship?" Again, make yourself open to receive whatever comes, without judgment.

7. When you have received a message from your own angel, ask the connecting angel if there is anything else you need to know.

8. Thank the angels and imagine a beautiful gift, one that contains the impressions and suggestions you've just received. Picture yourself handing this gift to the other person. Observe the other person's response.

Because we are all connected, any change in your heart will have an effect on your friend, lover, husband, wife, or co-worker. After you do this visualization, you may even find that the other person takes the initiative in making amends.

Patti is executive secretary and personal assistant to a brilliant tycoon, who is well known in New York City business circles. He's also quite gruff and has a notoriously bad temper. Shortly after Patti met her angel, her boss humiliated her in front of a large group of businessmen by yelling at her for some trivial matter. It was clearly a case of his throwing his weight around, since Patti is highly skilled at what she does and doesn't miss a trick.

When Patti returned for an angel gathering we held a few weeks after our "Opening to the Angels" workshop, we noticed that her usual brightness was subdued. She told us what had happened the previous week, and we suggested she do the candle visualization, calling upon the connecting angels. She phoned the next day. She did the visualization when she got home that night, and when she walked into the office the next morning, there were a dozen long-stemmed roses on her desk. The note from her boss didn't exactly apologize. It simply said, "Patti, you're great."

· OPENING TO THE ANGELS WITH
ANOTHER PERSON ·

One of the ways you can increase and expand your enjoyment of angelic encounters is by sharing the process with another person. Working with another to open to the angels brings in extra energy that makes it even easier to hear the voice of your guardian. It's been our experience with groups that the presence of others actually heightens personal vibrations—and it certainly brings in more angels!

You can share the GRACE Process with a friend, mate, relative, or colleague who also wishes to make the angelic connection. The same techniques you learned in Part II are adapted here for use with another person. The Releasing exercises (pp. 130–31, 133–34, and 138–39) can be used as they are.

Exercise 35:
GROUNDING WITH ANOTHER PERSON

Set up the same tranquil and serene atmosphere we've recommended before, eliminating any distractions. You will need the Introduction to Grounding and the Basic Grounding exercises that you've recorded on tape. Sit on facing chairs, with your knees six to ten inches away from each other.

1. Take a few minutes to just be with the other person with your eyes open. Allow yourselves enough time so that you go beyond any self-consciousness or judgments that may come up at first.
2. When you are ready, turn on the Introduction to Grounding tape and close your eyes. Go through this together.
3. Next, do the Basic Grounding Meditation.
4. When you have finished, share with each other what sort of rock, plant, and animal you were, and what you experienced in the other chakras.

Sharing your impressions and what you received with another heightens the enjoyment. It makes what happens more real, more vital and alive. Sometimes you'll find that you both got the same images, or ones that relate to each other. It's another sign of how we are all connected, all part of All That Is.

When Robert and Ellis compared notes after this exercise, Robert was a large rock in the middle of a field, surrounded by wild flowers. Ellis was a large rock formation lying near the shore of a beach, lapped by waves. They found that they both received images of birds for their animals. Robert saw himself as a sea gull, perched on a rock in the water, and Ellis was a hawk, circling a field. As they talked, Ellis recalled seeing a large rock and wild flowers.

Once you and your partner have grounded and shared, do the Spiritual Laundry Lists and Basic Releasing Exercise. Although you may have different things to release than your partner does, this exercise is most effective if you both release all the issues together, out loud, using the breath as forcefully as possible. Personally, we've yet to find an issue that we couldn't relate to!

Following the Releasing, you may want to take a little break. Get up and move around, rotate your shoulders, shake out your arms and legs, loosen up. Open a window and breathe some fresh air. You might even want to put some music on and dance to it for a bit. When you're ready to go on, sit down again—no more than ten inches away from each other. The following exercise will help you to align your energies, before you move into the Opening to Your Angel exercise (pp. 169–70). As with the others, we recommend that you record it, leaving pauses for you to follow the instructions.

Exercise 36:
ALIGNING WITH ANOTHER PERSON

This alignment will allow you and your friend to connect your chakras, creating a powerful energy field for angelic communication. Have notebooks and pens handy for the Opening process that will follow shortly afterward.

1. Close your eyes. Send roots down to the Earth and fibers up to the heavens.
2. Draw Earth energy up to your Root chakra and the celestial energy down to the Crown chakra.

3. When you have a clear feeling of the energies in your Crown and Root chakras, visualize a beam of light coming from these chakras and connecting in a straight line to your partner's chakras. Feel the light connecting you to your partner's Root and Crown chakras.

4. Open yourself to receive the beam of light from your partner and feel it connecting to your Root and Crown chakras.

5. When you have established a firm connection between you, move the Earth energy up to the Sexual chakra and move the energy from the heavens down to the Third Eye. Again, visualize a beam of light from these chakras connecting with those of your partner.

6. Receive beams from your partner into your own chakras.

7. When the connection is clear between your Sexual and Third Eye chakras, move the energies once again, this time to the Solar Plexus and the Throat chakras. Visualize beams of light flowing from them and connecting to your partner's chakras.

8. Receive those beams into your own chakras.

9. As the energies connect at your Throat chakras, tone together, making the sound of *om*. Keep toning until you both feel the tone resonating in your bodies.

10. Now move Earth and Heaven energies into your Heart and Thymus chakras. Send a beam of light from these paired chakras to your partner's paired chakras.

11. Receive the beam of light coming from your partner into your own Heart and Thymus chakras. Notice how you experience this. Allow yourself to feel it as deeply as you can. Be aware that your angels are already present, and open yourself to sensing their loving energy.

12. When you feel ready, open your eyes.

This connection with another is strong, and tender. Be with each other in silence for a few minutes, to allow yourselves the full measure of pleasure in your alignment. Be receptive to perceiving your angels' presence.

Rosie and Angie (who later resumed her true name, Angela) had never laid eyes on each other until they met at one of our angel workshops. When they decided to do this exercise together, Rosie was eager and excited, but Angie felt a little uncomfortable at first since she hardly knew Rosie. When they completed the Aligning, both young women were glowing. They hugged each other. Rosie, who's avidly interested in astrology, asked Angie when her birthday was. It was the exact same day as Rosie's.

When you are ready to go on with the Opening to Your Angel exercise, agree upon the question you wish to ask your angels. Asking the same question together is recommended to begin; on other occasions, you may each wish to ask a different one. A question that has proved fruitful is "What brings the two of us together?"

Follow the steps in exercise 13: Opening to Your Angel (pp. 169–70). When you have received your messages, thank the angels and share your transmissions with each other. You may find that there are similarities in what each of you got, words or images that were identical. Or you may find that they are very different. Enjoy them, and enjoy your mutual alliance with the angels.

Pat and Felicia are friends and enjoy exploring together many of the spiritual awareness programs and seminars that are so popular these days. They've both been in contact with their own angels for some time. They got together one day when both of them were feeling blue and decided to find out a little more about what was going on. They grounded, did their best to release their sadness, and opened to their angels. Here's what came through:

FELICIA'S ANGEL: Sadness releases the heart, expands it to nourish and nurture. When you cry and feel sad, you are in a space of surrender. You move onto a plane higher to calmness. Tenderness abounds. In this surrender, you let go of control and put yourself in a more open place to receive love, information, creative inspiration, messages. You allow yourself to listen more truthfully and share more with others. Your fears, your tears, carry you and move you to more serenity within.

PAT'S ANGEL: Weep gently and deeply with the sadness, and loosen yourself into knowing why it has come. A glass of water nourishes your throat and fills and flows as golden energy that penetrates the deepest regions of your emotions. Keep on and on; don't stop until the gentle hand of transformation quivers in your throat and you know the words, what they are, what has happened, what is to be.

After that, they both were able to experience sadness in a whole new way.

· ASKING THE ANGELS FOR MESSAGES FOR ANOTHER PERSON ·

Once you've made contact with your angels, you can open to receive messages for other people. You can do this with friends who've also learned to talk with their angels, having them ask the angels for you at the same time. Or, you can do this by yourself—but only *at the other person's request!*

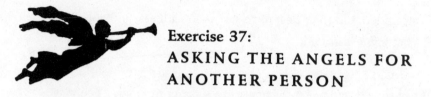

Exercise 37:
ASKING THE ANGELS FOR ANOTHER PERSON

For this process, you need to be grounded, released, and aligned. Have your notebook and pen nearby.

1. Sit quietly, with eyes closed, about six to ten inches away from your partner.
2. Invoke your angel and the presence of your friend's angel. Ask these angels to be with you as you open to receive information that will serve the highest good for all.
3. Bring up an image or a feeling of your angel. Whatever you get, welcome it as a manifestation of angelic presence.
4. Now allow an image of your friend's angel to come up.
5. See the angels interacting in your mind's eye. Imagine that they are greeting each other. How do they do that? Do they shake hands? Ruffle their wings? Dance? Bow formally?
6. Bring the image of the angels into your Heart chakra. Hold it there for a few moments until you begin to experience a warmth in your Heart and can sense the angels' presence.
7. Now place the image of the angels in your Third Eye and hold it there, too.
8. When the Heart and the Third Eye are filled with the energy of the angels, open your eyes and write down the question. Close your eyes and repeat the question to yourself, imagining that the words are written in your Heart and Third Eye.

9. When you begin to hear words, or receive impressions, open your eyes and write down what you are receiving.
10. When the words stop, remember to thank both your angels.

Take a few moments to appreciate the energy that surrounds you. Then read what you have written. If you find that the tone of the transmission is loving and accepting, if it does not give specific advice but gently guides, and if you would be comforted to receive that message yourself, share it with your friend. If it scolds or threatens or urges specific actions, there's a good chance your mind got in the way. Put it aside and ask for another message. Angels don't give orders; they encourage us to use our own faculties of mind, heart, and spirit, and to make decisions for ourselves.

Maria was having a terrible time with her boyfriend, José. He was always disappointing her in some way—and she often caught him in lies. She confided her troubles to Josephine and begged her to ask her angel what to do. Josephine had no trouble summoning her own guardian, but she wasn't sure she could make contact with Maria's. Nonetheless, she was willing to try.

Josephine asked Maria to sit with her, and she went through all the steps, listening to the exercise on tape. She got a clear image of Maria's angel, who looked very different from her own. And then she heard these words:

MARIA'S ANGEL: Maria likes illusions. She prefers illusions to reality. This is because her relationship with her father was so painful that she retreated into fantasy and picturing the world—and men—the way she wanted them to be. Maria has never wanted to be with the way things and people are. She has become attached to her illusions. This is why, whenever José shows himself to her as he really is, her illusions are shattered. She becomes disappointed and begins to criticize him and feel sorry for herself.

Josephine was startled, but she kept on writing, asking what Maria needed to do.

MARIA'S ANGEL: Maria needs to release her dance of disappointment, both with her father and with men in general, so she can be with them as they really are, flaws and all. Maria needs to know that José was not put on Earth to make her happy, and he is not responsible for her unhappiness either. When she accepts herself more fully and stops relying on others for her happiness, she will emerge into the bright and happy spirit that she is.

Josephine read the message over a few times before she decided that it was all right to share it with her friend. When she did, Maria began to cry. It was all true, she said; the truth had brought her to tears. Subsequently, Maria patched things up with José, and Josephine taught her how to contact her guardian and connecting angels herself. While the relationship still has its ups and downs, Maria has become more philosophical about it. With the help of the angels, she's learning to love José exactly as he is.

Sometimes, you may be tempted to ask the angels for someone who hasn't given permission. Here's what happened to someone who tried.

Ira was concerned about his business partner, Ralph, who seemed to be going off the deep end. Ralph was drinking heavily and acting so inappropriately that their business was threatened. Ira decided to ask Ralph's angel, "What can I do to help Ralph get back on track?"

Ira couldn't get an image of his partner's angel. All he saw was a murky gray cloud. Then he remembered that he hadn't asked Ralph if he could do this. Ralph would have laughed in his face if he tried. However, he still wanted some guidance, so instead of reaching out to Ralph's angel, he opened up to the connecting angel of their partnership. All at once he felt a warm, loving presence and quite unexpectedly he found himself relaxing. Within a few moments he "saw" the end of the partnership and realized that he could carry on alone. He never spoke to Ralph about it, but prepared himself so that when the breakup did occur, some months later, he was able to carry on the business and attend to the legal details without jeopardy.

You can also do this exercise when a friend is not present—but as we've seen from the example of Ira, only if he or she has asked you to do so! Simply begin with step 2, after doing the Grounding, Releasing, and Aligning. Many people find that when they first start conversing with their angels, it's even easier to get information for others. That's because you don't have a personal investment in the answer. Neutrality always brings clarity.

If you want to get information on your relationship with another person and do not have his or her agreement, consult with your personal guardian and with the connecting angel of your relationship.

In the chapter that follows, you'll learn how to share the angels with more people—family, friends, and groups.

Working with the Angels in Groups

Two or more people, working together, increase the energy that can be brought to bear on any issue or situation. Add the angels, and you've got a combination powerful enough to create miracles. In this chapter, we offer exercises and examples of how angelic alliances can contribute to the transformation and healing of ourselves and our world.

The angels tell us that certain radiations, emanations from nuclear waste, and various of the major planetary pollutants are particularly open to transformation by forms of spiritual alchemy. Guided visualization is one of these spiritual techniques, and it can be very much amplified by calling on the angels to add their considerable energies.

· ATOMIC MELTDOWN: HOW THE ANGELS HELPED ·

A true example of such an apparent miracle in action was witnessed by Timothy in 1984, soon after he'd started working extensively with the angels on global projects. In his own words: "I was in Great Britain in the winter of 1983, spending some time down in Glastonbury, known thereabouts to be the Heart chakra of England. It is a very powerful and sacred place, with a vigorous spiritual community.

"Word of a rather strange and terrifying nature came in sometime during the middle of the month of December. The dates are important because the whole affair has a very precise side to it. Apparently, the recently deceased mother (she'd been dead a few weeks, I believe) of a man in France, a Frenchman who himself was a devout atheist, had been coming to him in dreams and insistently informing him that there was going to be a meltdown in the atomic reactor on Cape de la Hague. And she gave exact dates: between January 16th and 18th of 1984. The nocturnal visitations became so urgent and disquieting to the poor man that he started telling a few people about it. Of course, his warnings were pooh-poohed extensively, mainly by the very people who were responsible and could possibly have done something about it—the scientific establishment.

"But, fortunately, among those he told there was one woman who had links with some people who would take such a situation very seriously indeed—people who believe in dreams. Thus, the word reached the spiritual community in Glastonbury,

England. It was soon discovered why. Just as the human body has energy lines called meridians that flow through it, so too does our planet. The great meridians of Earth energy that crisscross the face of our planet are called 'ley lines.' Glastonbury lies right on one of these main ley lines, which flows up the length of France, across the English channel, and north up into England. It so happened that the atomic power station on the Cape de la Hague was situated on exactly that ley line. Nobody knew quite what it meant, but it certainly carried feelings of foreboding.

"Conferences and meditations followed. The help of the angels and guides was requested, and a plan of action was developed. Individuals were dispatched to bury quartz crystals at key points along the ley line upon which the reactor sat.

"Come the predicted day, small groups sat in deep meditation together focusing their hearts' desires on guiding the atomic energies, and transforming them, with the help of our angels, into positive healing emanations.

"The result? A tremendous boost in regenerative and harmonized energy delivered to significant places of spiritual power. A sense among those participating of being able at last to do something practical about returning our planet to harmony and balance, and the report of an eight-year-old boy who saw hovering, right above the famous Glastonbury Tor, a hill near Glastonbury Cathedral, a small group of brightly shining flying discs at exactly the time of the maximum energy shift.

"Did it work? Was it all in our imaginations? Did the French atomic authorities have anything to say?

"Well, the reactor did not melt down in January 1984. Those who have ears, let them hear."

· ANGELS AND THE EMERGENCE OF
GROUP CONSCIOUSNESS ·

When any one of us takes a long and honest look at the state we've gotten ourselves into on this planet, we tend to be overwhelmed by the incredible complexity and the interdependence of all the factors that must be considered in a global transformation. No wonder it seems so impossible to conceive—or achieve.

Everything seems to be linked irrevocably with everything else. Dolphins die in the Gulf of Mexico because of the effluence of North American factories. Holes in the ozone layer at the poles open and close depending on what deodorant we use. Forests burning in Brazil affect the quality of air in Boston. The desire for aphrodisiacs in the Far East kills off the last remaining rhinos in Africa. The list is endless and growing daily. It all seems too complex for simple solutions.

Or is it? Is it possible that there's something so simple that it's staring us in the face—only we can't see it for the looking?

· CARING STARTS AT HOME ·

The answer *is* simple. It lies in human caring. The ability to feel concern for, and to care for, another's situation. And like much else, caring starts at home—with ourselves. For if we don't care for ourselves, how can we care about anything or anyone else?

If we cared, each one of us, about who we are and what our true purpose is, and if we cared about each other, about life in all its forms—about the waters, the air, the great forests, and the animals—then all the rest would follow quite naturally.

We all know what caring means. We know because we enjoy the feeling of being cared for when it occurs. But we allow ourselves to be hypnotized into forgetting to care. We let ourselves be dulled and numbed by fear. And it's fear that chases away caring—fear and ignorance.

But each of us can reverse this trend for ourselves. At any time, in any mood, we can begin by caring for what is right here, under our noses. If each of us does this, and continues to do it, this simple act will build a wave of caring that will indeed bring about the global transformation that all of us in our heart of hearts desire to see. When each of us remembers to do what we do with more care, and to do more of what we care to do—what we love to do most—then an immense and wonderful difference will be felt immediately, by each of us individually, and then by all of us together.

You may say, "Yes, the answer is simple. But how do we get there? How do we learn to care? How do we remember to care, when we have not cared for each other this way throughout all of our history?"

The answer to this question is also simple. It is the angelic way through. When we open to our angels, we open to a source of love that is endlessly abundant. And, after all, isn't it love that all of us are seeking?

· WORKING WITH ANGELS IN GROUPS ·

There are two ways in which the angels work with us in global healing and transformation. The first is through direct input, through sharing knowledge with us that will bring us to the next step in technology, culture, and consciousness. This occurs whenever we open to our angels and begin to dialogue with them. The second way is that by sharing their energy, we humans move into a collective consciousness—we become one heart, one mind.

Angels are collective beings, at the same time that they are very much individuals. For centuries we humans have been struggling to balance our individuality with our collective natures. In most cultures the individual was subsumed to the collective, but in the last few hundred years we have seen an increasing focus on the self, sometimes in opposition to the community, and sometimes at the expense of the community, whether this be family, city, or nation.

When we spend time with angels, whenever we bask in their energy, we take in by osmosis some of their capacity to be exactly who they are, in harmony with the whole—in harmony with All That Is.

The participants at our gatherings all come with differing beliefs. By invoking the angels, who are common to so many religious traditions, we cut across all these differences, creating a common ground, a unified field of consciousness. The energy of this field is deeper and broader than any one individual is capable of producing. Embraced in this field, which is held by the connecting angel of the group, it becomes very easy for people to meet their own angels.

Heartfully joined in this field, everyone's contributions add up to a wisdom and vision that no one person could have created by himself. Each individual tells another portion of the human story; each carries a part of the dream that all need to hear. Time after time, someone will express a thought, using the exact words that another person was about to say. It's refreshing and reassuring. You feel completely understood and heard. It doesn't matter out of whose mouth the words come, what needs to be said is said, and you know, with tremendous relief, that you don't have to do it all by yourself. You're not alone.

In our workshops, we've found again and again that magic happens when people come together in the company of the angels. There is laughter, sorrow, tenderness, sometimes fear—yet all of it is contained in the joy the angels bring. In writing this book, we found the same thing happening, too. If something needed to be done, there was always one of us who was ready to do it. Where one of us might be stuck or resistant, another of us wasn't. So the work went on, above, around, and through our individual blocks, as soon as we let in the joy again.

How many people dreamed about the nuclear disaster at Chernobyl, but did not have anyone with whom to share their dreams? As more and more of us open to our angels and work together with them in groups, we create communities like the receptive one at Glastonbury, able to work in harmony with the angels to avert disasters.

· ANGELS AND FAMILY GROUPS ·

Two friends who sit together with their angels make a difference in the world. Families who open to the angels make a difference in the world.

Our angels tell us that there have been cultures, in the long history of the planet, that have become aware of the celestial realms in such a gentle and heartfelt way that they were able to work with them over the centuries. One of the ways this was achieved was through families.

Sometimes, though, when a family would become aware of its presiding angel, perhaps even view it as a household god, the angel would withdraw. As we've seen, angels do not like to be worshipped. Yet, if the balance can be kept—as it was, so we're told, in the great Minoan culture that flourished on the island of Crete for fifteen hundred years without war, some two thousand years B.C.—then a highly advanced civilization can blossom.

Would your family, or those among them who are open to such things, want to come together to tune into your family's connecting angel? In times of stress and crisis such as illness or death, tuning into your family's connecting angel will facilitate healing and communication. If you are moving, expecting a baby, or are about to celebrate another joyous rite of passage, let your family's angel join with you and celebrate with you, too.

Tina and her five sisters and brothers grew up in San Francisco. Now they live everywhere from Hawaii to Maine. But they are all open to the angels, and every Sunday at the same time, wherever they are, they sit quietly for fifteen minutes and tune into their family's angel. By doing this, they've become so attuned to each other that when Tina went into labor, each of her brothers and sisters called her within an hour.

If, in reading *Ask Your Angels,* you have found that having a connection with the angels is healing for you, share it with your friends and family. But remember that you can work with the angels in groups even if everyone hasn't read this book. For example, when you come together at meals, feel the presence of everyone's guardian angels and feel the presence of the angel who watches over your entire family. You can invoke these beings, out loud, or simply to yourself, and thank them for watching over you.

Allan shared what he learned with his family soon after he did the angel workshop. Now, when they sit together at the dinner table, they all stop for a moment to acknowledge the presence of the angels. And his kids don't complain that he's not "present" anymore.

· BRINGING IT INTO THE WORLD ·

At work, at school, you can do the same thing. When you arrive, feel the presence of the companion angels of all your co-workers or fellow students. And feel the presence of the angels that watch over the entire store, company, office, or school. In conferences, staff meetings, or board meetings, invoke the angels of everyone present—and the connecting angels, too.

Allan hasn't quite gotten to the point of sharing his experience with the men he employs in his shop, but when he gets to work he invokes the angels. He's noticed that there seem to be far fewer mistakes now and that the jobs are getting done on schedule, a rare event in his thirty years of working experience. He tells us that through his angel he's developed an instinct for knowing what needs to be attended to before something goes wrong.

Everyone has a guardian angel, and everyone is moved by angels in ways that they may not understand. You may want to put a picture of an angel on your desk or bulletin board. Doing that is enough to touch a deep chord in everyone who sees it. And you don't have to say anything about it at all.

When you are sitting on a bus or waiting in line at the bank, feel all the angels, invite them to come closer. Think of yourself as a weaver of Heaven and Earth. Wherever you are, whatever you are doing, at any time of the night or day, when you open to the angels, you are doing your part to transform our world with caring and kindness.

To carry that caring a step further, we offer a process designed for a group. It is simple enough so that anyone can do it, whether they've made direct contact with their angels or not. You can do this exercise with one other person, but we suggest that you work with at least two others to securely anchor the angelic energy in the world. If the people in your group know about the Thymus chakra, invite them all to feel that a web of energy connects each person in the circle, from Thymus to Thymus to Thymus.

It's helpful to place crystals or stones that are special to you, a candle, a flower, or other significant objects in the center of the circle, to create both an altar and a lens to focus the group energy. A picture of the Earth or a globe is also very appropriate.

Exercise 38:
A GROUP VISUALIZATION FOR PLANETARY HEALING

As the group gathers in a circle, standing or seated, call upon the companion angels of each person to stand behind him, wings outspread, so that there is a circle of people on the inside and a circle of angels on the outside, enclosing them. Either prerecord this exercise, or ask one person to lead it.

1. In the circle, hold hands with the palm of your left hand—your energy receiving hand—up, and your right hand—your energy transmitting hand—palm down. Be aware of the presence of your angel behind you.

2. Use your Heart as a station for receiving and pumping the energy around the circle. As you feel the energy coming in through your left hand, through the person on your left, draw it up your arm and shoulder and let it pour into your Heart. Then send the energy out from your Heart to your right shoulder, down your right arm, and release it from your right hand into the other person's hand that you are holding.

3. Feel the energy moving around your circle all through this visualization. Breathe deeply in through the nose, and allow the exhalation to come out through your mouth, so that a very soft sound is made. This sound can be used to attune the group breathing, so that everyone in your circle is breathing in the same pattern. Become aware of the companion angels of the people on either side of you.

4. As the energy moves around the circle, picture angels hovering over the group, wings outstretched, creating a dome over all of you.

5. Maintaining the movement of energy, visualize an image of the Earth in

the center of your circle. See it suspended in space, beautiful, alive, and sacred.

6. Bring your attention to the land masses, the trees, and vegetation. Bring up pictures of lush, verdant rain forests, and healthy trees planetwide. See the soil, rich and fertile. From your Third Eye beam the picture of healthy, healed forests and a joyful Earth directly into the center of the circle. And from your Heart chakra beam the energy of your deepest love. Ask your angel to guide your energy to the correct places.

7. Now bring your attention to the waters of the planet—the oceans, rivers, lakes, springs, and reservoirs. Imagine them clean, clear, sparkling, and free of debris. From your Third Eye, beam out your Heart's deepest wish that the waters be clear and pure and energized again. Send out love from your Heart. Ask your angel to connect your energy to the waters.

8. As you send the energy of healing into the planet's waters, picture the whales, dolphins, sea lions, fish, and all the other aquatic species swimming freely and happily in the clean waters. See the corals, the algae, the forests of seaweed, and everything else living in the watery depths as healthy and flourishing. Send this picture from your Third Eye, and this wish from your Heart, into the Earth in the middle of your circle. Then conjure up images of the animals and birds on our planet. Picture them healthy and robust, their coats and feathers shining. Ask your angel to direct your energies to all the species that need it, as you beam out this vision and send out your love.

9. Now imagine blue skies and clean, clear air. As you do, breathe in the image and then breathe it out, sending a picture of that clarity of air into the circle from your Third Eye. Connect with your Heart's wish for

clean and healthy air, and send a burst of heartfelt energy into the circle, aimed at the Earth. Ask your angel to assist in the cleansing.

10. Finally, project a beam of light, love, and gratitude from your Heart chakra directly at your image of the Earth. See the Earth begin to gently spin now, basking in the light. See the waters clean and sparkling, the land and forests fertile and lush, the air crystalline and clear, and all species thriving. Ask your angel to help bring this image into reality. To ground this energy in your bodies, tone together at this point.

11. To close, release your hands and place them at heart level, with the palms facing toward the center of the circle, to feel the energy that has been generated by your loving intention. Collect this energy in your hands and then beam it back into your Heart, by placing your hands there. As you do, feel your angel surrounding you with its love. Thank all who participated in this ritual—yourselves, the angels, and the planet.

Afterward sit with your group and discuss your experience. What did you feel? What did you see? Observe how all of your different experiences weave themselves together into a larger tapestry. You may have received information on specific actions to take. In one gathering, several of the people felt called on to plant trees. In another circle, the participants were led to become involved with a neighborhood recycling organization.

Our friend, LiLi, who brings merriment and magic wherever she goes, joined us for this healing visualization at one of our gatherings. LiLi is a spiritual therapist and cosmic ecologist. By helping people to clear their minds and emotions, she's working to clear the World Mind. We'd asked everyone to be open to any messages that they might receive from the angels regarding the specific nature of the group that was assembled. With previous experience at our angel gatherings, she had pen and notebook ready. This is what LiLi received:

"You are part of a soul group, a core, which will bring to itself others whom you know and don't know, ones that you can see and can't see. Relax into this. In this there is no time. Only events and evolutions. Be at peace, we are with you. We are one. Smile and laugh. You are Ministers of Fun."

LiLi's calling card now identifies her as a Minister of Fun in the Church of One.

· CREATING ANGEL WORKSHOPS ·

Exercise 38 can be done in any group. The participants don't need to know their angels as you do in order to join in. You could share it with a prayer group, with your family, with friends. However, there are certain levels of human/angel interchange that require a direct connection to be effective. So, if you know other people who have opened to their angels, you may want to work with them. Or, you may find that you're being led to start an angel group of your own.

All the exercises in the second part of this book can be adapted to groups. Once

you have a clear and strong relationship with your companion angel, if you feel the urge to start a group, ask your angel for its advice and support.

Alma and Timothy began teaching their workshops because their own communication with the angels had proved so beneficial. They asked the angels to bring in anyone who would benefit from the experience. One hundred flyers were printed and distributed. Thirty-five people showed up at their first workshop in 1985. They had no formal structure in mind at the beginning, but they did know the importance of Grounding and Releasing from having worked with their own angels. As the group gathered in a meditation to launch the workshop, they opened themselves to guidance from LNO and Joy. Some of the meditations and processes in this book originated at that first gathering.

Andrew had been teaching individuals how to work with the angels for several years when Cathy and Mindy, two friends who owned a crystal store, asked him to teach an angel workshop there. He was nervous but excited about doing it. Announcements were printed and a dozen people came, plus many angels. That was in 1988. Since that time, Andrew has done many workshops, including a series for people dealing with life-threatening illnesses. Again and again, he's discovered how easy it is for these women and men to open to their angels.

Although the techniques that we'd been working with were different, when the three of us came together to write this book, we discovered that the principles that informed our work were the same. How could they not be, when they're coming from the same source?

Your work will evolve out of your own partnership with the angels. Ask them for their guidance and assistance. You can share what you've learned from this book with one person or a whole room full of people. With the advice of your angels, you can let the form create itself. You may want to record the GRACE Process exercises in the beginning of *Ask Your Angels,* or you may want to memorize them and lead your group through them.

Just as with talking to your angels, there's no one right way to do this—all the ways are right. Simply keep asking your angels for their input, as we have.

Be aware that there may be some rocky times. Just as the unified field of group consciousness leads people more directly to the angels, it can also bring personal issues to the surface. Often, one person in the group will magnetize all the negativity in the room. If you judge that person, you miss an opportunity to release for the entire group. When negativity is not acknowledged with compassion and released by all, it will be passed on, like a hot potato, from one person to the next.

Negativity can come up at any point, in the form of resistance, boredom, or spaciness. When it does, doing a group Releasing will clear the way for the work to go on.

· WORKING WITH THE ARCHANGELS— AND BEYOND ·

You have already met the archangels in chapter 8. While there are many of these overlighting presences, we introduced you to the four that are particularly involved in human affairs. As we said earlier, since all celestial beings are both male and female, you may use a feminized version of Uriel, Gabriel, Raphael, and Michael if you prefer.

Except for an occasional appearance to a rare awakened individual, the higher angelic beings have been remote from human experience. In the course of writing this book, Timothy spoke with David Spangler, one of the founders of the Findhorn community. Spangler's work has been involved with the angels who interact with the human evolutionary process. This has led him to observe that while the angels who deal with individuals and small groups seem to have a human quality and, indeed, take on human appearance from time to time, the angels dealing with larger groupings could appear, from our perspective, to be fairly impersonal.

The emergence in our bodies of a new chakra, the Thymus chakra, gives us an energetic link from person to person for the first time. This linking, and the gradual evolution of group consciousness, allows us to hook up with these beings in a new way. We may have been as blind to their presence as we once were to viruses and bacteria, but when we come together in groups, we generate an energy and consciousness sufficient to draw down hosts of archangels.

Why do we want to attract them? Is it some form of spiritual cop-out—an avoidance of our own responsibilities? Or could it be that they are the transformative energies for which we've all been praying? The ones whose depth of knowledge of planetary transformations will allow us to make these massive changes with elegance and grace?

When groups of doctors, for example, open to the archangels, they will be able to receive information on healing that will radically alter the way that we take care of ourselves.

Convocations of scientists who open to their angels will receive information far more advanced than anything they could hope to get from building billion dollar telescopes or particle accelerators.

Environmentalists and ecological experts will receive information on cleaning toxic waste and creating alternative energy sources that no one has imagined yet.

Politicians who gather together in groups, invoking the angels, will gain both insight and information on how to solve the major problems of our time.

Whether you're grappling with family or workplace matters, community or government issues, when you work with the archangels you upgrade the level on which you've been functioning, and you deepen the energetic web that connects you to the people with whom you are working.

· THE FUNCTIONS OF THE ARCHANGELS ·

Although their spheres of influence overlap and interconnect, each archangel has its own bailiwick. You met them in the Angel Oracle, and here we share with you more detailed information on their functions, so that you will know whom to tune into when you are doing different kinds of work.

Uriel brings transformative energies to the mind and is the overlighting presence to invoke when you are working with issues concerning science, economics, and politics. This includes such topics as pollution, toxic clean-up, new technologies, food and farming, housing and building, medical research, social equality, political reform, anything that involves organizations, systems, structures, and all work-related issues.

Gabriel is the guardian of emotions, relationships, and creativity. At a time when we are struggling with abuse, addictions, dysfunctional families, the struggles of sexual minorities to find love and be loved, Gabriel is the angel to invoke. In matters of the arts and any kind of creativity, call on Gabriel for its loving assistance.

Raphael is the overlighting presence in the realm of healing. This includes everything from surgery to herbalism, from the personal to the planetary. If you are a healer or need healing yourself, invoke Raphael. Its power can be brought to bear on physical, mental, and emotional illness.

Michael is guardian of the house of spirit and dreams, and is the archangel working for cooperation and reconciliation. It's time for us to learn to live in peace and harmony with others, to break down the barriers that have separated nations, political parties, religious sects, families, and individuals due to differences of opinion, fear, and selfish self-interest. All of us are citizens of Earth, regardless of our diversity. In the movement toward this level of cooperation, Michael is the being to invoke.

· MEETING THE GUARDIAN OF OUR UNFOLDING UNITY ·

Beyond the archangels is a group of beings often known as principalities or integration angels. They are the guardians of larger systems, from governments to multinational corporations. They are the ones who watch over our rulers, who see that governments function harmoniously and for the good of the planet.

According to Abigrael, among the principalities who work with our planet, there is one in particular who is reaching out to us so that we can work with it. Its name is Eularia, and it holds the blueprint for a harmonious and unified Earth. As more of us connect with Eularia, we will be supporting the rights of all of humanity, the peaceful cooperation of all world governments, and the emergence of a sane and stable world order that honors all of life. Because of this, one of Eularia's functions is to be the guardian of the United Nations, the seed center for world cooperation.

Looking at the world today, you might think that the principalities haven't been doing a very good job. But you have to remember that we're the ones who must open up to the angels. We are the only ones who can give them access to our world. They cannot work with our leaders if our leaders are not connected to them. But together, in groups, we can begin to draw the angels down into our lives, and create access wires for them to connect with us. In fact, groups are especially effective at connecting with Eularia, the patron angel of our emerging unity as global citizens.

· THE EARTH ANGEL ·

More and more people are becoming aware of the "Gaia Hypothesis," first formulated by James Lovelock in 1979 in his book *Gaia: A New Look at Life on Earth*. In it Lovelock resurrected the idea that the ancients and the indigenous peoples of the planet have believed all along—that our planet is a living being, a vast, self-regulating intelligence. Everything that lives on it and within it is a part of its beingness. Lovelock called it "Gaia" after the ancient Greek name for the Mother Goddess of all the life on Earth.

The more one thinks about the Gaia Hypothesis, the more logical and obvious it becomes. The Earth *is* alive. It's the parent of us all. And just as we have a guardian angel, a companion angel, so too does the Earth.

As our planet has a myriad of names—Earth, Terra, and Gaia being only a few of them—so too does the Angel of the Earth have many names, none of them known, but about to be discovered.

There are many orders of angels beyond the principalities. For example, the Earth Angel is a throne. All planets have guardians of this order, for in a sense, each world is a "seat" for the Creator, and these angelic beings reflect that.

If you were to try and visualize the body of the Earth Angel, you might find it to be a vast belt of light that covers the entire orbit of our planet—an elliptical shape,

595 million miles long. It takes the Earth a year to move around the sun, within the body of this being. When we connect to this angel, we experience a unity of time and space.

· THE HEALING OF THE EARTH ·

Our primary task at this time is Earth healing. The Earth surely knows how to heal herself so what we need to be able to do is to tune into our Mother Gaia, and the Earth Angel, and find out what the appropriate action for healing might be at any given time. As you do this next process, you not only send healing energy to the planet, but you let the nature spirits and the angels know that you're ready to work in harmony with all of them.

Doing this with others in groups is an important step toward the healing of our dear planet. If you know others who are dialoguing with their angels, or if you have begun to lead angel groups yourself, start to feel the collective energy of your group deepen and expand. When this happens, you'll be ready to work with the advanced angelic beings.

Exercise 39:
WORKING WITH HIGHER ANGELIC BEINGS

To establish a clear link with these beings, you will need at least two other people to ground your individual energies so that you can more easily climb the ladder through the angelic hierarchies.

To do this exercise, the participants will need to have a strong sense of their chakras. And they will need to have a familiarity with their angels. You can do this exercise sitting or standing. Again, you may want to tape the exercise, or choose one person to lead it.

1. Gather in your circle. Ground yourself, feeling your roots spiraling deep into the Earth and your Crown fibers reaching up into the stars. Sense all of your chakras. Feel yourself come into an open-hearted state. Now open your wings.
2. Hold hands—left palm up, right palm down. Feel the energy of your group moving from hand to hand and heart to heart.
3. Breathe together, in through your nose and out through your mouth. A soft sound is made each time you exhale. Use that sound to help all of you breathe together; this unifies your energy.
4. Close your eyes. Feel your companion angels standing right behind you, their wings outspread. Know that you are safe and loved.
5. Let go of the hands of the people on either side of you and turn to the east, invoking the presence of the archangel Uriel. Feel the light of its presence.
6. Turning to the south, invoke the presence of Gabriel. Feel the love of its presence.
7. Turning to the west, invoke the presence of Raphael. Feel the healing of its presence.
8. Turning to the north, invoke the presence of Michael, and feel the wisdom of its presence.
9. Now join hands again and into your circle invite the presence of the principality Eularia, guardian of the emerging new reality. Feel your entire circle being enfolded in its soft, golden, loving embrace. Speak to Eularia. Let it know that you are ready to work with it for global

healing and for harmony between humanity and all the life of Earth. Thank Eularia for its love and for giving you the opportunity to work with it.

10. If you feel there are places in the world at this time that are in special need of clarity and healing, think of those places. Call out their names. Visualize the angels of peace, working under Eularia, surrounding those locations and bringing them compassion and healing.

11. Now call out to the Earth Angel. Feel the way that our planet and all that live upon it and within it are floating in its enormous elliptical body.

12. Allow yourselves to feel the harmonious blending of time, space, and resonance that comes from connecting with the Earth Angel. Breathe all of that in together. And together breathe it out again, with a soft sound. Let the Earth Angel know that you will continue to connect with it.

13. Thank all of these angels for being with you. And from your heart, thank the Creator for having given you the miracle of life, the incredible gift of a physical body, and the chance to live in a time of great healing in a world of great beauty.

14. Focus once again on your breathing. Bring your attention to the hands you are holding. Open to experience the loving wings of your own angel wrapped around you. Move into the center of your circle, so that everyone can hug everyone else, and ground in all your bodies the energies that you have woven into yourselves.

The further out you reach, the more you have to ground yourselves, during and after the work. If there are people in your group who feel dizzy or light-headed after this exercise, have them stand with their feet slightly pigeon-toed and knees bent to bring the energy down into their bodies, while others in the group massage them very lightly on their arms, legs, back, and the back of the head.

Share your experiences with each other around the circle afterward. Did the angels have messages for anyone in your group? Did anyone see or feel something which should be expressed? Opening to these beings allows us to do major celestial work, and speaking about what you received helps to ground it in the world.

Now that you've learned to work with higher angels and with groups, we offer a last exercise. Just as a telescope looks out into space, you can use this vision to look ahead in time.

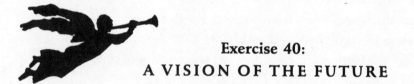

Exercise 40:
A VISION OF THE FUTURE

This exercise is a gift from Abigrael, who invites you to record it slowly, with long pauses after each step. You can play it at a gathering of your angel group, or by yourself, sitting in your sacred space. It's a good idea to ground yourself—and the others—before you begin. Keep your outer eyes closed and the eye of your heart wide open so you can receive the vision that comes to you through Abigrael's words.

Taste this vision. Touch it. Know that you are part of its creation. Feel the capacity for a new world rising up out of your relationship with the angels. Honor the work that you are doing in the unfolding of the Divine Plan. Know that all of us are co-creators.

1. Feel your breathing, and your heartbeat. Put your hands on your heart. Feel the presence of your angel right behind you, wrapping you in its wings, filling you with Divine love.

2. Float out of time and space with your angel. Just as the first man who walked on the moon changed the way we see the world, every single person who connects with the angels makes an even greater change, for all of humanity.

3. Feel the change that you and your angel are making. Hear the sound of your connection echoing in the heavens. Know that the work the two of you are doing is creating a world of harmony and love.

4. Picture a birthing room. Make it beautiful. It is your birthing room. You are about to be reborn. The lights are soft. The only sound you hear is your mother's regulated breathing, and the whispered encouragement of your father and the other friends who are present. As she breathes, your mother feels the wings of her angel wrapped around her, and feels the clear presence of your angel, too. For the last nine months she and your father and their friends have been getting to know you and your angel.

5. See how you slip into the world, into the hands of a midwife and the wings of your angel. Feel this angel, and feel the golden presence of the angels of birth, too, hovering over all of you, to give their blessings.

6. The sky is clear on this, your birth day. The air is pure, and the water with which you are washed for the first time is clean and pure, too.

Working with Uriel and with great teams of technology angels, humankind has cleansed and healed the planet.

7. See yourself as you fall asleep in your crib for the first time, your family gathered around you, in a room filled with angels. Feel this, and know that all through your growing up, they will support you in learning about the physical world, at the same time that you maintain your relationship with the spiritual realms.

8. You are a child now, sitting with your family at the dinner table. In your family, each meal begins with an invocation of the angels and a prayer of thanksgiving to the Creator. In this world there is much for which to be thankful. There are homes and food and meaningful work for everyone. There is no war. Together with the angels, politicians have created new forms of global interaction that honor the rights of all people on every part of the planet. There is respect for every race, religion, age, gender, sexual persuasion, and physical capability.

9. Watch yourself grow older and stronger, opening to creativity and to the blessings of life in a body. With your angel beside you, you move freely and joyfully in the world, with caring for all of life, from the microscopic to the cosmic.

10. Knowing the Universe is a safe place, you are not afraid to make mistakes, and not afraid to love. See yourself growing into adulthood, exploring feelings and relationships with a clear and loving heart. You know that love is the ground of all being. The angels are present in all your relationships.

11. In your chosen work, the celestials are with you. You know why you chose to be born, you know what you came here to do, and in harmony with the planet you watch yourself fulfilling your purpose.

12. There are challenges all through your life. But with courage and love, you face each challenge with enthusiasm and a sense of wonder at all that life brings. Your senses are all open, and you explore those senses with joy and delight—in friendship, love, work, and in the global community.

13. Having lived and loved and done God's work in the world, it is time for you to complete this life. You are filled with joy—joy at having touched and tasted the wonders of Earth. With your last physical breath, in a room filled with friends, you reach out to your angel again. Wrapped in its wings, you slip from your body with the same delight you felt when you were born.

14. Now breathe in the joy that surrounds you—and breathe it out again. Let your mind and your senses carry you beyond the angels, beyond the archangels, the thrones, beyond the cherubim and seraphim.

15. Hold this vision in your body. You are wise and strong and large enough to hold all of it. Feel this vision in every cell of your mind and your body. Feel it glowing in every part of you.

16. Now open your eyes again. See the world through this vision and know that as you do, you ground it in your body and make it real in the world.

Notice how you feel coming out of this meditation. Do you feel peaceful? Joyous? Hopeful? Content? These are the feelings that will empower us to create this new reality. This future belongs to us all—to our children, to our grandchildren, and to every living creature on our planet.

But we're not there yet. In the midst of the rush of our daily lives, and in reading the headlines or catching the news on TV, it's easy to lose sight of this vision. When this happens, come back and do the meditation again. Then, while you're still in a quiet place, open your notebook and ask your angel to show you what you can do right now to make this vision a reality in your own life.

Keep asking, from time to time, for more suggestions, support, and information. Notice how peace and trust, love, and caring are becoming part of your everyday life. In partnership with your angel, you are making this vision of the future the new reality.

Afterword

Most of this book was written in Alma's study, twenty-five floors above the city of New York. Looking out the window, you can see Central Park and the Manhattan skyline, with the Empire State Building rising above it all.

From this lofty perch we watched the ever-changing city landscape: traffic moving in a remarkably orderly fashion; the light changing from sun to moon; the seasons from winter to spring, and summer to fall. And in the process of writing *Ask Your Angels,* we watched ourselves and our relationships move and change, too.

How, we wondered, could we sum up the changes we feel we've experienced since meeting our personal guardians? For days we struggled to write this After-word. Finally, we remembered to invoke the presence of Abigrael and our angels.

You'd think after having written a whole book on the subject we would have done that sooner!

The moment we joined hands to invoke our angels there was a palpable shift of energy in the room. We might have forgotten about the angels, but they had certainly not forgotten us. We sensed their presence as a rearrangement of molecules in the air, like watching a crystal form all around us. After sitting quietly for a few minutes, the structure of this section became clear to us, as if it had already been written and we were simply reading it.

· ANGELS AND CHANGES ·

In comparing notes, we discovered that although the three of us had met our angels in different ways and under different circumstances, there were a number of unifying factors in our experiences.

Angels Appear in Moments of Radical Transformation. Each of us met our personal guardians when we were in some sort of collapse.

For Andrew, it was a collapse of his belief structure. His Buddhist-Marxist philosophy satisfied his mind, but his heart was missing the warmth and affection that the angels bring.

For Timothy, it was a physical collapse, a Near Death Experience that catapulted him into contact with the angelic realm, where he learned how much he valued his life.

For Alma, it was the collapse of her floatation tank business that precipitated her opening to her angel and beginning a new career.

Angels do not cause these radical transformations in our lives. Rather, they come to us at these times to help us move out of fear. They come to help us see vast and wonderful new opportunities.

Angels Increase Our Capacity for Trust. Before he met his angel, Andrew worked in a bookstore. He stayed there for two years longer than he wanted to because he was afraid to give up the security of a weekly paycheck. Several years later, after he'd met Sargolais, he decided to give up a thriving practice as a massage therapist so that he could write full time. This time, it only took two days—not two years—to act on his decision. He sold his first book a few weeks after he took that leap of faith.

Timothy had a persistent longing to leave New York City and live in a simpler, more natural environment. His angels, Joy and Beauty, encouraged him to trust his feelings and follow his heart, even though it meant leaving a life he'd spent more than twenty years building—and parting with friends and loved ones. He now divides his time between the deserts of New Mexico and the beaches of Australia doing what he loves best: writing, drawing, and swimming with dolphins.

Before she started collaborating with her angel, there were many times when Alma intuitively received information about a psychotherapy patient, but refrained from sharing her insight because it was just a "hunch." Since working with LNO, she's learned not only to trust this inner knowing, but to express it. And each time she does, her client will say something like, "Aha! Now I get it!"

Angels Revive the Innocence and Wonder We Experienced as Small Children. As a youngster, Timothy was a gifted artist. Later, he channeled this ability into architectural renderings, but eventually, his creativity had to give way to the technical demands of his vocation. But when he met his angels, all the wonder and delight he'd known as a child opened up in him again. The angels inspired him to return to his drawing, and for several years now he's been working on a series of visionary drawings of sacred sites all over the planet.

Angels Deepen Our Capacity for Compassion and Forgiveness. A woman that Alma disliked showed up at one of her seminars. But this time, before Alma fell into the old pattern of anger and resentment, she found herself thinking, "If she is here it must be for a healing." At the end of the evening, the woman came up to her. Without hesitation, Alma embraced her, feeling empathetically the deep wish the woman had for Alma to love, accept, and forgive her. In that moment, the only feeling she had toward the woman was that of the purest love.

The three of us agree that compassion and the ability to forgive are the greatest gifts we have received from our angelic friends. Again and again the barriers that exist between ourselves and others dissolve and disappear when we are open-hearted—a state that our heavenly partners help us to create.

Living with angels doesn't change us into someone different. It doesn't make us better or improve us. It simply allows us to be the person we always knew (or wished) we were, inside. That lost inner self lives in the heart, and it is to the very heart of ourselves that the angels bring us.

Some people think that if you're hanging out with angels you must be pretty flaky. On the contrary, all three of us feel we've become increasingly focused, that we've taken on more substance. Before we met our angels our actions were other-directed. We were governed by what other people thought we should be doing, from parents and teachers to partners and friends. Now, angel-tuned, we're inner-directed—

motivated and inspired by the promptings of our Higher Selves, moving in harmony with all of life.

· A TEXTBOOK FOR LIFE ·

Ask Your Angels is a primer for learning how to talk to celestials. Your own angel notebook is the advanced text—a textbook for your life. Use it to keep track of your changes and to consolidate your gains. Re-read your entries and acknowledge your progress and growth.

Notice how you've changed from the time that you made your first entry. What was going on in your life when you began? Where are you now? What did you think about angels then? And now? What are your own experiences of the unifying factors we discussed above? Record your observations in your notebook.

When you review what you've done over a period of time, looking at your notes all at once, a bigger picture begins to emerge. This lets you see through angel eyes and gives you an overview of where you've been and where you're going.

Ask your angels for guidance on the next part of your journey, remembering that the steps in the GRACE Process, plus all of the other exercises in this book, can be used again and again. The more you practice, the better you get at communicating with your heavenly helpers, and the deeper and more profound the information you will receive. Use what you've learned in your everyday life, and share the angels with others.

Just because you're partners with your angel doesn't mean that all your problems will miraculously disappear. What it does mean is that you will discover options and alternatives to help you solve them creatively. The angelic connection expands our human capabilities and extends our capacities.

· WE ARE ALL CREATING THE FUTURE ·

You opened this book to learn how to talk with the angels. When you did you opened yourself to limitless love as well. The power of limitless love—some people call it God—is what is healing our beloved planet today.

Our angels tell us: the future is now. Each action that we take in gratitude and grace weaves itself into the pattern we are jointly creating for generations to come. You and your angels are part of a growing spiritual task force. You are light-weavers, working together to bring the highest visions of our future into joyful manifestation.

Talking with our angels, connecting to the Divinity within us, elevates our personal awareness, which in turn improves our lives and circumstances. When we are able to connect with our own inner Divinity, it becomes easier to see the Divinity within others. The day we all see God in each other—we'll be Home.

When we interact with our angels, the energy exchange creates a special radiance within us. In art, this energy is often depicted as a halo. In our lives, it's the fire that ignites our dreams. As you move through your world, let your inner light shine forth for everyone to see. Claim your radiance. Honor your visions. Know that you and everyone you see are vibrant and radiant beings, connected in a luminous web of light that encircles our dear planet and shines out to the farthest reaches of the universe.

Further Reading

• ANGELS AND THE ANGELIC REALM •

Adler, Mortimer J. *The Angels and Us.* New York: Macmillan & Co., 1982.

Bittleston, Adam. *Our Spiritual Companions: From Angels and Archangels to Cherubim and Seraphim.* Edinburgh, Scotland: Floris Books, 1980.

Bloom, William. *Devas, Fairies and Angels: A Modern Approach.* Glastonbury, England: Gothic Image Publications, 1986.

Burnham, Sophy. *Angel Letters.* New York: Ballantine Books, 1991.

———. *The Book of Angels.* New York: Ballantine Books, 1989.

Carey, Ken. *Return of the Bird Tribes.* Kansas City, Missouri: Uni*Sun, 1988.

Corbin, Henry. *Spiritual Body and Celestial Earth.* Princeton, New Jersey: Princeton University Press, 1977.

Davidson, Gustav. *A Dictionary of Angels.* New York: Free Press, 1980.

Graham, Billy. *Angels, God's Secret Agents.* Waco, Texas: Word Books, 1986.

Hodson, Geoffrey. *The Brotherhood of Angels and Men.* Wheaton, Illinois: Quest Books, 1927.

Kaplan, Aryeh. *Meditation and Kabbalah.* York Beach, Maine: Samuel Weiser, 1982.

Leadbetter, C.W. *Invisible Helpers.* Wheaton, Illinois: Theosophical Publishing House, 1896.

MacGregor, Geddes. *Angels: Ministers of Grace.* New York: Paragon House, 1988.

Maclean, Dorothy. *To Hear the Angels Sing.* Issaquah, Washington: Morningtown Press, 1988.

Mallasz, Gitta. *Talking with Angels.* Einsiedeln, Switzerland: Daimon Verlag, 1989.

Moolenburgh, H.C. *A Handbook of Angels.* Essex, England: C.D. Daniel Co., 1984.

Newhouse, Flower. *Rediscovering the Angels and Natives of Eternity.* Escondido, California: The Christward Ministry, 1937. Reprint.

Solara. *Invoking Your Celestial Guardians.* Portal, Arizona: Star-Borne Unlimited, 1986.

———. *The Star-Borne: A Remembrance for the Awakened Ones.* Charlottesville, Virginia: Star-Borne Unlimited, 1989.

Spangler, David. *Revelation: Birth of a New Age.* San Francisco, California: The Rainbow Bridge, 1976.

———. *Links with Space.* Marina del Ray, California: DeVorss & Co., 1978.

Steiner, Rudolf. *The Influence of Spiritual Beings upon Man.* Hudson, New York: Anthroposophical Press, 1982.

———. *The Spiritual Hierarchies.* Hudson, New York: Anthroposophical Press, 1983.

Swedenborg, Emanuel. *Divine Love and Wisdom.* New York: Swedenborg Foundation, 1982.

———. *Heaven and Hell.* New York: Swedenborg Foundation, 1979.

Taylor, Terry Lynn. *Messengers of Light: The Angel's Guide to Spiritual Growth.* Tiburon, California: H. J. Kramer, 1990.

Urantia Foundation. *The Urantia Book.* Chicago, Illinois, 1955.

Valentin, Ann, and Essene, Virginia. *The Descent of the Dove.* Santa Clara, California: S.E.E. Publishing Co., 1988.

Ward, Theodora. *Men and Angels.* New York: Viking Press, 1969.

Wilson, Peter Lamborn. *Angels.* New York: Pantheon Books, 1980.

Wulfing, Sulamith. *Angels Great and Small.* Amsterdam, Holland: V.O.C., Angel Books, 1981.

Wyllie, Timothy. *Dolphins*Extraterrestrials*Angels: Adventures among Spiritual Intelligences.* Fort Wayne, Indiana: Knoll Publishing, 1984.

· AURAS AND CHAKRAS ·

Brennan, Barbara Ann. *Hands of Light, A Guide to Healing Through the Human Energy Field.* New York: Bantam Books, 1988.

Gregory, Laneta, and Treissman, Geoffrey. *Handbook of the Aura.* Norwich, England: Pilgrim Book Services, 1985.

Kunz, Dora van Gelder. *The Personal Aura.* Wheaton, Illinois: Quest Books, 1991.

Leadbetter, C.W. *The Chakras.* Wheaton, Illinois: Quest Books, 1927.

Mann, John, and Short, Lar. *The Body of Light.* New York: Globe Press Books, 1990.

Powell, Arthur. *The Astral Body.* Wheaton, Illinois: Theosophical Publishing House, 1925.

Sharamon, Shalila, and Baginski, Bodo J. *The Chakra Handbook.* Wilmont, Wisconsin: Lotus Light Publications, 1991.

· DREAMS ·

Delaney, Gail. *Living Your Dreams: Using Sleep to Solve Problems and Enrich Your Life.* San Francisco, California: Harper and Row, 1988.

Faraday, Ann. *The Dream Game.* New York: Harper Collins, 1976.

Garfield, Patricia. *Creative Dreaming.* New York: Ballantine Books, 1985.

Krippner, Stanley, ed. *Dreamtime and Dreamwork.* Los Angeles, California: Jeremy P. Tarcher, 1990.

Lang, Robert. *Decoding Your Dreams.* New York: Ballantine Books, 1988.

Maguire, Jack. *Night and Day: Use the Power of Your Dreams to Transform Your Life.* New York: Fireside/Simon and Schuster, 1989.

Reed, Henry. *Getting Help from Your Dreams.* New York: Ballantine Books, 1988.

Ullman, Montague, and Zimmerman, Nan. *Working with Dreams.* New York: Dell Publishing Co., 1980.

· RECOVERY ·

————. *Alcoholics Anonymous (known in AA as the Big Book)*. New York: World Services, Inc., 1976.

————. *Came to Believe (Stories from People in AA)*. New York: World Services, Inc., 1973.

Black, Claudia. *Double Duty*. New York: Ballantine Books, 1990.

————. *It Will Never Happen to Me*. New York: Ballantine Books, 1981.

Cruse, Sharon Wegscheider. *Another Chance*. Palo Alto, California: Science & Behavior Books, 1987.

Cunningham, Donna, and Ramer, Andrew. *Further Dimensions of Healing Addictions*. San Rafael, California: Cassandra Press, 1988.

————. *The Spiritual Dimensions of Healing Addictions*. San Rafael, California: Cassandra Press, 1988.

Farmer, Steven. *Adult Children of Abusive Parents*. New York: Ballantine Books, 1989.

Klass, Joe. *The Twelve Steps to Happiness*. New York: Ballantine Books, 1990.

————. *Living Recovery: Inspirational Moments for 12 Step Living by Men and Women in Recovery*. New York: Ballantine Books, 1990.

Schaef, Anne Wilson. *Co-Dependence*. San Francisco, California: Harper Collins, 1986.

Yoder, Barbara. *The Recovery Resource Book*. New York: Fireside, 1990.

About the Authors

· ALMA DANIEL ·

Alma Daniel is a healing practitioner and psychotherapist. In addition to her private practice, she teaches classes in spiritual development, hosts a weekly meditation group, and is the creator and facilitator of Inner Voyages, an intensive empowerment program. Alma is the mother of three grown children, Peter, Anthony, and Nora. She established and for many years ran the Human Potential Counseling Service and the Floatation Tank Association. A third degree Reiki healer, she has recorded a number of meditation and inspirational tapes, including versions of the Grounding and Releasing techniques used in the GRACE Process. For current information on her tapes and on angel and other workshops, you may contact:

Alma Daniel
c/o Eldorado
300 Central Park West
New York, NY 10024

· ANDREW RAMER ·

Andrew Ramer is a writer, artist, and healer. An alumnus of the University of California at Berkeley, with a degree in Religious Studies, he is also a graduate of the Swedish Institute of Massage in New York.

Andrew is the author and illustrator of *little pictures, Two Flutes Playing,* and *Tools for Peace.* Along with Donna Cunningham, another Ballantine author, he wrote *The Spiritual Dimensions of Healing Addictions* and *Further Dimensions of Healing Addictions.*

He has been listening to angels since childhood, talking back to them since 1982, and teaching groups and individuals how to communicate with them since that time.

· TIMOTHY WYLLIE ·

Timothy Wyllie was born in England during World War II and trained as an architect. He practiced in the United Kingdom and in the Bahamas before coforming a religious community and traveling with it throughout Europe and the United States. In 1977, he left the community and started a business in New York City. By 1981 he was able to devote himself full time to his lifelong interest in spiritual intelligences. His book, *Dolphins * Extraterrestrials * Angels* is widely regarded as a classic in that field. His most recent book, *Dolphins, Telepathy and Underwater Birthing,* is to be published by Bear & Company in 1993.

About the Artist

Yanni Posnakoff is an internationally known artist and illustrator whose personal vision is to draw, sculpt, or paint one million angels. Well on his way to achieving this goal, Yanni has created angels on sweatshirts, in stained glass, and in bread dough, as well as on paper and canvas. For a number of years Yanni was proprietor of the Angel Gallery, a studio-museum-shop in New York City that featured angel books, art, and music exclusively. Yanni illustrated the original bestselling edition of *Children's Letters to God,* and its sequel. He presently lives in Athens, Greece.